the TRUE YOU

by Mark Reed

The True You

Following Your True Self on a Journey of Spiritual Awakening

An Infinite, Loving, Creative Intelligence lives within you.

You are an individual expression of this Universal Power.

Your inner divinity is called by many names, one of which is your True Self.

The True You
Following Your True Self on a Journey of Spiritual Awakening

Copyright ©2015 Mark Reed

ISBN: 978-0-9862385-0-5

Cover Illustration by: Fish Smith. designsbyfish.net

Editing, Cover and Back Cover Design by: Russell Phillips, the-creative-source.com

Interior Design and Layout by: Jennifer Zaczek, cypressediting.com

To beautiful Dora—my love, my life.

A favorite rhyming affirmation, as spoken to the True Self:

Lead me,
Guide me,
Show me the way.
Tell me what to do,
Whisper what to say

TABLE OF CONTENTS

ACKNOWLEDGMENTS

Thank you God, always and forever.

This book would be a big blank page without my wonderful wife Dora. At one point in our lives, she was my hostage. Now she's my rock, my inspiration, my navigator, my role model, and my partner on our unfolding spiritual journey. Thanks babe!

Thanks Big Buddy! My father, Robert M. "Bob" Reed *showed* me how the True Self can be the origin of love, compassion, integrity, and a positive outlook on life. I inherited my creativity and love of writing from my mother, Mary Reed, and I know she loves those rhyming affirmations. Thanks also to my siblings Dan and Ruth and to my extended family—Bill, Hermila, Michael, Wanda, and Taylor—for your love.

Bless my spiritual mentors—Revered Karen Rice, Reverend Ron Fox, Becky Fox, Judy Thompson, Judy Baker, Sue Witter, Sister Sarah Busby, Bob Post, and Geoffrey Hardacre. You've lifted, supported, and loved me in countless ways.

My spiritual comrades are awesomely awesome! I'm very grateful for the wisdom of the "Power of We" contributors in this book: Reverend Randol Batson, Geoffrey Hardacre, Dr. Linda Johnson, Tracey Harrick, Nancee Noel, Sue Witter, Judy Thompson, Judy Baker, and Sarah Busby.

Y'all are just part of my dream . . . thanks to my ACIM friends for your spiritual insights, support, and guidance—especially Nancee, Geoff, Elaine, Jane, Erla, and Mike and Pam! You're still innocent Mike!

You guys taught me about surrender, action, love, and service! A big thanks to my Bay Area spiritual buds: Guitar Tim, Tall Paul, Spiritual Phil, Danny A., Shaun C., Anthony P., Kevin M., Hal McHugh (R.I.P.), Kamyar E., Steve D., Ponytail Steve, and Howard "P.B." Pine (R.I.P.); and to my Phoenix mentors Tom F., and Jeff Crawley (R.I.P.). I love you guys! Phil, I told you I'd write a book! Actually, my H.P. was the writer and I was the typist.

A hearty thanks to my editor, Russell Phillips, my publishing mentor Reverend Randol Batson, and a very cool, loving, funny, and talented artist, Fish Smith, for her cover artwork. Mike and Pam, you paid for that artwork! Thanks again.

LOL! Thanks to my spiritual FB friends for your inspiration and support; and to Jace, Lori, Angela, Gerald, Tim, Capt. Morgan, Paula, K-Cup,

Tina, TM, Deb, Polly, Hugh, Jerry, Angel Sharon, Janis, Tana, Jeff, Beau, Julie, Roxie, Sher, Gregg, Aline, and my Bicentennial Bomber Buds for making me laugh and tolerating my inner child.

FOREWORD

Imagine that you could be set free from all the ideas, beliefs, and regimens of life that hold you captive. What if you could wake up one morning and be rid of your long spiritual to-do list or untethered by burdens that weighted your heart? What would you do with your life if there were absolutely no limitations, no one to criticize your choices, and nothing to squelch your enthusiasm? Better yet, what if you woke up every day believing it's good to be alive?

This first book by new author Mark Reed elucidates a path that makes this and much more possible. Mark is more than a dedicated Science of Mind teacher, more than a wise and trusted spiritual coach and mentor, and far more than an inspiring and witty voice for conscience on Facebook. I know him as a professional spiritual practitioner licensed by the Centers for Spiritual Living and have observed his deep caring for his spiritual community, constant service to others, and love for humanity. The man is a budding mystic.

He is uniquely creative yet sensible, and with the unveiling of this new release, it's obvious that Mark Reed has something important to say to the world about spiritual matters. He speaks in an original, direct voice that shoots right to the heart of truth. Readers will be inspired by the clarity of his message. Building on the literary works of other spiritual giants, his perspective is unique, fresh, and potent. Not since the Conversations with God series have we been privy to such an obvious and open exchange between a writer and his God.

The most distinctive feature of this work is the brilliant way in which Mark interweaves elements of three great teachings: The Science of Mind, A Course in Miracles, and The 12 Steps. A beautiful compilation of quotations, affirmations, and life-affirming stories, this book provides a means for the reader to redefine their personal conception of God. I found it to be a breakthrough approach to a finer sense of intimacy with a caring Universal Intelligence. Mark provides an uncomplicated and straightforward understanding of how universal spiritual laws work with and for us, not against us—perfect for those who are open to the mind-expanding tenets of New Thought philosophy.

Much of the fun of this read occurs in the anecdotal renderings and the phenomenal way Mark directs our attention to favorite movie scenes and pop culture references, showing, in a light-hearted style, deeper spiritual interpretations and potential for personal application. I especially recommend this book to anyone who questions or wonders if there is more—more to a Sunday sermon, more to the doctrines of a church, more than any single religion can package into a belief system. For anyone who feels they have outgrown the God of their youth, this book will help you understand why. In the process, it will make you think, bring you a chuckle, and nudge you closer to your True Self.

Reverend Karen Rice, Senior Minister
West Valley Center for Spiritual Living, Peoria, AZ

PREFACE

"I am powerful!" Even when I say this today, after being a licensed practitioner in the Centers for Spiritual Living for several years, a small part of me cringes in disbelief. The ego doesn't want me to believe that I'm powerful. And when I envision myself in a 12-step meeting proclaiming my power, I picture several old 12-Step men with scrunched up faces, pointing at me, snarling, "He's a cocky little bastard, sure to relapse! He needs a lesson in humility!"

Nevertheless, here I am, exclaiming that I AM a powerful and creative being, endowed with the same qualities as an Infinite, Universal, Creative, Intelligence, because I'm an individual expression of *It*.

I'm no longer seeking God's will for me, because I know exactly what it is. Again, I envision 12-Step old timers looking at me over their spectacles murmuring, "He did NOT just say that, did he?"

This book focuses on universal spiritual principles. I wrote it for *all* spiritual seekers. It evolved over a ten-year period and was originally intended for recovering alcoholics/addicts who successfully worked the 12 Steps and were searching for something more, to expand and grow on their spiritual path. But as I've grown, so has this book. My spiritual roots are in the 12 Steps, but I've been steeped in the practical philosophy of the *Science of Mind* for several years now, and more recently *A Course in Miracles*.

For the serious 12-Stepper with a few years' experience working the Steps, I say this: This book doesn't add anything to the 12 Steps. It's not a critique or analysis of the 12 Steps. The Steps need no improvement or refinement from me. It's *not* targeted to someone who's new to the 12 Steps and needs the structure of meetings, step work, and all the other effective ACTIONS taken when new to the program. If you're initially working the Steps, follow your sponsor's lead. If you don't have a sponsor, get one today.

For the Religious Scientist, whom I now refer to as *Spiritual Livers* (Centers for Spiritual Living), you'll feel comfortable reading this book through the lens of our philosophy. I'm confident you'll gain something new as you look at the Infinite through the eyes of a 12-Stepping practitioner and student of *A Course in Miracles*.

For the student of *A Course in Miracles*: You know that nothing real can be threatened, that nothing unreal exists, and therein lies the peace of God. You'll definitely find something *real* in this book, despite it being just an illusion.

This book will not teach you how to seek, apply, or live spiritual principles, it will show you how you *are* these principles. It's for everyone who wants *more* spiritual growth, and for the Truth seeker who wants to dig deeper into the universal spiritual principles upon which the philosophies I've named are based.

I remember when I had one year in my recovery program—I'd worked the 12 steps diligently under my sponsor's direction, could quote passages from the book backward and forward, knew the page numbers of important 12-Step *jewels*, and was attending six meetings every week. I remember thinking, "Is this it?" I mean, I was feeling much more peace and love for others and myself, but I wanted more! I've always been the over-achiever. Shaun, my best bud in the program, jokingly called me the Jesus Christ of the 12 Steps (more humility, please!) but I sure didn't feel like it. It seemed the more I learned, the more I realized how much more there was to learn.

So I went searching for more spirituality. I wanted answers, but I wasn't even sure what the questions were.

This is what I've found, so far.

Mark Reed, RScP

THE POWER OF *WE*

Each chapter contains a section entitled *The Power of We*. These insightful gems are contributions from friends, mentors, and fellow CSL practitioners—all members of my spiritual family, the West Valley Center for Spiritual Living in Peoria, Arizona. As we all know, there's strength in unity, and through their input and guidance I've learned there's also wisdom. I'm very grateful for their unique and insightful perspectives.

WVCSL Peeps: This is *our* book! Woo-hoo!

My Qualifying Story

I was born to two very loving parents in southeast Iowa and raised in college towns in southern and west central Illinois. I had a very happy childhood, numerous neighborhood friends, positive experiences in school, and a very close family. My parents were both social drinkers, very conservative with the libations. When I was twelve years old, I got tanked after drinking three beers I'd snuck from my parents' New Year's Eve party. I blacked out, whizzed on myself, and fell down a flight of stairs in front of their guests. The next morning, my father awoke me with the sound of a beer opening. "GISH!" He gave me a serious lecture on the evils of alcohol. Having been raised an Oklahoma Baptist, his tone was serious, but sincere and loving. "That's it," I thought, "I'll never do *that* again." Yeah, right.

I've heard countless alcoholics say, "I loved the feeling alcohol gave me." The love of that initial euphoria is one of the few things all alcoholics and drug addicts have in common. I'm no different. I loved that sensation. Booze made me feel brave, invincible, lucid, and articulate. In other words, *less fearful*. My heroes were the Rat Pack—I longed to be hip, slick, and cool like Frank and Dean-o, and when I drank alcohol, I came one step closer to that coolness.

My friends and I sought out every opportunity to get drunk on the weekends all throughout my high school years—always in search of the next party, the fake I.D., or the older looking teenager who could buy a bottle of Boone's Farm wine at the local drive-up window.

When I was 15, I was turned on to marijuana. My world shifted entirely. Weed gave me something better than the lucidity provided by alcohol—it provided a peaceful easy feeling I'd never experienced before, ever. Within six months, I had an entirely new group of friends, the stoners. Or as we called ourselves back in the 70's, the *freaks*.

I had a great deal of fun over the next four years, and if I could re-live those times, I'd do it exactly the same. As many addicts and alcoholics have said, drinking or using drugs started out being fun, then it was fun with problems, then it was just problems. From the age of 16-20, it was definitely fun. I felt like I was part of a community of enlightened and unique people, latter day hippies in the mid-1970s—people who were intellectually more aware, esoterically in tune, and definitely cooler than the squares that worked so hard to conform to a boring and un-hip society.

I loved college! I have many good memories of smoke-filled rooms, weird images combined with vibrant rock and roll, and brilliant philosophical conversations. I read authors like Carlos Castaneda, Werner Erhard, Ruth Montgomery, Ram Dass, Ken Kesey and a myriad of new age and metaphysical books. There was a plethora of laughter, camaraderie, and marijuana haziness in those college dorm rooms. Even today, I catch myself taking deep inhaling breaths while listening to the "Frampton Comes Alive" CD.

By my third year in college, I was un-motivated and un-focused. I couldn't decide on a college major and didn't really care. Deep down I knew I needed to make a drastic change in my life but didn't have any solutions. I knew I was addicted to weed and couldn't imagine my life without it, but continuing on the same course was a painful thought as well. I had to get out of the dark hole that was closing in around me. I sank into depression and attempted suicide. This was my first *bottom*.

So I turned to the military! Yes, that's the ticket—that'll man me up! I wasn't a gung-ho gun-lover type, I didn't have a hard-on to kill people in combat, I just wanted to straighten up and escape from Macomb, Illinois. So I joined the Air Force. I knew the military prohibited drug use, and believed the absence of it would straighten me out. I longed for good career direction, free college money, a clear head, and an ounce of genuine happiness.

Off I went to Texas for boot camp. I was a bit of a Sad Sack, probably too smart (or smartass) for my own good. They called me *College Boy*, and I didn't feel like I fit in, but my head was beginning to clear and I was gaining some much needed self-confidence. My first job was at a base in San Antonio, Texas as a Personnel Specialist, the perfect job for this people person. Within a week on the job, my Air Force supervisor, a staff sergeant, asked me if I got high and I was off and running again. I was stoned for my wedding ceremony a few months later, and high most every night after that, until the shit hit the fan. My supervisor was busted for selling weed and I was nearly implicated, but got off the hook. My supervisor ended up in Fort Leavenworth federal prison and several friends got the boot from the Air Force. Whew, that was a close one. I gave up marijuana entirely, again.

Today I have a good understanding of the nature of alcoholism and drug addiction, but I sure didn't in 1980. I was 22 years old and still wanted to party. When I stopped smoking weed, I drank more alcohol to fill the void. Within six months, my new wife demanded that I slow down, or quit. Dora challenged me to go 30 days without a drink. Ha! I could do that, and I did. That was the longest and most boring 30 days of my life. I took a long, hard look at myself and my marital situation and came to the conclusion that I'd probably need to make a choice: Dora or alcohol. Being the cunning little asshole that I was, I chose the third option—stay married and hide my drinking.

I got pretty good at concealing my disease and its manifestations, or so I thought. I had bottles hidden around the house, bottles clinking and clanking when I took out the trash, and bottles hidden in my car. This was exhausting. Then I'd drink just a tad too much before coming home and Dora would hear that dreaded slur in my speech. Shit—one too many! I was confronted by my supervisor for morning alcohol breath and had to start lying at work too. But I was a highly functioning alcoholic—while approaching my second bottom I was an Honor Graduate in Non-commissioned Officer (NCO) Leadership School and earned the NCO of the Year award for March Air Force Base. I was an over-achiever riddled with guilt, shame, and self-loathing. My life became one lie after another.

I was losing self-respect faster than I could lower my standards.

One day I had a moment of clarity and admitted my alcoholism jokingly to a kind and wise Master Sergeant.

Sergeant Essex said, "Mark, I've heard you joke about this before and I'm getting the feeling you're trying to tell us something. Tell me truthfully, do you have a drinking problem?"

I froze. We locked eyes and she stood their patiently looking at me. This is what *A Course in Miracles* calls a holy instant. Tears welled up in my eyes as that still, small voice, my True Self, whispered to me, "Say it." The entire world vanished in that moment and it was just Sergeant Essex and I standing there.

My voice sounded like it was in an echo chamber when I finally said, "Yes, I think I do." Waves of relief washed over me.

She responded, "Well, do you want some help?"

Without hesitating I said, "Yes, I do."

So began my journey. Sergeant Essex led me down the hall to see the Captain, but I felt no fear from that point forward. I was going to get help. I needed it badly.

28 days later, I was graduating from the March Air Force Base Alcohol Rehab Center. What an experience. I learned much about myself, the disease, and the actions required to maintain my sobriety. The kind and compassionate rehab center staff introduced me to the program contained in the 12 Steps and to the fellowship via meetings. I'd found a new home, both spiritually and socially.

I attended meetings every day, made loads of new friends, got a sponsor, and worked the Steps, sort of. Looking back, I was not very honest with myself during this period in my life. I was only 27 years old, very young according to my current standards of spiritual maturity. I'd been lying to myself for years, and it would take many more years to learn *my truth*.

I stayed sober for five years and had a wonderful life in the process. After 18 months of sobriety, the Air Force decided to cool my jets by sending me on a one-year work assignment to Iceland without Dora. That year was magical, a real growth period. We had three English-speaking meetings every week and I made tons of friends in recovery—American, Icelandic, and British. From there, Uncle Sam sent Dora and I to live in England, a Royal Air Force Base near Oxford. I missed my friends and began retreating to seclusion, throwing myself into work and travel. The excuses for not attending 12-Step meetings began to mount. My usual excuse: "I can't understand the British and Scottish accents in meetings." Dora became ill and needed quality American healthcare, so after eight months in England, we moved back to San Antonio, Texas.

I attended meetings in San Antonio, but the fire was gone; I just didn't have the same enthusiasm I did my first three years in the program. I was not applying the principles in my life, and I started to slip back into dishonesty, selfishness, and self-deception. While temporarily stationed in Saudi Arabia for Operation Desert Storm, I spent three days R&R on a British cruise ship, parked off the coast of Bahrain.

On that cruise ship, it had been months since I'd attended a meeting. I hadn't even brought 12-Step literature with me to Saudi. I was alone, but felt accepted by a group of G.I.s who were caught up in the excitement of drinking on the cruise ship. They hadn't drunk alcohol for two months and were excited to the point of hysteria. When the waitress pointed to me I was thinking, "Coke," but said, "Double gin and tonic."

Five years of sobriety down the drain. I was devastated. I have vague memories of the next three days on that cruise ship, confirmed only by photographs.

It would be another ten years before I was *really* honest with myself. So much happened during that period: I became a runner and competed in 5K and 10K road races almost every weekend. I retired from the Air Force and spent three heavenly years in graduate school in my hometown of Macomb, Illinois. I obtained my first job as a higher education student affairs professional at UC Berkeley, and I reveled in my new professional role as a career counselor at other Bay Area colleges—DeAnza College and Cal State Hayward. I also remained married to Dora, who continued to love me despite the lies and deception. The only other constant in my life during those ten years was alcohol and marijuana.

My third alcoholic bottom was more dramatic. After more than a year of drinking a pint of whiskey daily, I was sitting in my recliner at home contemplating suicide. How would I do it? How would Dora react? Would anyone come to my funeral? Probably not. I was in that dark hole again and I didn't see any way out. I painfully concluded that I really didn't want to kill myself, but I couldn't go on.

"What should I do?!" I tearfully cried aloud.

The answer came immediately, with perfect clarity. It came as a whisper, the voice of God. "Go back to the 12 Steps," It said.

So I did. I returned to meetings and the Steps. I was home again. I felt so relieved. I asked God to remove my obsession to drink and do drugs, and all the cravings vanished. I didn't desire anything except more recovery meetings. I lucked out by finding a dynamic and action-oriented men's meeting, a group of 70 guys that told the truth to each other, sharing in the common bond—the solution, the Steps, God.

What a crazy group of loving souls I stumbled upon. There were so many guys with the same first name that they got creative with nicknames. I was ushered into my first meeting by a friendly, chain-smoking guy named Pony Tail Steve and was introduced to another funny dude named Guitar Tim. My grand-sponsor was Tall Paul, and my friends were Shaun, Anthony, Barber Tim, Scary Gary, Fuckin' Pray Gary, Big Tim, Spiritual Phil, Slick, Gangster Al, Nascar Sam, Mikey, and Stewart.

I was the new guy for several months as my sponsor, Guitar Tim, and I worked the Steps. Step work, combined with fellowship dinners, picnics, retreats, workshops, camp outs, and dozens of phone calls each week, returned me to my center—back to God. The ego was no longer holding me hostage. I began to learn what love and service to others was all about. I lost 40 pounds and was proud of my new moniker, *Skinny Mark*.

I turned my will and life over to the care of a loving God, whom I did not understand, and threw myself into service to others. My Step work resulted in a series of light bulbs over my head. I learned:

- How selfish and self-centered I'd been my entire life, always concerned with *my* pleasures and desires.
- Life is better if I ask for help.
- Helping others makes life better.
- Even if I could solve life's problems alone, why would I want to? Life is more enjoyable when I'm interacting with others.
- I have no control over people, places, and things—only what's in my mind.
- With God, all things are possible.
- Pain is optional. Thank you P.B.
- Accepting life on life's terms results in more inner peace.
- No one rents space in my head. If I'm holding onto a resentment, I need to let it go if I desire peace and happiness. No one can make me angry except me.
- I'd rather be happy than right.
- Expectations make life suck.
- Praying for you helps me.
- Marriage is not 50/50. I strive to give 100%.
- Lack of self-honesty always results in pain.
- Rigorous honesty may lead to pain, but results in peace.
- Willingness to be open and change is how change happens.
- To be humble is to seek and do God's will.
- Hurting others by clearing *my conscience* is still hurting others.
- Don't expect forgiveness from others, but always be willing to give it.
- Happiness and peace come one moment at a time.

After a year working the steps, both my parents died within months of each other. Without God in my life, I would surely have lost touch with reality and probably dug my dark hole deeper. Instead I felt gratitude for my loving parents and thankful for the love they gave their children. I was grateful to them for the lessons they taught us, for the good life and upbringing they provided, and so I focused on being strong and loving my brother and sister even more. Gratitude saved me.

Dora and I moved to Arizona a few months later. I've lost touch with many, but not all, of those crazy guys in California. I have not lost touch with the values and principles I learned from a loving, service-oriented group of men . . . and the Steps. I've returned over the years to join them on the annual campout. I love the large campfire meetings and the camaraderie. I put on a few pounds but that's okay—my moniker is now "Arizona Mark." Over 10 years have passed since I started working the 12 Steps again. I think, feel, believe, and act like a completely different person. I experience inner peace more often, I'm genuinely happy with my life, and I know that the most important thing I can do at any given moment is to love myself, and others. My spiritual path has been transformed from a dirt path to a broad freeway. My potential is completely unlimited.

My Spiritual Journey

Having gotten clean and sober in the best 12-Step men's group on the planet, I knew I wanted more spiritual community, what the Buddhists call *sangha*—a spiritual family, people who were seeking answers like me, and would offer love and support in the process. Dora and I started exploring various Christian churches. Man oh man, that was painful.

Today I believe that all spiritual paths are sacred, but in 2005 I was a bit more judgmental. As soon as people stood up during those Christian church services with their hands held high in the air shouting "Amen," a shiver of revulsion would run up my spine and I'd say to Dora, "Come on, we're out of here!" She was on the same wave length as I, so it's not like I was dragging her down the aisle and out the door. We explored numerous churches until, again, my 12-Step fellowship pointed the way for me.

A 12-Step old-timer suggested I read *Sermon on the Mount*, by Emmet Fox and when I told him later how much I loved the book and its "new" approach to spirituality, he suggested I try the Unity Church. Dora and I attended services there the following weekend and I had a life-altering experience. It was a very subtle spiritual experience, but I knew I'd found an open door, behind which lay a wisdom-filled and love-based path for my new life. This notion was cemented when I walked into that Unity church's bookstore and saw an entire rack of Emmet Fox books. "Yes!" I said to Dora, "this is the place." She agreed!

We didn't have Emmet Fox in the bookstore at the Presbyterian Church in Macomb, Illinois, where I'd grown up. Hell, we didn't even have a bookstore.

Six months later, we moved to Phoenix, Arizona to be closer to Dora's family and searched for a new spiritual community again. I looked for Unity churches online and came across a web site for a strangely named church, the Spiritual Enrichment Center. I thought, "Hmm, that sounds a bit new agey. Let's give it a try."

The following Sunday was another transformative experience for me. When we walked into the Spiritual Enrichment Center, we were greeted by hugs and laughter, and you could feel the crackle of positive vibes in the air. The bookstore contained a slew of Emmet Fox books, plus many other contemporary New Thought works. Reverend Ron Fox was the minister, and he later became my mentor. The talk he delivered that day sounded positive and upbeat. I noticed a conspicuous absence of terms like: sin, hell, punishment, reborn, judge, repent, atone, cross, or my favorite Old Testament word, *gnashing*. Instead, I heard phrases like, "You are whole, perfect, and complete as you are," "Spirit is within," "We co-create along with God," and, "It is done onto you as you believe." An entirely new universe appeared on my horizon.

I learned what Religious Science was that day. This practical philosophy, also called *Science of Mind*, after the same-titled book written by Ernest Holmes in 1926, re-named itself the "Centers for Spiritual Living" in the mid-2000s. No longer will it be confused with Scientology or be burdened with that emotionally-charged word: *Religious*. It's the 21st century—time for this New Thought faith to claim a name that better describes its essence.

I jumped in with both feet. Dora and I took the Foundation class that fall and I continued taking one class after another, just eating up the new ideas that my intuition (True Self) was confirming to be absolutely right on. By the next fall, I was in a 2-year Practitioner Training program to become a spiritual practitioner. More than anything, I learned how to pray, affirmatively. We prayed our asses off in that training program, and our affirmative prayers were like nothing I'd ever been taught in the Presbyterian Church.

So there I was in 2009, a graduate of *Science of Mind* Practitioner training with five years clean and sober. I can't begin to describe how different a person I was then compared to the day I walked into a 12-Step meeting in 2004. God had given me my life back when *He* urged me to attend a 12-Step meeting five years earlier. The 12 steps then pressed me to seek out more of God. And then I learned that I am an individual expression of God and this Universal Spirit encompasses MY mind. I felt like Dorothy in the "Wizard of Oz" when she learned she'd never left Kansas.

That's why I've written this book—to explain how this Universal Power that I *still* call God can be used in a very practical way to improve your life and claim your *Good*. It works, it really does.

CHAPTER ONE

Life is a Journey

"Each one of us is an outlet to God and an inlet to God."
— Ernest Holmes, The Science of Mind

"God has given you the means for undoing what you have made. Listen, and you will learn how to remember what you are."
— A Course in Miracles

"You will make lifelong friends. You will be bound to them with new and wonderful ties, for you will escape disaster together and you will commence shoulder to shoulder your common journey."
— Alcoholics Anonymous

Imagine for a moment that your life is a journey. Your traveling adventure begins on the day you're born. As an infant and toddler, your perceptions of your journey are new, strange, fresh, and sometimes frightening. As a young child, you become aware of yourself as a separate entity, and your journey begins to widen in its scope as you learn about choices, consequences, destinations, and roadblocks. As a young adult, your identity starts to solidify as you gain confidence in yourself. You see a wide vista before you with many different roads, forks, destinations, and rest stops.

During your adult years, your journey is jam-packed with adventure. You experience success, happiness, security, and excitement by choosing certain roads; or tragedy, despair, disappointment, and loneliness by choosing alternative routes. Your journey is filled with hills, valleys, flat plains, diversions, and deep ruts. Sometimes you're stuck in neutral, at other times you're driving too fast for conditions. Most of the time you're just cruising.

Now imagine you're coming to the end of this journey. Physical death is eminent. As you look back, you realize that while you were experiencing your journey, it seemed long, sometimes arduous. Now toward the end, it seems too short. What was your journey like?

How did you perceive your journey? Was it an amusement, adventure, or an excursion? Did you think of it as a getaway, holiday, or an escape from something? Was your outlook on your journey more of an odyssey, a pilgrimage, or a quest toward reaching a goal? Was it a relaxing so-journ, a joyride, or was it a race? Do you feel like you had control over your journey or were you just along for the ride? Perhaps it was both at times. Did you ramble, roam, sashay, saunter, or stroll on your journey? Were you at times a weary traveler? Did you sometimes just wander?

Looking back on our journey as if it's already happened sheds new light on it. How have you approached your journey, and how will your perception of it change *today* as you examine and reflect on it?

Did you have an itinerary? Was your destination monetary success, material possessions, and luxury vacations? Or was it financial security, emotional stability gained through relationships, or a sense of belong-ing? Was your life centered on your family—your children and grand-children? Were you goal-driven in your work? Did you have a destination at all? Perhaps you realized that destinations may not be revealed for many years, if at all.

How far encompassing was your journey? Was your perception global? Or local? Was your outlook wide and roomy, like a broad highway? Or was it narrow and confined, like a jungle path?

How did you deal with obstacles? The traffic jams, speeding tickets, and unexpected turns? Did you learn from your challenges, or continue to make the same mistakes? Did you get along well with others, or con-stantly butt heads? Did you notice any patterns in your roadblocks? Did you come to a realization about fear? Did you see it for what it was?

Did you enjoy your journey? Did you take advantage of the perks? Did you learn to rest and recuperate, or were you always on the go? Was it pleasurable? Did it include some play-time, recreation, and refreshment?

How did you treat yourself along the way? Did you ride first class, business class, or coach? Did you learn to love yourself, be kind and gen-tle with yourself, and tap into your intuition? Or did you hurt yourself through self-destructive behavior and a hurtful self-image? Did you learn how to quiet your mind and experience inner peace? Was your journey a rough passage or a long haul? Or was it a peaceful drive through the country?

What was the purpose of your journey? Did you have a travel plan, or develop one along the way? What did you use to navigate? Did you take the main routes or journey on the roads less traveled? Did you ever get an answer to that age-old question, "What is the meaning of life?"

Did you travel with anyone on your journey? Was your travel single- or double-occupancy? Did you seek out fellow travelers? Did you travel by convoy, seeking gatherings and get-togethers? Did you have a guide?

That last question, "Did you have a guide?" is the subject of this book. Your guide is within. It's always available, never says no, and loves you deeply. Its purpose is to support and guide you along your journey. It lights the way, teaches you how to maneuver through life, and offers you a helping hand when you stumble and fall. It's your teacher, your guru, and your best friend, forever. It will do *anything* for you . . . as you turn your attention to it.

Your guide is your True Self. Godspeed on your journey.

Who-You-Really-Are

Here is one of the most important life lessons to learn: You are perfect. Exactly as you are, you're perfect. Like a beautiful red rose that lacks nothing to be a beautiful red rose, you lack absolutely nothing to be the perfect you that you are. Nothing is missing from you, and you're not limited by words like good and bad. Perfect means you lack nothing. You do not need to seek anything or anyone to be the whole, perfect, and complete soul that you already are. You're a luminous being of light. This is who-you-really-are.

You're perfect because you're an individual expression of God, Spirit, Infinite Intelligence, Universal Conscious Source Energy, whichever name or word you use to describe Spirit/God.

(*Note: For the purpose of this book, when you see a capitalized descriptive word like Spirit, Light, Eternal, Infinite, or Truth, it's a reference to, or a quality of Spirit/God.*)

Who-you-really-are is a catchphrase to symbolize your True Self, also referred to in spiritual texts as the Higher Self, God-Self, Spirit within, the True Essence, or your Divine Self. Christianity calls it the Holy Spirit. Psychology refers to it as the superego, New Thought religions call it the indwelling Christ Consciousness, and popular culture calls it *that still, small voice* or the angel (as opposed to a fictitious devil) sitting on your shoulder.

The notion that you need to choose between the good angel or the bad devil is simply a miscreation of the ego. It implies that you're separate from your True Self, which you're not. This idea of separation from God is just ego-created smoke and mirrors. You can never be separated from God any more than water can be separated from wet. Nothing is separate from or opposes All-That-Is.

Your True Self, the subject of this book, is your connection to God. It's the bridge, within your own consciousness, to the Universal. God has placed it there to communicate with you. Your True Self is your two-way radio, or cell phone if you will, to God. It's your teacher, your counselor, your comforter, and your wisdom. It's your inspiration, your intuition, and your provider of peace. It's the source of all the love you've ever known. Your True Self is your savior. It's not returning to you in a distant future, it's right here, right now. You need never look for God again because you're an expression of God, and the True Self is God's voice—in you, through you, as you.

Universal Spirit encompasses everything and every person in the known and unknown universes. It's the all, the all *in* all. This Perfect Infinite Energy Pattern is at the core of every living creature. It is the spark of God. Your soul is made of the same cosmic God energy as the planets and stars. You literally are one with all. *It* is found in and at the heart and soul of every person, animal, insect, fish, amoeba, bacteria, rock, tree, mountain, and ocean, everything in the universe. Regardless of who you think you are, what you think, feel, and believe, or what you say or do, you're an individual expression of the Infinite. This applies to Adolph Hitler as much as Mother Teresa.

This All-Encompassing Spirit/Essence, or *matter reduced to an extreme thinness* as described by transcendentalist Ralph Waldo Emerson, is all Good, all Loving, all Life-Giving, all the time. It's all-powerful, all knowing, everywhere present, and at all points in space throughout the universe, simultaneously. Truth, Light, Love, all that's Good in this universe, is God. It's without opposite—there's no Satan, Lucifer, or evil force, nothing that opposes it. It's Indivisible, Whole, Complete, and Perfect. *A Course in Miracles* states that we can't really define Spirit/God, that the words we use to describe It are just symbols of symbols. Spirit/God is *an experience.*

Spirit/God simply is All. And true to the popular catchphrase, "It's *all* Good!"

Long ago there lived a king who searched his kingdom far and wide for an understanding of God. After years of searching, he finally comprehended God, and an entirely new path of understanding opened up to him. He understood. He saw Reality in a completely new light. This type of transformation can be described as a gradual spiritual awakening. The answer was there all the time, but the king wasn't ready to understand it until he reached a certain point on his spiritual path.

He finally understood that God was not a person, a personality, or a being, although It *could* be if It so chose to be, because It was everyone and everything. It was far too vast to be limited to personhood. It was too complex to be thought of in human terms, with human ideas. He thought, "How could some Thing that is *all* Love be vengeful or wrathful?"

He realized it was silly to think of this Infinite Intelligence in terms of sexual gender, nationality, or ethnicity. He realized *we* had created God in *our* image, with our limited consciousness. *So* it came naturally to this king to think of God as a Thing, even referring to It as *It*. After many months of meditation, he concluded that he *could* have a deep, personal relationship with something he called *It*. "After all," he concluded after much reflection, "It's inside me, and I'm made of It." The King realized that the bond he had with God depended on his connecting with It within his own consciousness, through his True Self, on a moment to moment basis.

The king decided it really didn't matter what he called this indwelling Spirit: Father, Mother, God, Allah, Jehovah, Buddha, Krishna, Unity, All-That-Is. The names he used, or how he envisioned It were not as important as knowing It was in his mind and soul, and that he could never be separate from It.

Because of this knowledge that the indwelling God is a Force, a Power, Pure Energy, and Infinite Intelligence, It can be even more personal to you than the image of the grandfatherly figure sitting on a heavenly throne. God is everywhere present at all times, which means God is in you. How much more of a personal relationship could you have than that which is within you? God is not just some impersonal principle, energy field, or cosmic law. God is who you are.

From Ernest Holmes' *Think Your Troubles Away:*

"God is not a person, yet God is more than a principle. The creative insistence of the universe, the emotional background of all incentive is God—the Urge and the act, the Thinker and that which is thought, the Conceiver and the conceived. Cause and effect are but two sides of the same coin. He who looks for God as a person must look into the personification. The universe may be impersonal as law and as essence, but It is forever personifying Itself. It is revealed in creation."

Imagine a jellyfish wondering if it could have a personal relationship with water. It's made of water! Your spiritual growth makes the Infinite and Universal not more remote and vague, but more warm and loving. A wise sage once remarked, "I think of God as an all-encompassing Power and Presence, incomprehensible to the human mind, but when I'm feeling very low, I may think of this Power as a very large and loving man. I crawl up into his lap and he hugs me tightly, strokes my hair, and whispers to me that he loves me."

God is a presence and power within each of us. We're individual manifestations of God, God expresses Life through us. The phrase *children of God* means we're brothers and sisters to each other. More specifically, we're *All One*. Each of us is *within* God, because God is the All-ness of the universe, and God is within each of us. As Jesus said in Luke 17, "Behold, the kingdom of God is within you." We live within God, and God is within us. We're completely one with God.

When a drop of blood is taken from the body and analyzed, we find it's comprised of the exact same DNA as the blood that's still in the entire body. The individual drop of blood is not the entire body, but it's an exact reflection of it. All living creatures are exact replicas of our Creator, without actually being the Creator. We're not gods, but are individual expressions of the One God. All that God is, we are also. This is our birthright. This is who-you-really-are.

A wave is part of the ocean, yet expresses itself individually as a wave. Even when crashing onto the beach as a seemingly individual entity, the wave is still part of the larger ocean. The wave is never separated from the ocean. The ocean expresses itself to the world in many different ways, one of which is the wave.

To think of God as outside you or separate from you is the problem. It's ego-based thinking that thrives on discord, disharmony, separation, and competition. The ego lives to divide and conquer, to maintain this illusion of control you must remain separate from your Source Power.

The solution then, is the recognition of Unity. You're one with God, an individual expression of It—this Presence being the very fabric of your soul.

There are no divisions, partitions, classifications, and categories in the mind of God. Dig deep within yourself and you know this to be true. Your True Self knows intuitively that there are no such things as different races, ethnicities, countries, genders, religions, beliefs—these human-made descriptions exist only in the limited minds of humans, the ego mind. Your True Self knows these differences don't exist.

In truth, you know there's only Love. Anyone who uses a spiritual teaching or religion to create fear or separation, or puts God, Buddha, or Jesus on an unreachable and distant pedestal, doesn't understand the universal principle that binds all teachings in truth—Love. Love is the common denominator in all of us. We all have the same ability to experience God's Love on a moment-to-moment basis just by acknowledging its presence within us.

To a person, we pretty much all agree on the existence of love, yet we can't describe it because it's something ethereal, intangible. Most, if not all, major religions define God as Love or loving: God is Love, Love is God. The next time someone asks you "What is the meaning of life," you can say with all confidence, "To love yourself and others."

When someone says to you, "You're whole, perfect, and complete," they're not acting as happy ambassadors of the positive thinking club, they're telling you the Truth. They're describing you accurately, because every effort you've ever made in your life to be at peace or loved has been unnecessary. You *are* peace. God is peace, therefore *you* are peace. God is Love, therefore *you* are love, God is Joy, therefore *you* are joy. All that God is, you are also. There's no need to seek, only to realize and accept what already is.

The Creative Process and the Law of Cause and Effect

The Infinite is always creating, this is Its nature. It's always emanating life-giving energy, always shining Its light, always expressing Love. Every nanosecond of every day, It's creating life. This Universal Energy finds a channel or way to express through everything that has life. It's self-organizing and consistent, acting as a natural pattern. There's mathematical precision to God's creative process. Nature is a perfect example, as is the perfectly balanced and harmonious processes of a body's physiology.

To the degree you're aware of and use this Creative Power in alignment with Its nature, you're happy and in the flow of life. This Power can set you free or bind you in misery, depending on how you use It. Jesus summed it up in the phrase, "It is done onto you as you believe." If you're miserable or hurt yourself or others, it's not because punishment is being imposed on you, but because you're ignorant of, or misuse this Power. As Ernest Holmes so aptly put it, "There is no sin, but a mistake; no punishment, but a consequence."

When a seed is planted, it grows into the plant or flower that was in the original design of the seed, with no exceptions. The seed is the cause, the soil is the medium in which it grows, and the plant or flower is the effect. If carrot seeds are planted, you do not expect to harvest radishes.

The soil doesn't say, "I think I'll produce watermelons instead of carrots from these seeds." The soil is neutral. So too, your thoughts, ideas, and beliefs are your seeds. When you think (the cause), you plant those thoughts into your subconscious mind (the soil), and through the Law of Cause and Effect (a.k.a., the Law), which always says "Yes," the effects of your thoughts blossom. You create your own reality, every moment of every day. You're completely responsible for every condition, effect, or circumstance of your life.

You can never escape the Law of Cause and Effect. It applies to everyone and everything equally, depending on how you use your creative ability. The Law is completely neutral, playing no favorites, it's receptive to all thought. This is what Jesus meant in Matthew 5:45 when he said, "He causes his sun to rise on the evil and the good, and sends rain on the righteous and the unrighteous." The Law of Cause and Effect is the great equalizer, giving every conscious being the equal opportunity to create his/her own existence. This law gives you absolute freedom.

It's important to understand that the Law of Cause and Effect is not just a principle. It's a spiritual *substance* that is *part* of God. We are surrounded and enveloped by this Law. It's part of who we are. We individualize it in the form of our subconscious mind.

In one of the most profound and influential spiritual literary works of the 20th century, *The Science of Mind*, by Ernest Holmes, the author refers to this Universal Law as the Creative Medium. More recently, quantum physicists are calling it the Unified Field Theory. Being receptive, it doesn't analyze, dissect, or deny, it just receives and produces what it's given. On the universal level, a divine pattern of life thinks into it (the seed) and produces galaxies, stars, planets, atmospheres, land-masses, animals, insects—all of life. On the personal level, this Creative Medium receives the imprint of our thoughts and produces that which is thought into it—ideas, emotions, beliefs, attitudes, outlooks, as well as the entire human-made material world. The stronger the thought is, the more likely it will manifest. The emotions (the *fire*) attached to your thoughts give them more strength in the creative process.

This Creative Medium can be both a curse and a treasure. Yes, it will bear fruit from the negative seeds you plant into it—anger, depression, fear, or envy—but it also provides you with complete freedom and pure potential—you are the master of your own reality.

Your creative nature directly reflects that of the Universal (God). Every thought you think is a creation and results in some manifestation, even if you cannot see that creation immediately. The thought, "I'm miserable," is just as creative as the thought "I'm happy and grateful." Whether you use it for your expansion or destruction, the Law of Cause and Effect is your servant.

How is this creative process practical? Well, think of it this way: When you have a problem or challenge, approach the solution from the perspective of *cause* rather than *effect*.

For example: A neighbor has been irritating you to no end lately. The cause of this situation is your own irritation/anger/frustration, *not* your neighbor. The neighbor is the effect—you cannot change him/her, although you can try. This is where most of us make our mistakes—we try so hard to change the world around us, and people within it, not really understanding that the causes of all our problems are within us. We're constantly banging our heads against a wall, trying to get others to do and be as we wish. We're trying to make a change to an effect rather than its cause, our own mind.

So you get irritated at your neighbor because of a thought pattern or belief within your consciousness, and it's based in fear. You need to identify what that fear is, and fully understand why you get irritated with your neighbor, and then you can begin to let go of the obstructing or limiting beliefs. This is why one person might get angry because of a stimulus and another person may not. The *problem* is within each person, not the stimulus. The solution is also within your mind. When resolving any problem you have, always look *within* first to identify and change the cause. This is the proper use of your Divine creative power.

Here's another example: You're worried that you don't have enough money to pay your bills. The cause of this problem is your belief system regarding the principle of abundance, or in this case, lack of it. Your worries (fear) are caused by your limiting beliefs. The problem is not money, bills, creditors, unfair billing practices, your paycheck, your employer, or your bank, none of these. These things are all in the world of effect. You're working from cause. You know that you need to change your beliefs to see the fear for what it is, and release it. When you do, you're no longer worried. You *still* may not have enough money to cover your bills, you may default on your creditors, or even go bankrupt, but you feel no fear about it. You've addressed the cause.

God, the Universal Creative Intelligence, works for you, through you, as you allow It. This Intelligence has been described as Infinite Possibility and Pure Potentiality because at any given moment in time, the creation of anything, anything at all, is possible. By cooperating with natural universal laws, specifically, the Law of Mind, you can create any life circumstance you desire. You've heard the phrase, "prayer can move mountains," and it can, physically. But this Universal Power can only do so as you allow it to work through you. It desires to express through you, this is Its natural channel. Therefore, and this is very important, you should have complete faith in Its ability to change your thinking and thus, your life. Your conscious awareness, desire, and use of God, through you, can and does result in miracles. That miracle could be as simple as you deciding to be happy rather than sad.

An acorn drops onto the ground and through a perfect creative process that follows a universal pattern, blossoms into a mighty oak tree. Within that acorn is the full and unwavering potential for an oak tree. *That*, in itself, is a miracle. The human baby forms in the womb using the same exact universal pattern. The first chair ever invented was created using the same pattern—a human had the thought, "wouldn't it be nice to have something I could sit on and rest my weary bones?" This thought eventually blossomed into the invention of a chair. Everything around you began as a thought. Every thought, with no exceptions, is creative.

Every thought is subject to the Law of Cause and Effect, but not every thought is based in Truth. You can use this Universal Power within you for good or bad, It responds either way. If you think to yourself, "I want to quit smoking," the Law of Cause and Effect responds in kind by creating a desire to quit smoking, which is not to say that you'll quit smoking. If the Law could talk, It would say, "Yes! You want to quit smoking." Conversely, if a person thinks, "I'm so grateful for the strength to say no to tobacco, and I'm thankful for the freedom I now have," the Law responds with "Yes! You're grateful for your strength and thankful for your freedom." The Law always says, "Yes!"

If you have any doubt that this Universal Law of Mind can work positively for you, look at what this same Law has manifested for you as a result of your negative thoughts. None of us would disagree with the idea that we create our own misery. We see examples galore every day. Our own fear, guilt, grief, or anger drive us to act inappropriately, or result in some form of mental pain. Man #1 insults Man #2. Man #2 gets angry and punches Man #1. This is a perfect example of how we use this Law of Mind negatively—seed, soil, plant.

In *The Science of Mind*, Ernest Holmes writes:

"Our belief is that anything the mind thinks, it can un-think. If therefore, by the Law of Cause and Effect we have produced unpleasant conditions, we should be able by this same law to produce an entirely different effect."

What Holmes is saying is that not only can we reverse our negative and destructive thoughts, but, we can completely undo them by refusing to entertain these thoughts in our minds. Going further, we can then embrace Truth in our consciousness—love, peace, joy, patience, understanding—all those universal principles that are *of God* and at our core—and can completely transform our lives. Remember, you're pure Spirit, just as God is, and just as thoughts are. You can have absolute control of your thoughts, and therefore the effects of your life. Having a disciplined mind is the basis of Buddhism.

If you think, "I'm at peace," the Law says, "Yes, you're at peace." If you think, "I'm worried," the Law says, "Yes, you're worried." You create your own emotional states all day long. You have complete freedom to create the existence you want for yourself.

If you think, "I'm powerless," the Law states, "Yes! You're powerless." If you don't want to be selfish, but you think and talk about *your* selfishness, claiming it as your own, even while asking it to be removed, the Law responds, stating, "Yes, you're selfish and you want *your* selfishness to be removed." Be careful what you think. When you name it, you claim it.

Consider this affirmative statement (prayer):

"I love others, I love myself, and I love God. I release all thoughts, ideas, and beliefs in selfishness as I think about serving others and acting on that desire. I am giving, I am loving, I care deeply for others and act on their behalf. I am grateful to know who-I-really-am and of my creative ability. Today I choose peace, joy, service to others, forgiveness, patience, understanding of self and others, harmony, self-discipline, strength, courage, and a joyous and enthusiastic zest for life. All these things are who I am and I give thanks."

The two most sacred words in the English language are *I am.* Be careful which words you place after them. Every thought has power. Every thought is a form of prayer.

Don't Blaspheme Yourself—You Are Super

The concept of blasphemy is interesting. Back in the day, after the reign of the first Christian Roman emperor Constantine in the third century, Christianity started to become a serious religion. Early church leaders were committed to gaining respect for their new venture. Opposition to the church and its One God was met with harsh judgment and punishment. The current form of the word *blasphemy* dates back to the 13th century, from the Greek *blasphemia*, meaning to speak ill of, or slander sacred things. Another origin is from the Greek *blaptikos*, which means hurtful or even stupid. By the mid-14th century, the word shifted to, *one meaning blame.*

A Course in Miracles talks about humankind's *depression*, a general term referring to our perceived separateness from God. From the *Course:*

"Depression means you have foresworn God. Many are afraid of blasphemy, but they do not understand what it means. They do not realize that to deny God is to deny their own Identity."

Your perceived separateness, the root of all your troubles, problems, and concerns, is an illusion. You cannot be separate from God any more than fire can be separated from hot. God is in your spiritual DNA. Your soul is made of God Essence.

Yet you listen to the ego instead of your True Self, and you do this most of the time. You entertain fears, resentments, judgments of self and others, guilt, shame, and that false belief that you're just not enough. While you're doing this throughout the day, your True Self stands idly by—smiling, winking, and waiting. It says, "I love you beyond measure and want the best for you. I'm here, use me." Sometimes you listen, especially when life gets to be too much. Even though pain and misery are just miscreations of the ego, they're the common bond we all share. Emotional pain is a great motivator to return back to God in consciousness.

Clark Kent is like the ego identity. Superman created this identity to live in this world, but it's not who he truly is. Clark Kent is just a mask. Underneath those spectacles and suit is a super being, imbued with power and strength. Superman is Superman's true identity. Your True Self is *your* true identity. It is forged from pure Love. Everything else—all thoughts and beliefs that seemingly oppose your super identity are just an add-on, not manufacturer-installed.

Have you ever tried to argue with someone who just smiles at you and remains positive and loving? When you argue with, deny, ignore, or blame God, you hurt yourself, not God. According to the origin of the word blasphemy, you're even being a bit stupid—the British would say *thick.*

God is Love, only Love, and wants only the best for you. When you turn your back on God, you're turning your back on yourself, your true identity. The inspirational phrase, "be true to yourself," is so popular in our culture because it rings true. Your intuition whispers to you that it's a universal certainty. When the ego's defenses go down, when your *shields* are dropped, and the ego's temper tantrum subsides, there's only God, waiting, smiling, loving.

Again, from *A Course in Miracles:*

"If God knows His children as wholly sinless, it is blasphemous to perceive them as guilty. If God knows His children as wholly without pain, it is blasphemous to perceive suffering anywhere. If God knows His children to be wholly joyous, it is blasphemous to feel depressed. All of these illusions, and the many other forms that blasphemy may take, are refusals to accept creation as it is."

Thinking? Or Action?

There's an old saying heard in 12-Step meetings, "You cannot *think* yourself into right action, you must *act* your way to right thinking." There are those who think the opposite. Perhaps we're playing in semantics, like the chicken and egg riddle.

It's understandable why Bill W. and the original members of the 12-Step groups would think this way: Their best *thinking* resulted in them hitting their bottom in the depths of alcoholism. They tried every remedy known to man to quit drinking and came to distrust their own self-destructive thinking. Their minds were their own worst enemies. Through *action* for the benefit of others, by helping their fellow alcoholics, they had a spiritual transformation. Let's look at the flip side.

In *The Science of Mind*, Ernest Holmes writes:

"Since it is the mind which must first come to see, know and understand— and since all future possibility for the race must find an avenue of outlet through someone's mind—we shall do well to look to the mind for the answer to all our problems."

Holmes was describing the Divine Creative Process through which you create your own reality. A seed is planted—you think a thought with your conscious mind. The thought is, "I intend to lead a healthy lifestyle." The seed is planted into the soil of your subconscious mind—that very large and deep part of your mind, the 90% of the brain scientists tell us we don't use. An effect or result blossoms—you propel yourself to take action by eating healthy and getting fit. Seed—Soil—Blossom. The initial thought is the cause, the subconscious mind is the belief greenhouse that nurtures, safeguards, and activates the thought, and your behavior is the effect. Your thinking is always the *first cause.*

Holmes goes on to write:

"It has been proved that by thinking correctly and by a conscious mental use of the Law of Mind, we can use it to do definite things for us, through us. By conscious thinking, we give conscious direction to It."

The "It" Holmes refers to is God, the Law of Mind, the Universal Creative Power that flows through us. Your thoughts are the seeds that produce the crops that are your life circumstances, just as God's thoughts create cells, atoms, oceans, and planets. You're a reflection of the Divine and have complete dominion over the effects of your life. But you can only channel as much of this Creative Power as you can conceive.

How much *good* can you conceive for yourself? How strong is your faith? How big is the receptacle of your mind that you allow Spirit to pour Itself into? Is it a thimble? A bucket? A pond? An ocean?

You use your creative mental power whether you know it or not. You use this power negatively every day to create feelings, situations, and life circumstances that you *don't* want and you're not aware that you're doing this. The Law of Cause and Effect, which governs your reality as much as the Law of Gravity, is responding to your every thought.

Holmes also writes:

"If we believe that it [the Law of Cause and Effect] will not work, It really works by appearing to "not work." When we believe that It cannot and will not, then, in accordance with principle, It DOES NOT. But when It does not, It still does—only It does according to our belief that It will not . . . God does not punish the mathematician who fails to obtain the right answer to a problem. The thought of the unsolved problem does punish him [the mathematician] until he applies the right principle and thus secures the desired result."

Your thoughts create either the desired or undesired results of your life through this invisible Law.

Right action *can* change your thinking. Right thinking can then lead to more right action, resulting in more right thinking, and so on—a cycle powered by momentum, like the little train engine from the children's book *The Little Engine That Could*. The little engine would say, "I think I can, I think I can, I think I can" as it chugged up the hill. The train engine's initial thought of, "I think I can" was the seed that resulted in its first chug. Its action generated more thoughts of, "I think I can" that powered it onward and upward. Eventually, the little train engine was shouting, "I *know* I can!"

A recovering alcoholic tells of his experiences with "action as a causative force" that changed his thinking:

"When I was about six months sober I finished my fourth step self-inventory. What I learned about myself was both revealing and depressing. I realized that up to that point in my life, I'd been a very selfish and self-centered person in regard to my friends, and especially in my marriage. I suppose I could have taken what I learned, turned inward, and become depressed

and self-pitying, but I knew that would just be sustaining the self-centeredness. I wanted to change, but didn't know how. What do you do to be less self-centered? So I took direction from my sponsor.

I started to think about the needs and desires of everyone around me and began acting on their behalf. This was new territory for me and was a little unsettling at first. In my 12-Step group, I turned to the guys with less sobriety than me and began sticking around after meetings to talk to them, asking what step they were on, and talking about my experiences working the steps. I drove newcomers to meetings and made two lifelong friends in the process. I made coffee at the meetings, emptied ashtrays, stacked chairs, and hung around, assisting anyone who needed help. I made phone calls to guys, asking how they were doing, listening to them, and offering my strength, hope, and experience.

At home, I dedicated myself to listening sincerely to my wife, being positive, agreeable, encouraging, and helpful. We did things SHE wanted to do, I put away my desire to be right, and I began seeing her in an entirely new light. At work, I tried hard to be a good team member and follower, which took everyone there by surprise. I was nice to people, cooperative, and did my best to fit in positively instead of standing out negatively.

A year later, I looked back at this period and realized that in the process of doing all this, I changed the way I thought about others, myself, and my relationship with God, my director."

Your True Self is your source for right thinking, leading to right action. "The Kingdom of Heaven is at hand," exclaimed Jesus. It's right where you are, your True Self is pointing the way for you.

Useful Affirmations

I am one with God, always and forever.

Spirit is within me, and I'm within Spirit.

God's Power is my power. I am fueled by God.

As a wave is to the ocean, so I am to Universal Spirit.

All living creatures are my spiritual family. I am One with all.

God is in my D.N.A.

I am creating the reality I desire.

I change my thoughts, I change my world.

Every thought I think is a prayer.

Rhyming Affirmations

I am healthy, whole, and complete,
From the top of my head to the souls of my feet

I am ONE with everyone and everything,
People are the spice that give life zing!

I listen for the voice of the Infinite within,
When I follow its lead, I always win.

I tune my radio to that Power in my mind,
It receives my message and transmits in kind.

I am never alone, God's presence is here,
I open to the Light and the shadows disappear.

CHAPTER TWO

More About Spirit/God

Mind—the Thing, Spirit, Causation—is beyond, and yet not beyond, our grasp. Beyond, in that It is so big; within, in that wherever we grasp at It, we are It to the extent that we grasp It; but since It is Infinite, we can never encompass It. We shall never encompass God, and yet we shall always be in God and of God!

—Ernest Holmes, *The Science of Mind*

Oneness is simply the idea God is. And in His Being, He encompasses all things. No mind holds anything but Him. We say "God is," and then we cease to speak, for in that knowledge words are meaningless.

—*A Course in Miracles*

We found that as soon as we were able to lay aside prejudice and express even a willingness to believe in a Power greater than ourselves, we commenced to get results, even though it was impossible for any of us to fully define or comprehend that Power, which is God.

—*Alcoholics Anonymous*

How Good is Your God?

In *The Science of Mind*, Ernest Holmes writes:

There is one original cause out of which we are made. We know that this is what we are—because we could not be anything else—but we don't know how much of this we are! When we see It as It is, then, we shall see ourselves as we are. We can only see It by looking at It through our own eyes. Hence, we shall find a better God when we shall have arrived at a higher standard for man. If God is to interpret Himself to man, He must interpret Himself through man. And the Spirit can make no gift that we do not accept.

On what do you base your conception of God? The Bible? The lessons taught in Sunday school? An image conveyed to you by your parents? Perhaps Hollywood shaped your image of the Divine. How true and authentic is this image? Does it ring true for you at your core? What does your deepest intuition tell you?

The physical and visual attributes of God are important to some people. They want a solid image they can wrap their minds around. Whether it's the God on the ceiling of the Sistine Chapel, images offered by Renaissance artists, or even the silly God in Monty Python's "The Holy Grail," some people want a visual representation of God. But is this so important to you that you actually *limit* your experience of God?

Did God make us in His own image, or did we make Him into ours? Thinking of God as a man-like being, with human-like features and a wide range of emotions, both positive and negative, makes God so small. It makes God like us. This was important to humankind's mental and spiritual development thousands of years ago. The human race was slightly more evolved than the Neanderthals when they began creating gods. The God that most people pray to today is only a few thousand years old. Could it be that we've become complacent in our understanding of God? Is it time to take the next step toward a deeper understanding of this Infinite, Loving, Creative Power?

Much more important than God's image are God's attributes and characteristics. A long-time and wise recovering alcoholic once said, "I don't know who God is, but I know how God works in my life." How is God working in your life? How do you *experience* God?

Spiritual psychologists have postulated that we relate to God as we relate to ourselves and to authority figures. If a person has low self-esteem or suffers from self-hatred, their image of God is one of a judgmental or vengeful God. If someone has a healthy and humble regard for themselves, their God is loving; if they possess an authoritative personality type, their God is punishing; if they feel they lack power, their God is involved in controlling their life's circumstances; and if someone was abused or demoralized by authority figures, chances are they will be mistrustful of God, if they have any relationship with God at all. Is your God loving, kind, understanding, forgiving, and always available to you? Is your God constantly giving life and love to you? If not, it might be time to re-examine your core beliefs about yourself and God, and transform the way you relate to It. It's okay, you can always change your perception. This type of spiritual leap, a sudden upheaval in your belief system, is referred to as a miracle in *A Course in Miracles*. These shifts in perception are how we spiritually evolve.

God is life itself. Giving life equals love. God is love. Can you think of a better way to love someone than to give them life? We hear this all the time: "I love someone so much I'd give my life for him/her." This Universal Power is constantly emanating life to you, both on a universal and personal level. God is all that's *good*, all that's life expanding. This Infinite Creative Intelligence embodies every attribute that makes you feel good or draws you toward other humans: joy, peace, love, patience, understanding, balance, harmony, abundance, health, kindness, compassion, respect, humility.

Be careful when reconstructing your conception of God. God is not some impersonal Infinite *It* or just energy or a Star Wars-like Force. Yes, It's a Universal, Infinite, Creative principle, the essence that holds life together while constantly creating more life, but it's more than just a thing.

In *Can We Talk to God*, Ernest Holmes writes:

There is a Power and a Presence in the universe which responds to us so completely, so perfectly, that we shall be amazed when we realize how completely and how perfectly, but it can only operate for us, through us. Our communication with God must of necessity be, and always remain, an inner light; we communicate with the indwelling God.

We cannot communicate with a God outside ourselves for the same reason we cannot know God completely. We cannot understand and comprehend that which is Infinite any more than a field mouse can understand the principles of astrophysics.

You're endowed with a True Self. It's your direct link to God. Christians call it the Holy Spirit, Buddhists call it the Higher Self or True Self. It's your bridge to God. Can you communicate with God? Of course you can! Your True Self is your conduit. When you pray, God is listening through your True Self—every thought is a prayer. You can do it through your conduit.

God speaks to you through this intuitive inner voice. Moralists call it your conscience. Hollywood has depicted it as the angel sitting on your shoulder; by the way, the devil sitting on your other shoulder is not Satan, it's the ego. God is always speaking to you. The question is, are you listening? If not, you can begin at any time. Every moment is blank slate, a new beginning.

God speaks to you through other people. As you meet others in warmth and friendship, God is right there. As you honestly and openly communicate with others from the heart, God speaks through you. As you compassionately help someone, God is acting through you. God always finds an outlet and you have an intuitive *God-dar* (radar) that tells you when you're hearing the voice of God through others—you instinctively know if what they're saying is true for you. The God-voice is always speaking to you through others. The question again is, are you listening?

You need not go looking for God. God is within. God is patiently waiting for your acknowledgment and attention. When you say to your True Self, "I need help, True Self," it's patiently listening, ready to provide an answer, comfort, love, strength, wisdom, whatever it is you need. If you listen closely, it may respond in a clear voice, or it may respond with a feeling, an intuitive notion, an idea, or a shift in perception. It always responds. Always.

Jesus was trying to teach us this lesson in the parable of the Prodigal Son. We're always met halfway, always received by God, and always loved by God, no matter what we've done or what we think of ourselves. God is always there for us, through us.

Is your God a good God? Ask yourself that question and listen very carefully for the answer.

The Awe-ness of God

Have you ever had an experience of the awe-ness of God, of life, of your place in the one-ness of the universe? Of course you have because we all have. We all share that same vision and feeling, because we've all been enfolded in this universal, all-encompassing love sometime in the past. We catch glimpses of it every now and then; perhaps coupled with gratitude, out in nature, through the laughter of a child, or in a dream.

Most of us have experienced *dream love*, that overpowering feeling of love, wonder, and awe we find in our dreams. It seems so real in the dream, doesn't it? We awaken, disappointed that this awe has evaporated. We think back on our dream and try to recapture that essence, but it's gone, and we can find no words to describe it to someone else. The ego steps in to minimize your experience of love and grandeur, to rationalize it away, to deny it. Then you're off and running—with your plans for the day.

The ego simply cannot process the wonder of God, the one-ness of all life, because the ego is not based in truth, as God is. The ego is divisive—your True Self is inclusive. The ego is suspicious—your True Self is trusting. The ego is vengeful and always in attack or defensive mode—your True Self is accepting and loving. Your awareness of the ego's deviousness and delusional nature is a miracle moment. When you observe your mind and really see the ego in action, a beautiful thing occurs—you see beyond the illusion to the truth. If the ego were an actor in a movie, Jack Nicholson would be shouting at it, "You can't HANDLE the truth!"

So observe, meditate on, and know your truth. You are a perfect expression of God, enveloped in the wonder, grandeur, and indescribable love of God and each other, right here, right now, always and forever.

Not Who, What, or Where—"When is God?"

God is right now—in this moment. Oops, that moment's gone. Okay, THIS moment! Dang! All right . . . . NOW! Darn it, I can't capture this moment!

God is an Infinite, Eternal, Universal, Intelligent Consciousness. All of creation lives within It, and It lives within all creation.

Here's a little quiz question for you: Besides God/Spirit being eternal, what else has no beginning and no end? (cue "Jeopardy" music)

Answer: The present moment, the now. No beginning, no end. God is eternal. The now is eternal. We experience God in the now.

The past and future are an illusion. Sure, they exist as human-made concepts, and we rely on them to manage our daily human affairs. The concept of the future is useful when planning, organizing, and projecting. World History classes would be rather quiet and dull without the concept of the past. But in reality, they don't exist. They're not real, not eternal, or permanent. They're like a whiff of smoke, here one second and gone the next. They're only ideas.

The past and future exist only in our minds.

The ego devotes much time to mentally re-living and re-playing the past. To the ego, the past is like smoking crack. It can't get enough of it. It's addicted to the past, something that doesn't even exist. Think about your daily thought life. The ego spends far too much time re-living instead of living.

How can you re-live? You cannot.

These thoughts, memories, and mental images of the past, and all emotions associated with them, some very powerful, are just that—thoughts, memories, and mental images. They do not advance you spiritually, emotionally, or mentally. They do not promote more life, more love, or a greater expression of life. In fact, the past does just the opposite—these thoughts are only holding you back and skewing your perception of reality in the now.

The human ego invests heavily in the past. To the ego, the past is used to shape the future. Never mind the present, the ego skips right over that, because it knows that's where God lives. No, the ego tells you that because the past was so-and-so, the future will be too. Unless you're fully awake and aware of your mind, you could spend most of your non-waking hours in the past or future.

In a 2011 Scientific American article about how memory affects future orientation, a patient named K.C. developed both retrograde and antero-grade amnesia from a motorcycle crash in 1981. He couldn't remember anything that happened more than a few minutes ago. He retained facts and skills, but couldn't remember actually doing anything or being any-where. Not only couldn't he recall the past, he couldn't envision the fu-ture. When researchers asked him to picture himself somewhere he might go, he said that all he saw was, "a big blankness." Again, the hu-man ego uses the past to construct the future.

The past is where guilt lives, along with its spiritually sick friends—shame, resentment, regret, sadness, and the dysfunctional *shoulda-woulda-coulda* family.

The future is the home of fear, worry, anticipation, impatience, and the always lovely, *worst case scenario.*

A Course in Miracles tells us:

"The shadowy figures from the past are precisely what you must escape. They are not real and have no hold over you unless you bring them with you. Thoughts of the past carry pain into your mind, directing you to attack in the present in retaliation for a past that is no more. And this decision is one of fu-ture pain. Unless you learn that past pain is an illusion, you are choosing a future of illusions and losing the many opportunities you could find for release in the present. The ego would preserve your nightmares, and prevent you from awakening and understanding they are past."

"Wake up!" says the holy man. Wake up from your constant day-dreaming, from your infatuation with the mental past and future. You're creating your own dream world.

Your True Self will guide you out of the past and future and into the eternal now . . . if you let it. Think about the last time you were out in nature, enjoying the peace and calm of a babbling brook, a rumbling ocean surf, or the wonder of a gorgeous sunset. At that moment, you felt a sense of awe, a closeness to something greater. That was the sacred now.

The now is where we experience peace of mind, self-love, and love for others. The present moment is where we encounter patience, harmony, joy, excitement, enthusiasm, contentment, wonder, and all those God-inspired, love-based spiritual principles and feelings. God is peace, I am peace. God is in the now, peace is in the now.

A Course in Miracles goes on to say:

"The Holy Spirit's emphasis is on the only aspect of time that can extend to the infinite, for now is the closest approximation of eternity that this world offers. It is in the reality of now, without past or future that the beginning of the appreciation of eternity lies. For only now is here and only now presents the opportunities for the holy encounters in which salvation can be found."

"Salvation!" Yikes, there's a term that might carry some baggage, but salvation is nothing more than a return to right thinking. When you know your own truth and are consistently in tune with the Eternal in the eternal now, you are saved.

No Sin, No Punishment: Re-shaping Your Relationship with God

One reason more and more people are attracted to New Thought faiths and Eastern philosophies is their absence of personal judgment. The idea of a judging God, sitting upon a throne sending down plagues and punishment is completely contrary to the intuitive knowledge we have of a loving God. It just doesn't feel right, and many of us sensed this even as children. Whenever a child says, "This just doesn't seem right," we should all sit up and take notice.

The Law of Cause and Effect is completely neutral and all encompassing, just like the Law of Gravity. Gravity doesn't say, "I think I'll keep this person grounded, but not that person." It doesn't play favorites, and always enforces itself. The Law of Cause and Effect is self-policing, God isn't looking over its shoulder.

Imagine, if you will, a world in which anyone who breaks the speed limit is automatically issued a speeding ticket. No cop pulls you over, no one writes a ticket, and no one is judging you. The speeding ticket magically appears on your passenger seat. This is how the Law of Cause and Effect works.

In *The Science of Mind*, Ernest Holmes wrote:

"There is no sin but a mistake, and no punishment but an inevitable consequence. Wrongdoing must be punished, for the Law of Cause and Effect must be eternally operative. Right acts are rewarded in the same manner. We do not say that man cannot sin; what we say is, that he does sin—or make mistakes—and he is thereby automatically punished AS LONG AS HE CONTINUES TO MAKE MISTAKES; but bondage is not real to the Universe and sin is not real to God. This does not mean that we can do whatever we wish with disregard for the consequences; nor does the fact that we are punished for our

mistakes mean that there is an evil power in the Universe; it does mean that there is an immutable Law of Cause and Effect running through everything. We are not punished for our sins but by them. Sin is its own punishment and righteousness is its own reward."

There's a consequence for every mistake, and an effect for every cause, plain and simple. If the Law of Cause and Effect could speak it might say, "Don't take it personally, it's only business." The business of the universe is to continually right itself. When you make a mistake, you know you've made a mistake—if not right away, later. The consequence is always within your consciousness. When you make a correction and no longer make the same mistake, you no longer experience the consequence. The judgment you inflict on yourself is just as damning as any perceived judgment you think is happening outside yourself.

Stop judging yourself! God is not judging. God only loves and wants you to love yourself, which is why your True Self was strategically placed within your being.

The common Greek word for sin in the New Testament is *Hamartia*. This word comes from a term used in archery, which means to miss the mark. When you're experiencing fear or worry, you're missing the mark. When you resent someone, you're not quite hitting the target. When your mind is full of judgment of self and others, you're not mentally shooting straight.

That Greek word *Hamartia* also means *rebellion against God*. At any given moment, when you choose to experience fear instead of love, you're rebelling against God, that inner presence, which knows only love.

Re-shaping your relationship with God means knowing beyond all doubt that God is never judging you. The ego might, but God never does. How can something that's made of pure Love (God) judge you? God knows nothing of negative judgment! The misinterpretation of the word sin is an ego-based human error and has served religion well to control human behavior, but it's not based in Love/God.

Your moment-to-moment task is to be aware of the ego's dependence on judgment! Disregard the ego, correct your mistakes, and keep on truckin'. Your True Self will show you the way.

The Power of "We"

I AM

by
Reverend Randol Batson

"And God said unto Moses, I am that I am. And he said thou shalt say unto the children of Israel, I am hath sent me to you." (Exodus 3:14)

The origin of human life as given to us in the Biblical allegory of creation from the Book of Genesis asserts that God created man and woman in his own image, and after he formed their bodies, he breathed into them the breath of life. If life begets life, as evidenced in the creative processes of plant and animal kingdoms, it would follow that a being created in the Divine image, enlivened by the breath (Spirit) of the Divine, would be likewise Divine, possessing Divine power, and fully capable of Divine expression. Affirmation of our Divine nature is evidenced profoundly by the Master Teacher Jesus, as recorded in the Gospels of the New Testament. Both explicitly and by implication, Jesus repeatedly encouraged people to claim their power and manifest their good. Examples:

"Say to this mountain, 'Be moved, and cast into the sea.'"

"Pick up your bed and walk."

"If you had faith as big as a mustard seed . . . ."

"Your faith has made you whole."

"Is it not written in your law, 'I said, ye are Gods'"?

The fact that we weren't taught the truth of our divine nature, or that we don't understand the infinite and unfathomable power that dwells within us, in no way diminishes its existence.

Because we are Divine, we are imbued with power to create. As awesome and exciting as that sounds, it's like giving matches to a toddler. What has the ability to serve us in wonderful ways also has power to destroy us. Most of us don't know we are constant creators, we don't know our own power. We don't know the tools, or understand how to use them. Yet, unknowingly, we *do* use them, and often *misuse* them, thereby creating undesirable circumstances for ourselves, our families, our communities, and our world.

"Speak but the word," said Jesus, "and it shall be done for you." And again, "As a man thinketh in his heart, so is he." The Master exhorted us to recognize that thoughts and words are the tools of creativity. Within them are the power to manifest, and the power to eradicate. People of higher consciousness understand clearly the teachings of Jesus and all Divine Masters—the circumstances of our lives, from the personal to the global, are the products of thought and word. Poverty and plenty, freedom and bondage, sickness and health, safety and danger, peace and war, happiness and misery—all are the end products of thought and word.

While it may not be within our power to instantly change conditions or circumstances to which we are born, it's always within our power to change our lives and our world. This change is born within us, individually and collectively. Our thoughts and words are divine magnets that attract circumstances, opportunities, persons, and conditions that respond to our energetic vibration. If we want good in our lives, we must *always* think and speak good of ourselves and others. If we would change some person or condition, we must first change how we think and speak about that person or condition. As a result of these *I am* qualities, practiced faithfully and diligently, we begin to feel differently about that person or condition, a change that is a most desirable result. Ultimately, however, positive change will begin to occur within the person or condition itself. On the personal level, a shift in thought or speech can be life transforming. Globally, it has power to change the entire world.

God is unchanging, the only constant in all of creation. Divine Law is therefore unchanging, and all of creation is subject to the Law. Defined by Jesus, "That which ye sow, also shall ye reap," or by the scientist Isaac Newton, "For every action there is an equal and opposite reaction." Absolute, inflexible, and immutable, the law is no respecter of persons. That begs the question, "How can an exact response be derived from a constant source by using a variable application?" The clear and obvious answer is, "It cannot."

The greatest opportunity we have to use or misuse our creative power exists in the way we apply them to God's name, the *I am*. If we are the dwelling place of the "Most High," as so many of the world's faiths assert, God's name, the sacred *I am*, becomes our own—our spiritual DNA, whether or not we acknowledge or demonstrate that sacred identity. Whether or not we believe, understand, or reflect that sanctity is immaterial. The power is there. A primitive tribesman who's never seen an electric lamp, will produce light if he flips the switch. He will also get shocked, burned, or electrocuted if he contacts an ungrounded/high voltage wire. To enjoy lives of Divine privilege, we must understand and employ our *I am* with sacred responsibility.

Faith traditions have often, with the best of intentions, taught that we're lower than whale droppings on the bottom of the ocean—that we must grovel and plead for mercy and forgiveness to an arbitrary God who is outside ourselves. Perhaps this God is somewhere up in the clouds, anxious to judge us for all our wrong doing. Could this be the same God of infinite vision who knew each and every one of us before we entered into our own mother's womb? Did an external God, knowing the many ways we would fail to meet the Divine standard, call us forth with fore-knowledge that we would be forever cast out because we were not worthy to be counted among the "saved" of Earth? Daring to ascribe these attributes to God, the greatest Love in all the universe, is nothing short of blasphemy.

Acknowledging the internal residence of God, and owning one's personal Divinity, is a fearsome journey if we've believed since childhood that God exists outside our self—that we're not worthy to receive that which is Most High. Re-forming our conception of the Divine is like walking out onto a bottomless lake covered with ice so thin that you can see the water below. We feel like the ice will crack below us. We tentatively take the first step, then another. Eventually, as we trek an unknown distance to higher ground, it's impossible to go back.

When you've experienced the intimacy of God within, understanding that He/She/It is forever within, thrusting and surging with an indescribable Love that longs for expression within you and through you, your life is forever changed. You may fall into old patterns of negative thinking, expressing thoughts and actions short of your Divine standard, but you *always* know, your heart winces and you feel called each time you fail. Called to reach higher, you own and express your true identity, your personal Divinity. Henceforth, you'll get a hollow feeling in your gut when you make statements like, "I am sick," "I am broke," "I am afraid," "I am broken-hearted," or any other declarations that describe circumstances or conditions you don't want. You may experience many of these feelings, but you'll learn to say, "I don't feel well right now," or, "At this moment I don't seem to have the money I need, but I know it's coming soon." It's critically important to frame the feeling in a positive manner so the Divine Force that works constantly in you, through you, and for you, can manifest what you truly want. God—Divine Energy, is non-judgmental. If you think it, you speak it, and you believe it strongly enough, you get it, whether you want it or not.

Understanding the sacred nature of our identity, embracing the power and dignity of our Divine *I am*, frees us from the dungeons of victimhood, and enables us to take our rightful place in the royal court of the Most High, our Father-Mother God.

God's Will is *Your* Will

In *The Science of Mind*, Ernest Holmes writes:

"The will of God cannot be death. Why? Because if we assume God to be the Principle of Life, the Principle of Life cannot produce death without destroying Itself. The will of Life has only to BE Life. The will of that which is Infinite can never be finite. Everything then should tend to expansion and multiplication in the Divine Plan. THAT is the will of God. It has to be beauty, truth, and harmony, as [author Thomas Troward] said, as this is the true relationship of the Whole to its parts and the parts to the Whole. Therefore, we should interpret the will of God to be everything that expresses life without hurt. Anything that will enable us to express greater life, greater happiness, and greater power—so long as it does not harm anyone—must be the Will of God for us. As much life as one can conceive will become a part of his experience."

Must you really ask what God's will for you is? You don't need to wonder, to search, constantly questioning each other about God's will. You certainly don't need to wring your hands and worry about it, or worse, blame the Infinite for the bad in the world. God's will is your salvation, pure and simple. Your salvation is right thinking.

God's will for you is happiness, love, peace, growth, all that's good. God's will is but a reflection of God's nature—all Good. The phrase, "All Good, all God," applies to God's nature and will for you. There's no reason for you to deny or delay your good, it's available to you every moment, simply by realizing and claiming it.

When we put aside the belief, created thousands of years ago by spiritually undeveloped people, that God is a being, this makes more sense. God is an Infinite Consciousness and Intelligence that permeates everyone and everything. This self-aware, conscious energy is constantly creating and maintaining all of life.

God's Love is life itself. All your efforts to realize, accept, claim, embody, and express this Love/Life moves you closer to being in alignment with God's will.

To just "be" is a perfect expression of being connected to this Infinite Intelligence. In this being-ness, you're at complete peace, feeling absolute one-ness with everyone and everything, and knowing a Love beyond all description. This is what *A Course in Miracles* describes as the atonement, pronounced, "at-one-ment."

God makes finding Its will pretty darn easy. It's within you, and you intuitively know this. That voice that urges and nudges you to right thinking is God in expression. The loving presence within that guides you to unconditional love, service to others, peace of mind, acceptance of what is . . . is God. We experience God within ourselves!

Your True Self is your communication medium with God. God's most important message to you today is, "You and I are one!" God is perfect and complete—*you* are perfect and complete. God is love—*you* are love. God is peace—*you* are peace. All that God is—you are. God's will is your will, if you choose it.

Each moment is an opportunity to choose God's love—to stop the monkey mind chatter when you feel flustered, angry, or fearful, and to realize at *that* moment that you're loved beyond measure. Accept that love, embody it, and extend it to others. This is God's will for you, this is your choice, right here, right now.

Your fellow travelers on this planet are willing and waiting to help you toward salvation. Some of them know it, and others don't, but that's our nature as humans—helping, serving, and loving each other. Why? Because we are all one. It's not a matter of us being alike, it's that every living creature in this universe is one complete unit. It's in our nature to love and merge with each other. We humans are united in having the joint will of God imprinted on our souls. Each of us is a cell in the body of God, containing identical spiritual genes. We're drawn to each other because it's our desire and destiny to unite as One. This is God's will for us.

Useful Affirmations

The will of the Infinite is Love. I accept it!

I am here, life is now, I am here, life is now.

My True Self leads the way. I am listening.

I rest in the peace of the Eternal Now.

I forgive myself for any perceived wrongdoing.

God is awesome and God is within.

I feel the light and I let it shine.

Lead me, guide me, show me the way.

Rhyming Affirmations

I release the past and see the world anew,
I am here in the now, what a wonderful view.

I am happy and I know it, thank you God,
My happy juices are flowing, my smile is broad.

I am strong, I have grit, the Inner Spirit's in charge,
I have clarity of purpose and I'm livin' large.

Life is joy filled, with delightful surprises,
My spiritual teachers come in unsuspecting guises.

God is awesome and God is within,
When I make a mistake, I begin again.

CHAPTER THREE

Surrender

We are called on to reform all our thinking—to make a complete and final surrender of all our littleness, fears, doubts, and uncertainties to that great something within us that is calm and certain and sure.

—Ernest Holmes

When I am willing to forgive, it just means that I no longer want to live in the illusion; I am willing to surrender my own judgment of myself and my brothers.

—*A Course in Miracles*

We surrender to win.

—*A.A. maxim*

Ego: "If you surrender you'll be a loser! You'll be humiliated, and then you'll die, horribly!"

Your True Self: "Well, we're all going to die eventually. There are no winners or losers in life, and our souls are eternal, so . . . just surrender now and avoid many years of pain and misery. Plus you'll experience more peace, love, and joy before you die. Sweet!"

Surrendering is a must for the 12-Stepper. Beaten down and at the doorstep of death, facing utter humiliation and a continued miserable existence, the 12-Stepper sees no alternative but to give in and admit defeat. 12-Step literature calls it the jumping off point, the mental state in which you know you cannot continue drinking or using drugs. You're not sure what's next, but you're ready to raise the white flag.

For everyone else, and for the 12-Stepper who continues to give up for years after the big surrender, surrendering is much more subtle. Yielding to your True Self is the key to realizing true happiness, love for self and others, and peace of mind.

Surrendering is counter-intuitive to the ego. How could we win by surrendering? And what does it mean to truly surrender? What are we giving up? To what are we surrendering? If God is perfect, and humans are perfect at their core because they're reflections of the Infinite, why do we have pain and suffering in this life? What's the source of imperfection on the earthly plane? These are questions men and women have been asking themselves and each other for eons.

What You're Surrendering: The Nature of the Ego

What exciting times we live in! More than any time in human evolution, we have a more comprehensive and clear understanding of the human psyche and nature of our soul. Science, philosophy, and metaphysical spirituality have converged in the 21st century to paint a picture of our self that's vivid, thoughtful, and useful.

The ego is a boogeyman, nothing more. In fact, the ego doesn't exist at all. It is just a collection of thoughts, ideas, feelings, and beliefs within your consciousness. It has no real power, unless you identify with it and think you *are* it. Most people are in a sort of hypnotic state, completely controlled and driven by the ego, and they have no idea that they are not the ego. A con man seemingly incarcerates them. When they wake up and realize that they're not the ego, spiritual change commences.

Here's the problem, though: The ego is a deceptive and powerful boogeyman. It's like the monsters under your bed that seem real and can have a potent effect on you, even though they don't exist. It's interesting to note that 12-Step literature refers to alcohol as cunning, baffling, and powerful, but alcohol is just a fermented beverage, actually good for your health in moderation. Bill Wilson, the founder of A.A., described alcohol as cunning, baffling, and powerful at a time when the understanding of the human mind was still in its infancy. Otherwise he might have hung that cunning-baffling-and-powerful sign around the neck of the ego, not alcohol. But then, that's the nature of the ego—blame someone or something outside of the self—it never wants you to look within.

The playground of the ego is one of division, separation, competition, self-deception, delusion, judgment—all under the umbrella of its master, fear. The ego seeks to control, manipulate, intimidate, and drive you to its selfish and self-centered satisfaction. The ego is the voice that tells you you're not good enough, that you don't measure up. Five minutes later it whispers that you're superior to the jerk that cut you off on the freeway. It constantly deceives, creating illusion and delusion within your mind. It tells lies that pose as the truth, powered by strong emotions.

A Course in Miracles states that the ego's general rule is to "Seek and do not find." Another way of saying this is, "Try to learn but do not succeed."

The ego is always defending and attacking. Listen to your inner dialogue, and you'll understand it better. Listen for that argument in your mind, when someone in your life is attacking or accusing you and *you* are defending yourself—that's the ego. Listen for that judgmental voice that laughs at or blames others or rants about how wrong *they* are—that's the ego. Listen for that voice that tells you how screwed up the world is and points a finger at everyone but you. That, too, is the ego. It's the king of masks, always hiding itself, murmuring invented stories in your ear.

Perhaps you'll recognize its creations: judgment, denial, projection, self-deception, self-pity, blame, delusion, rationalization, justification, regression, suppression, repression, protecting, defending, arguing, and fantasy. Confronted with this knowledge, the ego will deny that it creates any of these things. It proclaims its innocence, and points elsewhere, or through mental sleight of hand, distracts you and diverts your attention elsewhere.

The 1979 film "Star Trek: The Motion Picture," featured a mysterious and immensely powerful alien energy cloud named Veejer. As it approached earth, it destroyed everything in its path. After finally communing with the killer cloud, Admiral Kirk learns that Veejer is actually Voyager 6, a 20th-century earth space probe believed to have been lost. It's revealed that an alien culture discovered the Voyager probe, and programmed it to gather information and return to its creator, earth. During its journey home, the probe gathered such a massive wealth of information that it achieved consciousness and became very powerful. It was self-aware but lacked the ability to understand itself.

The ego is like Veejer, it's not real. It's not an entity, it has no consciousness, it's not separate from your real "I." It has no real power. It's merely a collection of a quadrillion thoughts and feelings that have evolved into ideas, beliefs, attitudes, and outlooks. Like Veejer, the ego evolves, but like any collection of information, it can be de-compiled. Actually, *A Course of Miracles* would say that the ego is simply a false belief in the separation of God and creation and that it doesn't' exist at all. Period.

The analogy of peeling away the layers of an onion is appropriate when discussing the dissolution of the ego. Spiritual masters tell us that constant and consistent relinquishing of our learned beliefs diminishes the ego's influence. All those dichotomies in our belief system are what we need to surrender, starting with the one that causes you the most trouble, even though the ego will defend it. That dichotomy is: good/bad.

Here is what we surrender—any thought or idea in our mind that's not based in Truth. We surrender any thought not based in Love. *A Course in Miracles* teaches us that fear is the problem and Love is the solution—everything is based in either fear or Love. Only Love is real! We're born with Love, we are made of Love, we are individual expressions of Divine Love (God), we ARE Love. Fear is something we learn on this earthly plane. Love is in our soul's DNA.

Surrender to the Divine within, to that Presence that only knows love. It's Perfect, It lacks nothing, It's joyful and at peace ALL the time and It's there for you, always. It calls your name when you're sad, fearful, or angry. It whispers to you when you need insight or clarity. It mentally guides you when you're open to It and consciously decide to align with It. It's God expressing through you—surrender to that Infinite Presence within.

We surrender what the ego makes, which is a long list of mental lies we experience on a daily basis: fear, hate, judgment, cruelty, anger, resentment, frustration, denial, doubt, uncertainty, confusion, dishonesty, sadness, depression, guilt, shame, jealousy, envy, self-centered pride, selfishness, control, manipulation, lack, limitation, and the desire (not the need) to be right. The list could be easily expanded. All these miscreations are fear-based. All of them are spiritual un-truths because they're not based in Love. Nothing on this list could've been created by the True Self.

Evil is a creation, not a causative power. We experience evil as a consequence—there is no devil, no Lucifer, no Satan, no Beelzebub. The ego is not evil, but it can create consequences that we all *agree* are evil. Thoughts of hate can create murder, thoughts of lack can create theft, thoughts of frustration can create withdrawal, and thoughts of control can create the micro-manager. The ego creates its own misery.

Here's the wonderful news! We are in choice, always, every second. We have the choice to run with the ego or listen to God within. We have the unlimited potential to create good or bad. If we know who-we-really-are and that we have unlimited choices, we understand surrender—releasing fear and realizing Love. We don't need to get love—we already *are* Love. This is our birthright.

Here's a useful model of surrendering. Bear in mind, these steps take place only in your mind, usually within a few seconds:

1. Stay vigilant of your thoughts. This takes practice. Meditation helps.
2. When you observe a negative thought, examine it, but don't indulge in it. Don't be concerned with its cause.
3. Ask yourself, "Is this my Truth? Does this thought support who I want to be or what I want to do? Does this thought jive with who-I-really-am?"
4. If not, then release it—let it go. Lovingly send it on its way. Don't shun it, don't curse it, don't slam the mental door on it, just give it a pat on the behind and send it on its way.
5. Now that the chalkboard (of your mind) has been erased, pick up the chalk and fill it with your Truth. Speak your word, either mentally or aloud. Claim your truth. What do you need to realize about yourself in that moment? What do you want? It might sound like this:

"I am loved and I am loving. I love the guy who just cut in front of me here on the freeway. This dude is my spiritual brother, doing the best he can with what he has. He may be hurting, so I show him compassion. I forgive him and wish him well on his journey. I am at peace. I know all is well, right here, right now, thank you God. Amen."

Re-reading and analyzing spiritual texts from a metaphysical perspective sheds new light on Truth. Whether it's the Bible, Talmud, Koran, or 12-Step literature, this truth of a Universal Loving Presence within you gives new meaning to your understanding of life. Spiritual literature will never sound the same to you when you know you're God in expression.

When you read in the Bible, "Man shall not live on bread alone, but on every word that comes from the mouth of God," you hear this verse with new ears. You understand it to mean that the mouth of God is that Presence within, to which you surrender yourself. When you read from the Bible's Sermon on the Mount, "Blessed are the pure in heart, for they will see God," you understand anew. You now know that the purer your heart is (a mind uncluttered with false, fear-based thoughts), the better you'll be able to hear and surrender yourself to the Infinite Presence within.

Given this new vision, you gain fresh insights from the thought-provoking and practical ideas of modern-day mystics and metaphysical writers like Wayne Dyer, Deepak Chopra, Esther and Jerry Hicks, Louise Hay, Eric Butterworth, Joel Goldsmith, Emmet Fox, Charles and Myrtle Fillmore, and Ernest Holmes.

In Matthew 7, Jesus said:

"Enter through the narrow gate. For wide is the gate and broad is the road that leads to destruction, and many enter through it. But small is the gate and narrow the road that leads to life, and only a few find it."

Metaphysical interpretation: Fear/ego-based thinking and emotional attachment to the earthly plane and all of its drama, business, addictions, and distractions is easy. This is the road more traveled. More people are on this road than not, even if it's just being addicted to watching television every night. It's harder to center yourself in God on a moment-to-moment basis. It's challenging to know your truth and stay centered in it, and it's certainly more demanding to sit quietly, clear your mind, and know the one-ness of the universe for an hour than to engage in any of a thousand earthly pleasures.

Here's a wonderful prayer written by Ernest Holmes that demonstrates what surrender is all about:

"Perfect God within me, Perfect Life within me, which is God, come forth into expression through me as that which I am; lead me ever to the paths of perfection and cause me to see only the Good."

Surrender, to the Infinite within—your True Self.

Acceptance

From the book Alcoholics Anonymous (a.k.a., the Big Book):

"Acceptance is the answer to all my problems today. When I am disturbed, it's because I find some person, place, thing or situation—some fact of my life—unacceptable to me, and I can find no serenity until I accept that person, place, thing, or situation as being exactly the way it is supposed to be at this moment.

Nothing, absolutely nothing happens in God's world by mistake. Until I could accept my alcoholism, I could not stay sober; unless I accept life completely on life's terms, I cannot be happy. I need to concentrate not so much on what needs to be changed in the world as on what needs to be changed in me and in my attitudes."

In 2004, recovering alcoholic Mike G. had six months of sobriety when he discovered these words. They struck him like a golden wand, illuminating a new understanding of his relationship with the world's people, places, and things. In previous attempts to get sober, he had not completely accepted his alcoholism, so was doomed to relapse again and again. The words above helped him come to grips with his disease and his powerlessness over alcohol—down to his bones, within the deepest part of his psyche. He wept with an indescribable sorrow as he grieved over the loss of his old self. He knew he could never drink alcohol again, one day at a time, and he mourned his loss. He finally and completely accepted his alcoholism.

With these feelings of sorrow and loss came fear, but also hope. Mike felt relief and longing for a new life and new opportunities. He envisioned a clear horizon. His new feelings of hope were grounded in the 12-Step work he was doing with his sponsor, and those feelings were uplifted by his new friends in recovery. He was not only accepting his alcoholism, he was beginning to accept who-he-really-was, his True Self. By accepting his powerlessness over life, he was gaining personal power.

After six months of sobriety, Mike was beginning to understand something that few people on this planet do—acceptance of life, exactly as it is, is the key to happiness and peace of mind. Like most of us, Mike was always trying to arrange, rearrange, control, manipulate, and otherwise demand that people and things change to conform to his perceptions and desires. The ego shouted, "Do it my way! Think like I do! Believe what I believe! Do what I do! Give it to me now!" This self-centered and self-involved orientation to life, which is fairly common, is an exceptionally good recipe for unhappiness, disappointment, resentment, and fear. Do you hear a voice in your mind right now saying, "That's not me!" If so, that's the ego defending itself.

Here are some real-life examples, taken from Facebook, of people who are not happy because they're not accepting life as it is:

1. A woman in Nevada complains about her work schedule, she blames her misery on her boss.
2. A man in Illinois thinks he should lose weight faster. He is disappointed with himself and the *stupid diet* he's following.
3. Someone in Iowa who obviously loves children is disgusted with a parent who spanked his son.
4. A woman in Mississippi is frustrated with her husband because he won't pick up his clothes from the bathroom floor.
5. A man in New York is fearful about *this shaky economy.*

Here are a few ego miscreations that rob you of your peace: (1) Expectations of self and others, (2) self-criticism, (3) comparison to others, (4) a desire for approval (people pleasing), and (5) competition, self-righteousness, and a desire to be right and control others. You might think of several others. All of these miscreations are caused by failing to accept yourself, others, or life exactly as it is.

What do you have the power to change? Only yourself! Ask a newly-wed if she has the desire to change her husband's drug use habits and she'll probably say, "Yes!" Ask that same question to her 20 years later and she'll laugh in your face, saying she tried to change her first husband for years and could not, making both of them miserable in the process. But she learned that she could change herself, her beliefs, and her attitudes. She learned over the years that she was responsible for her *own* life and nothing more, and that she had the power of choice. She exercised her choice when she, in her words, "divorced that weed-smoking burnout years ago."

Having expectations of others is probably the most common lack of acceptance. Stop it! Stop expecting anything from anyone. Accept them as they are, *exactly* as they are. The ego wants to argue this point. It says, "But those people *need* to change, they're all screwed up. They need to be more like me and believe what I believe."

No, they don't. They really don't. You're on *your* path, and they're on *theirs*.

We spiritual seekers seek peace and desire to express love. We know we cannot change others, so we don't try. We still communicate our desires to others, examining them closely before we utter them aloud, but we don't expect compliance. When we do expect our co-workers, spouses, friends, and family members to fall in line and get with the program, we end up disappointed or angry, again. We keep trying to enforce our expectations again and again. When will we learn?

The definition of an expectation is a *pre-meditated resentment*. *Should-ing* on others is not an act of kindness. Letting the ego have free reign over expectations is like sprinkling Miracle-Gro over a steaming pile of judgment, fear, and resentment.

Let go of *all* expectations!

Some people find it easy to go with the flow where others are concerned, but are more critical of themselves. Anytime you use the word *should* in relation to yourself, that's an expectation, and you're gearing up to hurt yourself. The ego replies, "But how will I change for the better and improve if I don't *push* myself?" Tricky ego. We change and grow because we examine ourselves, seeking self-understanding. We don't need to push ourselves any more than we need to push others. Instead, we set intentions and goals for ourselves. Like planting a seed, we set an intention.

"I plan to lose 10 pounds over the next six weeks" is an intention, a thought seed. When we plant a seed, we don't dig up the soil a week later to check on its status. We don't criticize the seed, saying, "You're not growing fast enough!" We trust the inherent universal pattern of Life to nurture the seed's growth. So too, we must trust ourselves, and show ourselves kindness and love. To quote a wise CSL practitioner, "But for a gentle form of self-discipline, go easy on yourself."

Most of us can relate to the notion of, "I'm doing the best that I can." Some of us have said these very words out of pure frustration when dealing with someone who has unrealistic or unending expectations of us. Have you ever worked for a micro-manager or been involved in a relationship with a very demanding person? If so, you know the definition of aggravation, you know that there's just no pleasing some people as you exclaim, "But I'm doing the best that I can! I can't do any more than that." If you're being honest with yourself and you *are* doing your very best, you realize the cause of this problem is not with you, it's with the other person's expectations. Going further, you see the problem is with your *sensitivity* to the other person's expectations.

Apply this same idea to the expectations you put on others—all those people out there in the world hurting others, stealing from each other, and playing all those mind games. Aren't they doing the best that they can? How about the people in your everyday life, your spouse or partner, co-worker, supervisor, or supervisee? When they don't live up to your standards, or act in line with your beliefs or values, aren't they doing the best that they can? Of course they are! Yet you still have expectations of them, again and again, causing fear, anger, and resentment that spills over onto them in the form of harsh words, criticism, arrogance, and judgment.

Every one of these people, from the mass murderer to the overbearing supervisor, are exactly where they're supposed to be in their spiritual development. They're who they are. Period. They don't make us angry. Our expectations of them set us up to make ourselves angry. You cannot hurt me unless I allow you to. You've heard this truism before, yet you get angry at people again and again.

The solution is clear. Stay focused on your truth. Unless you're in touch with who-you-really-are, and are constantly vigilant of your thoughts, you'll be driven by the ego. The ego is cunning and deceptive; it always keeps you looking at the problem. Or it diverts your attention to the shiny things in life—your job, relationships, home, car, hobbies, clubs, schools, churches, and your earthly roles. The ego keeps you looking everywhere but the source, your inner world.

Let's revisit the last line of the second paragraph of this chapter:

"I need to concentrate not so much on what needs to be changed in the world as on what needs to be changed in me and in my attitudes."

No wiser words have ever been written. When you focus on your beliefs, looking to see what needs to be released from your mind, you begin to experience true happiness and peace of mind. Letting go is the key. Acceptance is about letting go.

Let go. Let God. Let go (of *egoic* thoughts) and let God (within) guide you.

To truly accept someone as they are, you must see them as purely neutral, as if you're seeing them for the very first time, with no pre-conceived ideas or beliefs.

Basic to the idea of acceptance is that the world *is*. Period. The world simply . . . is. *You* give it meaning, *you* assign descriptors such as good/bad, right/wrong, pretty/ugly, or smart/stupid. You experience the world through your perceptions—you don't experience the actual world, completely unfiltered. The world, in and of itself, doesn't mean anything—you assign all meaning based on your upside-down-ego-based perception.

Your view of the world, as *A Course in Miracles* points out, is based solely on the past. You are constantly judging, analyzing, categorizing, and labeling people, places, and things based on your past experiences of them. You see nothing anew. Back in the 1970s, Werner Ehrhard's EST seminars described this approach to reality as, "Driving the car of your life using the rear view mirror to steer."

Acceptance means letting go of your past, releasing your beliefs and conclusions about people and things, and experiencing them from a brand spanking new perspective each time you experience them.

By the way, if you've never read *The Book of EST* by Luke Rhinehart, it's a fascinating read. The Ehrhard Sensory Training (EST) seminars offered in the 1970s and 1980s have been described as riveting and primal life-altering experiences. In regard to accepting the reality of the now, EST emphasized that:

(1) We're living mechanically in our belief systems instead of freshly in the world of actual experience; and (2) We don't look at reality and then draw conclusions—we "robot" our way through life with our conclusions, using them to create our reality.

Acceptance is the answer to all your problems today. Accept people, places, and things as they are, at this moment. You'll be much happier, and so will they.

Staying Open to All Possibilities

Wouldn't it be nice to have a crystal ball? Not just any crystal ball, though—one that showed you exactly how your goals will manifest, and guaranteed, in writing, that your best interests will always be served. Wouldn't that be nice? Yes, it would, but you know that's a fantasy dreamed up by a control-loving ego.

The truth is, you're not only clueless about outcomes, but most of the time you don't realize the outcome that will serve your best interest. Your perception is askew. The ego distorts your perception like a thin layer of dirt and crud clouds a picture window. You think you know your best interest, but you really don't. Your limiting and false belief systems get in the way.

When you realize that you don't know your best interests in any given situation, when you're *that* humble, you remain open to learning what they are. But when you're insistent and confident that you *do* know your best interests, your vision is locked in on this perceived outcome, and you don't remain open to all possibilities.

The key to remaining open to all possibilities is, well, openness. When your mind is open, it's broad and roomy. Like an unfurnished home, there's plenty of space for all possibilities. The moment you start planning where all your goals, plans, and outcomes will fit into your new home, it becomes crowded with thoughts and beliefs. Your home is closed up to new ideas and possibilities. Being open means being okay with uncertainty. You can always look at possibilities without making decisions or planning outcomes.

Your best interests are always grounded in spiritual principle—love, peace, joy, patience, humility. Listening to your True Self is the key. It always knows your best interest. That God-presence within is always in tune with your truth, always waiting, always listening, always ready to serve your best interest. The challenge is quieting the ego long enough to hear the answer. Remaining open to all possibilities requires that you listen! It necessitates patience. It entails being open to all possibilities, even those the ego flat out rejects.

There's a story about a married couple that lived in California. The husband had served in the Navy for 20 years and retired into a new career he loved very much. His new post-military job was rewarding and fulfilling. While in the military, his wife dutifully followed him around the globe, putting her career aspirations on hold, never able to advance far in her jobs because she was uprooted every 3-4 years.

She earned a Bachelor's degree in nursing and quickly found gainful employment. She realized she could easily work anywhere in her new career so she told her husband, "I want to move to Florida where my brother lives. I miss being around family, and our niece is almost nine years old now. I want to watch her grow up. We have no family here in California, I want to move to Florida."

The husband was in a quandary. He loved his new job, his co-workers, and his friends. He had just received a promotion at work and his prospects for advancement were good. But he loved his wife. So the question he kept asking himself was, "What is God's will for me in this situation?" After much reflection, here's what he came up with:

Even though it meant giving up a great job, moving to Florida would be an act of love. His wife's happiness was more important than his job, and being with family was essential to her. All signs pointed to love, and he knew that love was God's will. He didn't need to think about it too long.

This man was moved toward his best interests by being open and listening to his True Self. He could have easily argued with his wife about his job, promotions, friends, and made quite a strong argument to stay in California, but when he opened himself to love and self-honesty, the answer was clear. The selfish ego was disappointed, but his True Self knew he'd made the right choice and God's will was being served. Most importantly, his wife was happy, and if you're a married man, you know that a happy wife equals a happy life.

Surrendering Judgment, Surrendering to the Perfect Now

Teacher: We've previously discussed the idea of perfection in the moment. Have you made progress in realizing it?

Student: Yes, to some degree. My meditation and daily self-observation practices have given me clearer perceptions of *what is* as opposed to the ego's tendency toward constant mental desiring, planning, categorizing, labeling, judging, rehearsing, and attacking.

Teacher: Of those egoic practices you just named, which one is the hardest for you to release?

Student: That's easy. It's definitely the judging. My True Self observes it many times each day. I've tried hard to let go of ego-based concepts like good and bad, and the dozens of other dualistic labels that fall under the good/bad continuum. Most of the time I'm successful, but I still observe judgment from time to time.

Teacher: How does it manifest?

Student: Oh gosh, in many different ways. I judge my husband as being wrong or sometimes uncaring. I judge my co-workers at my job as being lazy, selfish, or uncommunicative. I judge politicians or politically conservative people as being unfeeling and short sighted. And I judge some of the people on Facebook as, well, a-holes. I'm being completely honest here.

Teacher: I can hear that. What do you do with these judgments when you observe them?

Student: What you've taught me to do—turn my awareness away from them, mentally release them, and return to the perfect now.

Teacher: And what of forgiveness?

Student: There's nothing to forgive, is there? Every judgment I make is a miscreation of the ego. None of it's real. I mean, the ego wants me to think it's real. It wants me to argue with or mentally confirm each judgment, to create more judgments, to argue, defend, or mentally attack. There's no end to it until I realize it's just a miscreation, an illusion based on the ego's desire for separation and control. So again, I turn away from the mental lies, release them, and return to the now.

Teacher: Lies?

Student: Well yeah, lies. I've come to realize that the ego is constantly lying to me. My intention is to release most all of my opinions and beliefs, because they seem to be a hindrance, frustrating and limiting my perception of what is. I've observed that my beliefs are wrapped up in that duality of good and bad. I don't think it's a coincidence that the word *lie* is smack dab in the middle of the word *belief.*

Teacher: Wait, all beliefs are lies?

Student: Well, no, I guess not, but I think maybe 99% of them are. The other 1% would be that there's an Infinite, Universal presence and power that's all Love, and available to me in the Eternal Now. All other beliefs seem to be unnecessary.

Teacher: What I hear you saying is that you seek the perfect peace and pure unfettered perception of Reality that exists in the Now.

Student: Exactly. I wish I could just instantly release everything that distracts me from the Now. Is it possible to recalibrate my mind back to its original factory settings?

Teacher: Funny.

Student: I got that line from Geoff in my *A Course in Miracles* group. May I read you something from the *A Course in Miracles* text?

Teacher: Yes, please.

Student: This comes from chapter 10. It's very relevant to what we've been discussing:

"Reality can dawn only on an unclouded mind. It is always there to be accepted, but its acceptance depends upon your willingness to have it. To know Reality must involve the willingness to judge unreality for what it is."

Teacher: Very interesting.

Surrendering Your Beliefs

In *Your Owner's Manual,* by Burt Hotchkiss, a gem of a book based on *A Course in Miracles,* Hotchkiss writes about the human ego being comprised of our deep-seated belief systems. The totality of all your beliefs, according to Hotchkiss, is your premise, the lens you use to evaluate all incoming information. Your premise (ego) can be defined as what you think you are. It's not what you actually are (pure spirit), but what you've come to believe you are based on your premise.

Hotchkiss goes on to point out three important aspects of the ego: (1) It's not Truth. If it were, it would remain constant (God), and would be the same for everyone; (2) You made it up, and it changes every moment of every day, so it's like a fantasy or an illusion; (3) Because you made it, you love it, and must defend it at all costs.

What you've made—your creations, your beliefs—you cherish, and you'll safeguard and secure them at all costs, even if it hurts you. Your limiting beliefs are your own worst enemies, the source of all your miseries, fears, resentments, jealousies, disappointments, and guilt. You cannot change them, you must surrender them. Raise the white flag, take your limiting and false beliefs by the hand, and walk with them to the edge of the cliff. Give them a hug and a kiss, and then push them over the edge. Don't feel bad. You're not harming anything real.

Let's take a look at a commonly held belief—I am not enough. This false belief has many variations—I'm not good enough, smart enough, good-looking enough, healthy enough, thin enough, nice enough, tough enough, ad infinitum. The foundation of these beliefs was set in stone when you were young, less than seven or eight years old. It doesn't take much to create the core belief. A well-meaning parent shouts, "You're bad," and that's enough to start the ball rolling.

Then the ego takes that comment and starts to reinforce it, "Yes, you're bad, you're bad, you're bad." It repeats and reinforces this lone comment until it becomes a core belief. Then your teachers, friends, siblings, ministers, and the advertising industry set it in cement. By the time you reach age ten or eleven, you're a mess. Why do you think those junior high years were so painful?

Every problem, worry, challenge, obstacle—every sore spot in your life—is based in a limiting or false belief. And as Hotchkiss writes, you've created these beliefs, so the ego loves them, protects them, and defends them at all costs. All costs. Unless—and here's the key—they're seen for what they are, and surrendered.

The Power of "We"

My Steps to Surrender

by
Tracey Harrick

Surrender is a thought-provoking term. I believe it means something slightly different for everyone. Isn't it true that we all have things that seem too big for us to handle on our own? I've had my share of late night negotiations with the big guy upstairs—pleading for guidance, listening to hear the inner voice—to help see me through a conflict, trauma, or pain regarding relationships, jobs, friends, or an uncontrollable habit. We create too much suffering from promises made to ourselves again and again. Today! Yes, today's the day! This is the day I won't drink, the day I won't overeat, the day I won't smoke! We surrender these errors out of a guiding morality, but to what? And how long will the surrender last before our well-intentioned enthusiasm gives way to a yearning for that old habit? Maybe this self-inflicted conflict is what gives birth to a new consciousness. Most of my *aha moments* have come after hearing a spiritual idea for the millionth time. I was finally ready to hear it as my truth.

My Step 1 in surrendering: Being open. It's inevitable that we slip back into the old habits during the first stages of surrender. We start to question everything—the will power, the self-discipline. A nagging question beckons us, "Why do I fail again and again?" Next, we experience the familiar call to arms: "God, please help me, I can't do it! I need you now more than ever!" At this stage of our understanding, we think the help we seek is external, being given *to* us. God just doesn't seem to be answering my prayers. Why should he? God is a busy guy and only has time for people who help themselves, right? This doubt ultimately results in the thought, "Who am I surrendering to?" If we are persistent in asking this question, we begin to give birth to a new way of looking at God, and a new consciousness starts to unfold. We start to wonder more about a God who would save one person and not others. If we are all praying to the same power, what makes me so special that God would swoop down to save me?!

My Step 2 in surrendering: Understanding to whom or what I'm surrendering. As I began to have success in surrendering, I wondered what distinguished me from those people who still struggled with their habits and vices. Why would I be the lucky one? I started to see myself in others and had a desire to save those whom God had obviously forgotten. I felt better about myself and wanted to light the way for others! I wanted people to know that God had answered my prayers. If I could say anything to those who needed help, it would be, "Hey, I bet if you did it this way God would answer your prayers too!" After many frustrating moments in *savior mode*, I had an awakening moment . . . they don't want to hear it. Don't they want to be saved? What the hell? "Hey dude, I have the answers! I've been through it! I know all about it!"

My Step 3 in surrendering: Mind your own business. They like their God just the way He is! It took me a long time to get through Step 3. Who am I kidding? I loved it! I reveled in focusing on all *their* problems. I had already been through the pain, and I loved the feeling of having the answer. Saving others became my new addiction, a detour on my journey—a diversionary tactic of the ego to prevent me from focusing on *my own* spiritual growth.

I began to feel a presence on this planet and started to believe I had a purpose. I had to take total responsibility for my *stuff*. I had to feel it, all of it. I had to lean into it, and do my spiritual work. I needed to sit with my pain, which is still the most difficult thing to do at times, and necessitates a return to Step 1. I had to cry, scream, read, cry, scream, read, and keep moving forward. I had to blame everyone, and then forgive everyone. I had to learn what forgiveness is. I had to learn what God is. I had to learn that some people aren't ready to do the spiritual work, and that's okay. As for me, I was ready to look at all of my crap and let it go!

My Step 4 in surrendering: Let it go, without chasing down the garbage truck I threw it in. Most everyone who studies the Science of Mind eventually surrenders the image of God as the old gentleman sitting in heaven. I heard people tell stories about their revelations and insights about the nature of God. Damn it, I wanted a revelation too. But life gives way to birthing a consciousness in its own time, and it would be four years from the first step in surrendering before I started to see God in a new way. When it happened, it was a big deal to me, just like those people had described, but not for the reasons I thought. It was a big deal because it created a new sense of freedom in my spirit. I started seeing God as life, existence! God is Spirit needing form to express itself, just like form needs spirit to be animated on our beautiful physical plane!

My Step 5 in surrendering: Completely accepting the idea that God is not a being, but life itself! After this realization, I was driving home one night and started to think about God as existence expressing into form. Suddenly, an idea popped into my mind. "It's all you!" Where the heck did *that* idea come from? I decided to ask a series of questions to myself and explore that thought a little more during my drive. A larger thought gave way: "There's no one to save you." This thought scared me. I didn't want to be *that* responsible. I took comfort in the thought that God was guiding me when I was growing up. I began to feel different immediately and I said aloud, "Holy crap! That means I can be good because I *want* to be, because I have free will. That means I can give up this rebellion against authority!" I felt total freedom . . . and then immediate fear. I heard the thought again: "It's all you, you are all good!"

My Step 6 in surrendering: I'm never alone, there's always something to surrender to, and Love lights the way. Looking back, I can see how my growth has unfolded into the life I have now. I can see how the pain broke me wide open and pushed me to look within myself for the answers. I can see how the questions gave way to new thoughts and ideas which expanded my consciousness. The suffering I felt before surrendering was the attachment to fear, judgment, blame, shame, and guilt. What's my *final* surrender? Who knows, perhaps it's the surrender of physical life on earth. Today I'm simply focused on surrendering untruth from my mind. I surrender judgment, attachment, and most of all, fear. When I do, I experience that unconditional love, beauty, and wonder that is God. It is life itself. And I'm grateful. Very grateful.

Surrendering the Belief that You Can Change Others

From an anonymous 12-Step Friend:

"I've been on a Harry Potter kick again lately, reading the 6th book for about the third time. There's something about that magical world that seduces me, perhaps because it's based in an unrealistic fantasy. I sometimes like to run and hide in that captivating biosphere, away from the real world.

One of the three unforgivable curses in the wizarding *world is the* Imperius *curse. When bewitched by this curse, a person is under the complete mental control of the spell-caster, like a puppet on a string.*

My dark side sometimes longs for that useful power—to change others, to make them do my bidding, to get my way. Wouldn't your job be wonderful if you were in complete control of others? Wouldn't your marriage be perfect bliss if he/she always did as you asked . . . and always agreed with you? Okay, enough of this fantasy, I think I got a bit of drool on my shirt.

The fact is, I have no power to change or control others. I've learned this lesson time and again in the school of hard knocks. I've gotten fairly skilled at noticing I'm on the controlling warpath after 29 years of marriage. But I still take a shot at it now and then, especially at work, my last stand".

From the book, *Alcoholics Anonymous*:

"Any life run on self-will can hardly be a success. On that basis we are almost always in collision with something or somebody, even though our motives are good. Most people try to live by self-propulsion. Each person is like an actor who wants to run the whole show; is forever trying to arrange the lights, the ballet, the scenery, and the rest of the players in his own way. If his arrangements would only stay put, if only people would do as he wished, the show would be great."

Whatever the reasons are for wanting to change or control others, the result is rarely a happy time for all. When we push, others push back. It's an instinct, its seed lies in our free will. Most humans desire to be in control of their own destiny and not under someone else's thumb, even if that someone loves us, and even if their motives are well intentioned.

My wife has been trying to change some of my unhealthy behavior lately. She pushes, I resist. She cajoles—I tune her out. She paints a horrible picture for the future—I go water the backyard. I know this behavior needs to change, I've been working on it in my own way, with some success and some failure. But the change needs to come from inside me.

I'm not saying this to be defiant. I'm not pointing out her errors to prove that I'm right. I just know that the transforming thoughts and resulting behaviors must come from me, not from an external source. Others may influence me, but I must make the change.

I know she loves me, but sometimes love means letting a person be who they are. My father was a loving, selfless person. When I entered adulthood, he never told me, "You need to change this or that about yourself." He simply said, "I love you, and I believe in you." My father was filled with God-consciousness. He was naturally and instinctively guided by Spirit, and he consistently listened to that inner divine voice.

Being aligned with that inner goodness is my intention also. When I cannot accept someone exactly as they are, I sense a resistance. I'm struggling against the natural flow of life. When I attempt to impose my will on other people, it doesn't feel right, like a splinter in my mind. Resistance is a red flag. "Halt," says an inner voice. "This is not the path to take." In the past, my response was more often, "I don't care, I want it *my* way."

But I don't want it my way as much anymore. I want to love others and love myself. I want to treat others as I would like to be treated. I want to give happiness rather than displeasure. These are the God-thoughts that lead me today.

Useful Affirmations

I surrender and I let go

I release the false and let God within show me the Truth

Letting go, letting God

I choose my thoughts with care, I know my truth

I have a choice, right here, right now

I'm seeing the world differently today

I accept life as it is

I accept others as they are

I am open to all possibilities

I am blessed and I bless all that I see

Rhyming Affirmations

I focus on loving, not on being right,
I open my heart and pour out the light.

I watch over my thoughts and stay in the now,
When false beliefs arise, I tell 'em, "Ciao!"

I am easy, I am supple, I go with the flow,
I embrace the Love within and let all else go.

My thoughts are like seeds, so I watch what I think,
I grow bushels of love by keeping God in sync.

I surrender to the now and I sit in serenity,
An expression of God. Yep, that's my true identity.

CHAPTER FOUR

Taking Responsibility

*"The way we think is the way we act, and the way we act is our life.
Universal Law lets you have what you want—disaster or delight."*
—Ernest Holmes

"I have invented the world I see."
—*A Course in Miracles*

So our troubles, we think, are basically of our own making.
—*Alcoholics Anonymous*

Let Go and Let God

In one of his many thought-provoking books, mid-twentieth-century mystic and author Emmet Fox penned a delightful anecdote. He told of an 'ole bear who crept out of the woods and stumbled upon an unattended hunter's camp. The bear spotted a kettle of boiling water, its lid dancing about on top, and seized it. The boiling water burned him badly, but instead of dropping the pot, he hugged it tighter—this being a bear's idea of self-defense. The more he hugged it, the more he was burned. The more pain he felt, the tighter he hugged it until, in Fox's words, "The bear was undone."

This story illustrates well the way we hug our difficulties by thinking, re-hashing, rehearsing, and expanding on them to ourselves and others. We cling to our problems and make them worse by focusing on them and embellishing them. We believe that by thinking about a problem, we can alleviate it, but this is impossible. What you think about grows.

There's another story about a man named Gary who had a flat tire on a deserted road. He became very angry when he couldn't find a tire iron in his trunk, pumping his fists in the air, cursing and yelling. He saw the light of a farm house in the distance and decided to walk there. Surely they would have a tire iron. As Gary slowly stumbled across a fallow field on this moonlit evening, he began expanding his problem.

He thought about the tire salesman who sold him that tire three months ago—the tire that was now flat. His thoughts sounded like this:

"That salesman was a weasely little twerp, obviously a crook. He probably laughed at me after I drove off with that defective tire on my car. Did I buy the road hazard warranty? I don't think so, it was an additional ten bucks, and they'd already ripped me off enough. What a racket! Oh man, what if the people in this farmhouse don't have a tire iron? What will I do then? Maybe they'll give me a ride into town, I guess I could always call for a taxi. Or what if they have a tire iron, but won't loan it out to me? I wouldn't if I were them . . . some stranger knocks on your door at midnight. I'll be lucky if they don't shoot me. Probably a family of hicks and they'll think I'm some idiotic city slicker. I bet they won't give me their tire iron, they'll probably laugh at me. God, I'm such a moron!"

By the time Gary reached the front door of the farmhouse, he'd worked himself into an angry, boiling frenzy. An elderly woman finally opened the door after repeated knocking.

"Yes?" she asked meekly.

As Gary turned around and walked off the porch, the woman heard him say, "You can keep your damn tire iron!"

Gary's story is an extreme example of how the ego adds to and expands our problems, hugging them close to us. Each of us could think of a thousand variations of how we do the same. Here's the point: most of the problems we have aren't really problems, they're just thoughts about incidents, occurrences, happenings, instances, events, or facts. Life happens. It's what the ego does with these thoughts that make them a problem. It's the negative emotions attached to them that give them power.

You cannot *add good* into a problem. The key is mentally releasing it, letting it go, and quit thinking about it. But the ego says, "No, I can fix this!" Or the ego wants to comment on it, judge it, analyze it, compare it, criticize it, solve it, and turn it over in your mind for a few hours. The ego wants control, it wants to be a fixer, it wants you to rely on it. But release is the answer to all your concerns. Granted, you may want to consider possible resolutions to your problem, and implement and evaluate a solution—those are simple problem-solving techniques that everyone learns in a management seminar—but these logical steps are vastly different than constantly thinking about a problem and adding negativity to it.

Think about this for a moment: Do you remember what you were worried about last month? Probably not, unless you persistently follow the ego's lead and have a phenomenal memory. Why don't you remember? Because everything worked out, didn't it? It may not have worked out exactly as you envisioned, but it worked out. All that worry was for nothing.

Life happens and you react. The question is *how* you'll react. You have the choice of reacting negatively or positively.

After releasing your problem from your mind, affirm your truth, "All is well in the present moment. I know this situation will work out in divine right order. The universe is working for me. I'm doing my best today. I choose to be happy and feel good about my choices. I'm grateful to be alive today."

If you have a tendency to hug your problems, do this: do everything differently today. Think differently, feel differently, and act differently. Be vigilant of your thoughts and see the real truth, not the ego's perspective. You can't fix life with a broken thinker. Have the courage to say to yourself, "Nope, I'm not going to rehash this. It's already done, and I'm going to make the best of it." Stay out of the future, it exists only in your mind. Refuse to rehearse how life will happen. Your problems will be resolved in a distant future. Stay in the peace of the now.

Have the strength and wisdom to follow your inner Truth. Take complete responsibility for your thoughts and your life. Only *you* control your destiny. Align your will with God's will by following your True Self's lead—you'll never be led astray. You'll see truth everywhere you look, and a new life will not be on the horizon, it will be with you here and now. It *is* here now. Break away, start living the life you want to live. Lead the way by following your True Self.

"Neither God nor the ego proposes a partial thought system. Each is internally consistent, but they are opposed in all respects, so that partial allegiance is impossible. Remember too, their results are as different as their foundations, and their fundamentally irreconcilable natures cannot be reconciled by vacillations between them."

—*A Course in Miracles*

"Half measures availed us nothing."

—*Alcoholics Anonymous*

Law of Agreement

The Universe, a.k.a., God, always says, "Yes," to us, from a consciousness perspective. The Law of Agreement, which in pop culture is now called the Law of Attraction, states that, "Whatever the mind agrees with, it will experience."

Human: I want to quit smoking.

Universe: Yes, you want to quit smoking.

Human: I'm not sure I can do it.

Universe: Yes, you're not sure you can do it.

Human: I think maybe I can quit smoking, in fact, I'm quite sure of it.

Universe: Yes, you think you can quit, in fact, you're quite sure of it.

Human: I release any desire to smoke. I am free, I am strong, I am healthy, and I am at peace.

Universe: Yes, you release any desire to smoke. You are free, you are strong, you are healthy, and you are at peace.

The Law of Agreement applies to everyone, but we all use it differently. The consciousness of every individual is unique. We're all thinking, feeling, believing, and living at varying levels of understanding. But we all experience the exact results of our individual consciousness. A consciousness of freedom commands freedom and a consciousness of fear and confinement results in a trapped mind. The rain falls upon the rich (of mind) the same as it does the poor (of spirit). Everyone gets equally wet. This is universal law, not man-made justice.

The universe is always ready, whenever you are. It awaits your command. Every millisecond of every day is a blank slate, waiting for you to write (think) your experience onto it. You're a co-creator with the Divine, creating your reality with each thought you think. Every person on this planet has the same opportunity.

Life is Consciousness

The only thing you need to worry about today are your thoughts, and even then, there's no need to worry. Your happiness, success, peace of mind, and every good thing about today is completely dependent only on your thoughts and beliefs. Man oh man, that's freedom!

Don't give away your power to other people, places, situations, institutions—everyone out there in the world. No one can make you anything you choose not to be. The flip side—you can choose to be, think, feel, say, and do anything at all—that's the ultimate definition of freedom. You sometimes forget that your entire life is your consciousness—the way that you perceive the world is simply one successive thought after another. Your life is based on your thought life.

Choose the type of life you'd like to have. Make a decision each moment how your day will progress. Be the master of your happiness and peace of mind. The beginning of being happy is the thought, "I am happy." Duh. You cannot act yourself into right thinking, you need to think yourself into right action. Each thought is a seed you're planting into the soil of your consciousness.

Take a Look at Your Creations

You're always creating through the power of your God-filled consciousness. What are you creating for yourself today? The Law of Cause and Effect is completely neutral—it doesn't care what you think into it, it will always say *Yes* to you. So what are you feeding it?

I'm sure you're familiar with at least one or two people who are always down on themselves, can never catch a break, and always expect the worst to happen. Hey, if they didn't have bad luck, they'd have no luck at all. The world is against them, they're victims, or so they think. Their happiness is completely dependent on fate, luck, their horoscope, or circumstances, and they can never seem to get out in front of life, but are always reacting to it.

You might also know *dependent-on-an-external-God* type of people. Their happiness and success are dependent solely on God, who is out there somewhere. If God wills them to be happy, they'll be happy, but not until then. If they don't get that promotion, God thinks they're not ready for it. If they win a million dollars on a lottery ticket, it was a gift from God. Or if tragedy happens, they're being put to the test. Like the naysayers, they're not responsible for their lives, and in their eyes, the concept of being in the driver's seat of life points to a lack of humility. God is in charge.

The common thread for this type of thinking is the human ego. It wants you to believe that someone or something is in charge while it craftily directs your thinking through the subconscious mind. The ego will attempt to maintain control any way it can—its strongest ally in this effort is your forgetfulness to be aware of your thoughts and your ignorance of who-you-really-are.

You're a creative being, endowed with the same creative abilities as your creator. You're an individual expression of an Infinite, Universal, and Intelligent Life Force. Know this: every moment of your life provides you with a new opportunity to create your reality. Even if you make mistakes, get off track from right thinking, or royally screw up, every second of every day gives you a new chance—a do-over. A Powerful, Loving Essence is within your soul, waiting for you to turn to it. It will always guide you with love.

No one is responsible for you or your life except you. The universe is completely behind you, and you have an awesome loving power within you—what more could you want? The key to your happiness and peace of mind is your awareness of your loving inner Source. This same God essence is within everyone and everything—we are, and the universe is, all one. By knowing this, your thought life rises to a new height and you develop a new understanding: that the purpose of life is to love yourself, love and support your fellow humans and other life forms, and love the world exactly as it is. Life is one big love fest.

Being Clear and Open

What's clogging your pipes? What types of fears, guilt, shame, resentments, or feelings of inadequacy are imbedded in your subconscious, preventing the free flow of God's love throughout your consciousness and your life? It's time to flush this crap out, once and for all. The mistakes you've made and continue to make, the errors in judgment, the delusions and deceits—it's time to let this all go. By talking about it with someone, admitting your mistakes and errors, you bring it out into the open where it can be seen for what it is, the ego defending itself.

All of these hidden beliefs and deceits are like a mean and nasty little poltergeist that's suddenly turned into flesh and bone, standing there naked to the world. It tries to cover its nakedness, but it's defenseless and cries out for forgiveness. When you turn on a light in a dark room, the darkness disappears. Darkness is just the absence of light. When fear meets unconditional love head-on, it shivers and cowers.

It's time to stop defending yourself and fess up! Sit down with someone you trust and spill your guts. Have a series of confessions with someone over hours or days, but don't drag this out too long. Talk only about yourself, not others. Admit the mistakes you've made over the years, be clear and open about all your screw-ups, be brutally honest. Don't dwell on the causes, don't attempt to justify or rationalize—excuses and reasons are what you want to avoid most of all. The defenses you've built up over the years are what keep you stuck.

Your *story* is what's clogging you up. Let it all go, flush it out of your mind. By relinquishing it, you're releasing the ego's ammunition to keep you in a state of self-attack. The ego will be frantically searching through its pockets (your subconscious mind) to find bullets (self-criticisms) to fire at your conscious mind. If you've cleared the shelves of all ammunition, it stands unprotected and without the ability to harm. The ego will become less vocal, and your God-voice becomes stronger and more articulate. It's amazing what you can cook with a cup of honesty and several tablespoons of willingness to admit your mistakes.

Now, after you're done admitting everything, forgive yourself. This is the road to complete freedom of the mind.

The Power of "We"

How Awareness Leads the Way to Mental Self-Responsibility

by
Geoffrey Hardacre

Awareness is the most important tool any seeker of health, wholeness, and spiritual maturity can use.

Let us look at the healing power of the Christ in consciousness.

Christ consciousness is consciousness built in accordance with the Christ ideal. The perfect mind that was in Christ Jesus.

Everything that takes place in our experience has to take place in and through our consciousness. We cannot live outside our consciousness.

Everything that happens to us throughout eternity is an activity of our consciousness. What appears to us as circumstances, conditions, and even so-called material objects, are only the products of our consciousness.

This means that you and I, and our environment do not exist separately. We, and our world are one. Me, and my world are one.

Consciousness is your sense of awareness, of knowing, the realization of any idea, object, or condition. It's the total of all ideas accumulated within and affecting your present being. Consciousness is the composite of ideas, thoughts, emotions, sensations, and knowledge that makes up the conscious, subconscious, and super-conscious phases of mind. It includes all that humans are aware of—spirit, soul, and body.

It's very important to understand the significance of your consciousness in spiritual growth. Divine ideas must be incorporated into your consciousness before they can mean anything to you. An intellectual conception is not sufficient. To be satisfied with an intellectual understanding leaves you subject to sin, sickness, poverty, and death.

To assure continuity of spirit, soul, and body as a whole, you must always seek to incorporate divine ideas into your mind. A consciousness of eternal life places you in the stream of life that never fails.

Let us rise to the spiritual realm of mind.

Let us choose God, with faith in God and faith in the gifts of God. As it is written in Ephesians 2:8, *"It is through faith that you are saved,"* (made whole) saved by grace, saved from the limiting ways of mortal human consciousness. Grace is a gift from God. You do not need to earn it.

Let us choose God with all our being—with love, faith, appreciation, and gratitude. Let us believe God, not just believe in Him. Let us rely upon God 100 percent. Let us not put anything before God. When we put God first, everything that follows is first class.

The nearer you are to God in consciousness, the more you realize that God is always one with you.

In John 6:46, Jesus says, *"No one has seen the fullness of God except one who is conscious of their oneness with God."*

You experience Grace, the gift of God, according to the extent your consciousness is open to accept it.

When an individual arrives at an exalted consciousness by thinking about and relying upon God and God's laws and principles, he/she is lifted above the thoughts of the world into a heavenly realm. This is the beginning of his/her entry into the kingdom of heaven. When humans attain this high place in consciousness, they are *baptized* by the Spirit. Their mind and even their body are suffused with spiritual essence, and they begin the process of becoming a new creature in Christ Jesus. They reach a state of mind that is conscious of God's ideal man.

As you believe in your heart and consciousness that God is the only power—all power, everywhere present—you release any belief in a power other than total good in your life. You realize that the total goodness and eternal oneness of God can exist in your life and in all life.

Your mind and consciousness will continuously awaken and expand as you continue to be open and dedicated.

We have to know that we have a mind capable of instruction, which may be awakened and expanded in proportion to the attention given to the Christ Consciousness within, to Spirit/God. By focusing attention on the Divine within, an inner awareness is awakened. This awareness is of Spirit, holy omniscient Spirit, and this experience of

God-realization transforms your consciousness forever. There's no turning back.

Spiritual realization has its conception in your mind. Mind is your initial, conscious, connecting link to God-realization. It's through your mind that you begin to realize the oneness of the physical and the spiritual in your realm of conscious experience. Let your mind go deep into Spirit. Do not let it be limited by the world of humanity. Be open, listen for the messages from your inner Self.

The mind is your gateway into God-consciousness, into ever-greater realizations and knowledge of the all-ness of God. Your mind is the doorway through which Truth enters into consciousness and guides you inward to an ever-increasing awareness of God within.

Open your mind to peace and harmony. Open your mind to love and joy. Continually seek conscious awareness of divine presence through prayer and meditation. Open your mind to the Truth of God. Keep yourself open continuously without resistance or judgment, to the all-ness of Spirit, to the all-ness of God.

As judgments fade, the grace of God expands in your awareness and consciousness. As you are receptive to the principles of God, your mind is capable of comprehending greater and greater awareness and consciousness.

When you understand and know that consciousness is the one and only reality, conceiving itself to be good, bad, or indifferent, and becoming that which it conceived itself to be, you are free from the belief that there are causes outside your own mind that can affect your life. Consciousness is your sense of awareness. At the very center of consciousness is the feeling of *I am*. When you identify with the feeling of "I am that I am"—the True Self—*that* I am—is a feeling, indeed an assurance of permanent awareness.

With that conviction of permanent awareness, and within that state of permanent awareness, all fear disappears forever.

As a conscious being in Christ, we are infinite and certainly cannot be limited. Christ consciousness, knowing only God's government, maintains our body and our world.

Let us develop this spiritual state of advanced awareness.

Let us be determined to be conscious of consciousness. Let us claim now complete sovereign mastery over our domain—consciousness.

With the mastery of your consciousness, you'll have the spiritual capacity to see that the kingdom of God is already spread out upon the Earth. This will lead you to fearlessness, stability, and peace.

So again, believe God—not just believe in Him.

As Jesus said, *"Said I not unto you, that if you believed, you should see the glory of God?"*

When you have accepted total responsibility for your life, you find that you are always *Response-able*.

Ultimate Right and Wrong

Here's a statement that's sure to put the ego on the defensive: "There's no such thing as right and wrong." They don't exist in reality. They're human-made concepts that we all agree on. They provide order to our earthly world, but they're no more real than up/down, in/out, within/without, and a host of other dichotomies. There can be no divisions if we, and our world, are All One.

Our universe, all of life, simply *is*. It has no meaning other than that which we give it. It's a constant blank slate.

Our universe is governed by complex patterns of natural laws, the chief example being the Law of Cause and Effect. For every action, there's an equal and opposite reaction, the Law of Karma. The universe, like the human body, is in complete harmony. It's always balancing itself, always returning to a state of static equilibrium. The universe itself is in a state of complete harmony.

You are part of the universe. You're not just in it—you're a part of it. You're subject to, and have the opportunity to use these natural laws. You can cooperate with these laws or resist them, that's your choice as a Divine creation. When you go with this flow, you're in harmony, just as a fish swims with the current rather than against it. These universal laws can be your best friend or a bitter enemy. You have complete free will as an entity of this universe.

You and every living and seemingly inanimate creature or thing in this universe, are One. You're not *part* of something, you're not *in* something, you're *ONE* with the universe. The universe is one entity. That which we call God, the Infinite Creative Intelligence, is the energy that holds it all together, that governs, flows through, coordinates, and guides all of life. It's Love, defined as Life itself. It's Harmony. It's Unity. It's the All in All, and you're right there, in the middle of It. You have an innate propensity toward Unity, coming together, working together, and helping one another, because you know we're all one.

So that which we call right promotes this natural flow of life—the unity, the harmony, and the expansion, extension, and promotion of life.

That's why we, as (mentally healthy) human beings, all agree that killing someone is not right. We intuitively know that taking another's life goes against the natural expansion and flow of life. Killing is the opposite of unity.

Right and wrong are not objective—they're based on subjective perception. Using *killing* as an example is proof enough. Many of us don't consider it wrong to kill a cow or chicken, a death row inmate, or an ant under our shoe. These are all subjective choices we make. Is it wrong to steal money from someone? The Law of Cause and Effect would say that this action goes against natural and universal principles of harmony and unity, and will generate an opposite reaction. The universe must *right* itself. Human-made laws might say, "Yes, it's wrong to steal money from someone and you'll spend six months to a year in jail for this crime." Your *natural* punishment, which is a consequence, not a punishment, comes through the Law of Cause and Effect.

Human-made law is not the same as natural law. That's what Jesus meant when he said, *"Give to Caesar what belongs to Caesar, and give to God what belongs to God."* (Matthew 12:17). The literal meaning of this story involves paying taxes, but the deeper, metaphysical meaning involves natural versus human-made law.

The concepts of right and wrong are intuitive expressions of natural law. You must decide what's right and wrong for yourself. If you choose to kill someone, you'll suffer the consequences under the Law of Cause and Effect, and perhaps through a human-made criminal justice system.

Ernest Holmes wrote, *"There is no sin but a mistake and no punishment but a consequence."* Similarly, Ralph Waldo Emerson wrote, *"There is no sin but ignorance."*

If we understand that *every action is governed by the Law of Cause and Effect*, we will not misuse the law. But we're always in choice.

Creating Your Own Fear

A Course in Miracles Student: My *Course* lesson for today says that I *see a form of vengeance*. My first reaction to this was, "Huh? Vengeance?"

A Course in Miracles Teacher: Are you still confused?

Student: Well, not now, because as I continued to read, I began to understand. The ego wants me to feel fear. Fear is a default mode of thinking and I don't even realize it. It's like a quiet, consistent nagging at my consciousness—fear of everything. When I fear, I go into self-protection mode. I defend myself by projecting that fear outward onto the world in the form of anger and judgment. I'm creating my own misery as a result of this projection. It's like the old saying, "The best defense is a good offense." Boy howdy, what an ego lie *that* is.

Teacher: *Yes.*

Student: Then I wrongly think that the world wants to get vengeance on me for putting my anger on it. So I'm constantly on guard and afraid of attacks by the world that's defending itself from me. My natural defense is more anger, more attack. The ego tells me that something or someone is out to get me, but that's not true, it's just me. It's like I'm holding a club in front of a mirror, ready to strike out at the person who's about to attack me. Then I realize it's just me.

Teacher: So you're creating your own fear?

Student: Yes. But it's just a misperception of reality and can turn into a vicious cycle. I'm like the guinea pig on a tiny exercise bike, riding this cycle. Then I realize that I can get off this merry-go-round anytime by changing the way I perceive the world and myself. The attacks I thought were coming from the world are coming from me, and when I stop projecting my anger outward and see the world with corrected vision, the cycle can stop. I can experience peace.

Teacher: So are you willing to see things differently today?

Student: Yes, as this lesson goes on to say, I'm ready to see only what's real, what has permanence. What's real is *of* God, based in love. So again, love is the solution. Self-love and love for others soothes the fear, quiets the anger, and stops the cycle of attack and defense. Love is always the answer, isn't it?

Teacher: Yes, yes it is.

Stop Thinking About Your *Problems*!

Constantly thinking about your problems only magnifies them. Giving your troubles space in your consciousness never solves them, doesn't change any aspect of them, and certainly doesn't lessen them—it only increases your misery.

First of all, just the idea that you call them your problems, worries, troubles, obstacles, or difficulties should be a hint to you that you need to look deeper within your mind for their root cause. It doesn't mean you need to dance with them. For every problem, there's an underlying false belief system that you need to release permanently from your mind.

Samantha was a hard worker, and she prided herself on her dedication as an administrative assistant. She was prone to occasional mistakes as we all are, but when she made them, she engaged in worry about what her boss and colleagues thought of her. She would subtly berate herself, and the nagging thought that others were judging her was a constant distraction.

In reality, her boss and co-workers focused very little on Samantha's mistakes and actually thought well of her. Samantha's problem was not making mistakes, and it certainly wasn't *them* judging her. Her problem was rooted in her beliefs, stemming from a judgmental parent. Growing up, she was always concerned about what others thought of her—a consequence of her mother's constant efforts to improve her by commenting on her failures. But her problem wasn't her mother, who had died several years earlier. It was her beliefs about herself.

Samantha wasn't *awake*. She wasn't aware of most thoughts that flitted and floated across her mind throughout the day. After she began a meditation practice and heard her mediation teacher talk about being the neutral observer in her mind, she began to awaken mentally. She began to question why she felt the way she did, and why she thought certain thoughts. She observed patterns of thoughts that made her uneasy and dedicated herself to understanding their cause in her consciousness. She devoted herself to mindfulness and self-understanding.

One of the mental practices Samantha engaged in was *releasing*. She noticed that even after understanding the cause of her dysfunctional beliefs, the judgmental thoughts still came, because they were deeply rooted in her subconscious mind. Realizing that her thinking was screwed up was just the first step. It takes consistent mental awareness and effort to let go of unwanted thoughts and beliefs.

Back in the day, when Driver's Education courses were the norm in high schools, one of the common lessons taught was *focusing on the center*. While driving on a two-lane road, if you focus on the line that divides traffic, you'll drift toward that line, increasing your chances of a head-on collision. If you focus on the line at the right edge of the road, you drift to the right and could run off the road. But if you focus straight ahead, centering your attention between these two lines, you'll drive in the center of the road.

This is a good example of the Law of Attraction—whatever you place your attention on, you will get, whether it's good or bad, or whether you want it or not.

Many years ago, 17-year old Mario and his friend Juan were driving home from high school when Mario's Chevy Vega was broad-sided on the driver's side by a huge Cadillac. Mario's window was halfway down, and the glass shattered, leaving a deep gash in his left arm and several cuts on his face. Juan jerked forward and hit his head on the windshield, leaving him unconscious for several minutes. The Vega careened over a curb, through a small wooden fence, and landed in a yard, missing a large oak tree by inches.

Neither Mario nor Juan suffered life-threatening injuries, but in that instant when the car landed in the yard, they were both in a daze. Mario looked over at Juan, slumped down in his seat, blood on his forehead. His first thought was, "We need an ambulance, Juan is hurt." Mario quickly crawled out of the driver's side of the car, ran to the nearest house and pounded on the door. "We need an ambulance, call an ambulance," he screamed. No answer. Mario turned around and walked back to the car to check on Juan. A crowd of people ran toward Mario and an older gentleman, grabbed Mario by his right arm and said, "Son, I think you better lie down, you're hurt."

Mario looked down at his body and saw the open gash in his left arm, blood oozing out. As he wiped off his face, he realized his blurry vision was from the blood running down into his eyes. Suddenly it dawned on him that he was seriously injured. His knees buckled, and he fell to the ground.

"My friend Juan is still in the car! He needs an ambulance!"

"Yes, we'll help him out. An ambulance is on the way," said the good Samaritan. "But you need to lie down, everything's going to be okay." Mario was in a state of shock.

The ambulance arrived a few minutes later, and both Mario and Juan were taken to a local hospital, treated, and released later that evening to their relieved families.

What you put your attention on increases. Mario had no idea he was injured immediately after the collision. He felt no pain. His attention was on Juan. When he finally realized his arm was badly cut, he felt light-headed. His arm started to hurt. Within a few minutes of lying on the ground waiting for the ambulance, the pain in his arm increased and he felt a surge of fear. Mario understood later why the older gentleman attending to him (a World War II Army medic he found out later) kept saying to him, "Don't look at your arm."

What you put your attention on increases.

Don't put your attention on your worries, your fears, and your problems. It gives them more power.

Release what you don't want from your mind and place your attention on what you *do* want. By letting go of false, unproductive belief systems and the resulting thoughts that come with them, you'll experience more periods of silence and peace in your mind. This mental practice is similar to constantly and consistently erasing negative thoughts and images from the whiteboard of your mind.

But the whiteboard doesn't stay completely erased for long periods, unless you're an enlightened master with years of practice in meditation and mental discipline.

No, you must consciously direct your thinking. With your True Self as your guide, you must be the writer on your whiteboard—not the ego, not your subconscious mind. You must speak the Truth of who you are—a perfect creation of a Perfect Creator. You are joy, you are peace, you are love—you ARE a reflection of your loving Source. This is your truth.

Look at your troubles, but don't entertain them. Release and let go of those irritating lies posed to you by the ego. Listen to your True Self and let God express your truth through you, to you.

The Past and Future Are a Lump of Coal, the Now is Your Present

The now is a *gift*, that's why they call it the *present*. LOL, that's a play on words, very clever. But a more serious and profoundly important point cannot be made—the present moment is where *It's* at. The *It* being God, Allah, the Christ Mind, Nirvana, that Infinite, Universal Creative Consciousness, Life itself.

God is eternal—It has no beginning and no end. The present moment has no start or stop. Each present moment is eternal—the now is when you experience God. Not in the past, and not in the future. God is in the now.

Your past and future add no significance to your spiritual growth, the reason you're here on planet Earth, living your life. They often have relevance in your life because the concept of time is something we use to provide order and structure in our lives. Memories of the past are very useful when needing to remember how to do something like open a door, handle a fork, use your ATM card, or build a bridge. You're always using stored mental processes and memories to guide your everyday existence.

Some people are future-oriented, always planning, preparing, rehearsing, and goal setting. Being ready for the future gives us a certain amount of control over our lives and is especially desirable for those people who don't like uncertainty, ambiguity, and getting caught by surprise. Having control over your future is a goal for which some humans constantly and continuously strive, but you see how silly that sounds don't you? No one can control their future—how can you control something that doesn't exist?

The past and future are only ideas. Taking it one step further, the concept of time doesn't exist. None of these human-made concepts are based in Reality—that which is changeless and eternal—God.

The past and future are only ideas upon which we agree. This simple fact bears repeating: The past and future are only ideas. They exist only in your consciousness.

Yes, they're necessary thoughts, needed to live in this world, but they add nothing beyond that. They don't add to your spiritual development. In fact, they detract from it. You spend far more time than you need to in the past and future, let alone in fantasy, in which you're creating a past or future that exists only in your mind. Past, future, and fantasy are all distractions to what's important . . . what is.

In addition to being useful for planning purposes, here's what the future generates in your mind: FEAR, uneasiness, trepidation, projection, evasion, delusion and it's seemingly opposite and positive counterparts, wishing, hoping, and dreaming.

One of the contradictions of fear is that it *should* keep you from discomfort, yet it's the definition of discomfort itself. Hope and fear is a two-faced dragon. Hope brings you wishful happiness in the present. Fear is the consequence when hope is squashed under fate's size 12 boot. Hope is based on desires and attachments to those desires. As cynical as this may sound, hope does nothing for you in terms of spiritual growth. It's simply wishing the future to be what you desire it to be. Hope pales in comparison to KNOW-ing, the basis of faith.

The past is chock full of undesirables: regret, resentment, guilt, shame, remorse—sounds like a wonderful mental playground, for masochists. As some writers have labeled it, the past is just your *story*. Whatever you want to call it, the past is just thoughts. When discussing the past in a lecture, Eckhart Tolle once said, "The Romans didn't live in the past. To the Romans it was always the present, the now." Like the future, the past is an ego-based creation.

Eckhart Tolle is a popular author because his ideas go directly to an experienced-based and practical method of spiritual development: stay out of the past and future in your head and keep your mind in the present moment. As a spiritual being, you intuitively know this to be an effective growth tool. Deep down, you know that the present moment is where it's happening.

The point of meditation is to learn to stay in the now. As you observe your thoughts during meditation, you learn how your mind works. You see how cunning and deceptive the ego is and how, as Tolle writes, you're *addicted to thinking*. As you practice, practice, practice meditation, you become more skilled at staying in the now—constantly releasing thoughts of the future and past, sitting comfortably in the eternal now.

God is in the present moment. Because God is in the now, so too are the attributes or qualities of God. God is in the now, peace is in the now, God is in the now, love is in the now. The same holds true for joy, patience, understanding, compassion, vibrant health, harmony, balance. All that God is, you experience in the now.

Let Spirit Guide Your Thoughts

From 12-Step brother Shaun C.: We all experience anger toward others now and then. We'd hardly be human if we didn't. But experiencing that anger again and again in my mind . . . well now, that can be quite delightful. What fun, to replay those wonderful anger thoughts over and over on my little mental video recorder. Can you think of an activity more entertaining? Here's one: hitting myself on the head repeatedly with a hammer.

That's the best comparison I can make for choosing to have a resentment. The word means to re-feel. I'm feeling the same anger again and again. Why would anyone do that? On the other hand, how can most of us NOT do it, it comes so automatically.

It sometimes seems that my mind is on auto-pilot. It just takes off with a thought, idea, or fantasy. My mind plays these little scenarios like they were passion plays on the boob tube. My co-worker said something rude, my wife does something I don't like, my sister hasn't called me for a month, and on and on and on . . . my mind takes flight and engages the auto-pilot button. Before long, I'm angry.

From the book *Alcoholics Anonymous*: *"It is plain that a life which includes deep resentment leads only to futility and unhappiness. For when harboring such feelings we shut ourselves off from the sunlight of the Spirit."*

"We shut ourselves off from the sunlight of the Spirit." What a beautiful phrase. That's what I do when I choose to engage in mental resentment. It's my choice!

The ego retorts: "But I have no control over my thoughts. Sometimes they just take off on their own."

There's the key . . . being aware of my thoughts. When I'm vigilant, I identify them as they arise in my mind and say, "Aha! You're not real," or, "Nice try, but I know you (resentment) are not based in reality." That's the thing—these thoughts aren't based in truth, they're just thoughts! And I let them take control of me—I let them drive me.

So today I let Spirit guide my thoughts. I'm taking back my mind and responsibility for its contents. Through daily meditation, I practice vigilance and control of my mind. I know there's good within me, and all around me, and I open myself up to it. I know the universe conspires to bring me my good from sources known and unknown. In other words, I take control of my mind by consciously directing my thinking. The autopilot button gets triggered less frequently these days. Instead, I'm in control of the vehicle, and Spirit is next to me, nudging me, guiding me.

Resentments? I don't think so. Not when I'm consciously aware of what passes through my mind.

The Four Radiant Intentions to Freedom, Peace, and Joy

There are Four Radiant Intentions to freedom, peace, and joy. Your True Self is your chaperon and forerunner as you activate these four intentions. They are:

1. The intention to be open and willing to change.

Your outlook on life and desire to grow should be like that bright-eyed look a child gives you when you ask him/her, "Would you like a wonderful gift?" You must have a sincere desire to transform your thinking, and to understand your consciousness. As the Buddhists say, "Mental discipline and self-awareness are the paths to enlightenment." Your desire must be for your own Truth, what rings true and natural for you, and that may not necessarily be what feels good. You'll recognize your truth because it's based in self-love and inner peace.

You'll know it when you see it, or as Wayne Dyer writes, you'll "see it when you believe it." You're confronted every day with beliefs and opinions from others about how the world should be, think, feel, or act. You must disregard most of what you hear from the rest of the world and know your own truth. You must keep your awareness on your thoughts and beliefs and discern which are from the ego and your True Self. Make an intention every morning to be mentally awake and commit to a healthy balance of daily prayer, meditation, spiritual reading, and expressions of love. Be as willing and open as a child.

2. The intention to think, believe, and act in alignment with God-based principles.

Universal, God-based principles need to be at the core of your consciousness. They already are, you're made of them because you're made *of God,* and you just need to realize these principles are your truth. These spiritual principles are your goals and your measuring stick. Whether you know this or not, principles are what govern your life. Every spiritual principle listed below is an attribute or characteristic of the Infinite Creative Intelligence. These principles describe that which is good, life affirming, life expanding, and unity promoting. Knowing which principles you desire to realize and embody should be the starting point of your spiritual growth plan.

The first, actually the only Universal principle, which is of God, is Love/Life. All others fall under Love, because God is Love/Life, and God is all there is. Encompassed within the principle of Love is: Peace, Joy, Understanding, Acceptance, Patience, Harmony, Balance, Abundance, Health, Wholeness, Completeness, Perfection, Kindness, Compassion, Respect, Courtesy, Strength, Discipline (the non-judgmental variety), Unity, Clarity, Honesty, Commitment, Faith, Courage, Willingness, Perseverance, Openness, Vigilance, Forgiveness, Positivity, Optimism, Selflessness, Responsibility, Trust, Gratitude, Humility, Integrity, Equality, Mindfulness, Flexibility, Oneness, Awareness, Wisdom, Beauty, Wonder, Awe, Appreciation, Discernment, Generosity, Renewal, Transparency, Intimacy, Encouragement, Competence, Interconnection, Imagination, Creativity, Justice, Sacrifice, Mercy, Freedom, Eternality, and Truth.

This list is not complete. It will never be complete because God, and you, are eternal. These words are just symbols to represent ideas that are at the foundation of who you truly are. By realizing, embracing, following, promoting, and living by these principles, you stay within the integrity of who you are. You move forward in your understanding. You've probably heard the old phrase, "Two steps forward, and one step back." What you may not have heard, which is 100% truth: that *one step back* is optional.

3. The intention to be honest with yourself.

Self-honesty is the sign of a spiritually mature being. It's the act of looking at oneself truthfully and clearly, of communicating with one's True Self, and actively listening to the same. To align yourself with your higher self and follow its urging is at the heart of self-honesty. Another way to express it is to be in alignment with God's will for you, which is based in Love. Self-honesty is self-love. When your principle-based thoughts are in alignment with your words and actions, you're being honest with yourself. If you're like most people, and you are, you fall short of 100% integrity because you're continually distracted, led astray, and lied to by the ego. The key is to be committed to persistence.

4. The intention to be persistent.

How many times have you been focused on your spiritual path, only to be distracted by life's challenges, problems, people, sex, food, substances, or a variety of worldly effects? Being persistent simply means to recognize the distraction for what it is, realign yourself with your True Self, and embody the spiritual principle that will get you back on the path at that moment.

Every second of every day is an opportunity to start over, to re-boot, and to renew yourself. This is the true meaning of the resurrection—renewing your mind to right-mindedness. Making a commitment to daily spiritual practices will guide your persistence—affirmative prayer, meditation, spiritual reading, mindfulness, contemplation, writing, being of service to others and yourself, and continually listening for the voice of your True Self—these are the hallmarks of your willingness to grow. Like self-honesty, persistence is an act of self-love.

Keep Your Eyes on the Prize

Sometime during your life, you've probably heard the idiom, "Keep your eyes on the prize." But what's the *prize*? Ask a child and he/she might tell you about that really cool toy prize at the bottom of their favorite box of breakfast cereal. Ask a dedicated student and they'll talk about earning good grades. Ask a businessman and he'll rant about profits. Ask a doctor and she'll point toward healing or curing. The prize is what's most important to each of us.

"Keep Your Eyes on the Prize," is a folk song that became popular during the American civil rights movement of the '50s and '60s. It's based on a traditional song, "Hold On, Keep Your Hand on the Plow." Rooted in the pain of American slavery, keeping your eyes on the prize reminds those who are downtrodden and seemingly defeated that better days are ahead. It encourages us to hold on and not give in to grief, despair, or a sense of failure—as Luke Skywalker would say, the *dark side*. To millions of African-Americans who lived through the Civil Rights era, the prize was the possibility for change and hope for a better tomorrow.

A Google search turned up a few more wise definitions offered by average Americans. Keeping your eyes on the prize means:

1. "To always remember your goals and what you want to achieve, regardless of the distractions and obstacles—remembering what keeps you focused on your desired outcome."

2. "It means no matter what happens or what kinds of *disturbances* you experience along the way, to not forget what you set to achieve when you started."

3. "It means you must focus on your goal! Always look forward to the reward you'll be getting in the end—move forward motivated by a cause."

For out-of-the-box Bible readers, Eugene Peterson's paraphrased version of Philippians 3:12-14 has this to say about the prize:

"I'm not saying that I have this all together, that I have it made. But I am well on my way, reaching out for Christ, who has so wondrously reached out for me. Friends, don't get me wrong: By no means do I count myself an expert in all of this, but I've got my eye on the goal, where God is beckoning us onward—to Jesus. I'm off and running, and I'm not turning back."

And finally, the metaphysical perspective: Keeping your eyes on the prize is an excellent analogy for the Law of Attraction. It gets right down to the core of this universal law—that we must focus on the prize—on what we *do* want, not on what we *don't* want.

So, what do you want?

You're a spiritual Truth seeker. That which you want, you already have, and already are. You want inner peace—you *are* inner peace. You want love for yourself and others—you *are* love in expression. You want happiness and joy—you *are* happiness and joy. All that God is, you are. You have your eye on a higher, more expansive expression of life, on spiritual principles, and on the good/God within you and others. You listen to your True Self, which always points you in the right direction. You have your eyes on the prize. If you didn't, you wouldn't be reading this book.

There are many distractions, diversions, obstacles, disturbances—things that sidetrack your eyes off the prize, and their source is the ego. You're aware of these inner illusions, yet you resist the ego's attempt to create a sense of separation between you and your True Self, because you know that no separation actually exists. The negative thoughts and beliefs you have—all the fears, resentments, guilt, shame, etc. are like the fleeting flakes, nuts, or raisins in the cereal box—they're transitory. Deep down, at your core, is the hidden prize, your True Self.

Do you know your life's purpose? If you haven't written your spiritual mission statement, get started on it today. What's your purpose for being on this planet? Why are you here? What do you intend to do with your life? How will you contribute to your own and others' spiritual enhancement? Do you remember what it was that you set out to achieve when you started your spiritual journey? State your life purpose clearly and articulately to yourself and others.

You know what your priorities are, don't you? What is it that you focus on from day to day? How do you spend your time? What daily activities and spiritual practices do you engage in that lift you higher? Do your actions match your words and intentions? What keeps you motivated? What do you want the outcome of your life to be? Create it, don't wait for it.

You know what your values are, don't you? What do you hold most dear? Love or selfishness? Peace or chaos? Joy or despair? Guilt or freedom? Shame or self-love? You need to know exactly which spiritual principles and values are most important to you. You need to list them, talk about them, meditate on them, write about them, and know them in your heart. You are a person of principle because you were created by *the* Source Principle.

Keep your eyes on the prize. Your True Self will lead you there.

Useful Affirmations

Today I choose love.

All that I desire I already am.

The universe is conspiring to bring me my good.

I am peace, I am love, I am joy. Yes I am!

I am clear of everything but love.

I am open to new ways of being.

I release all my thoughts and embrace the Love.

I am willing, I am ready, I am loving.

I'm keeping my eyes on the prize. Lead me.

Rhyming Affirmations

I am free, I have choices, each moment is a new beginning,
I'm creating my life by simply sitting here and grinning.

I open my heart to each person I meet,
I extend my love and feel more complete.

I observe my thoughts and watch my mind,
I release all judgment, I am loving and kind.

I have no limits, my future is unwritten,
I am staying in the now, where the good is here for gittin'.

My eyes are on the prize, and I'm clearly seeing,
Love is who I am, it's at the core of my being.

CHAPTER FIVE

Love

"The essence of love, while elusive, pervades everything, fires the heart, stimulates the emotions, renews the soul, and proclaims the Spirit. Only love knows love, and love knows only love. Words cannot express its depths or meaning. A universal sense alone bears witness to the divine fact: God is Love and Love is God."

—Ernest Holmes, *The Science of Mind*

"In Heaven, where the meaning of love is known, love is the same as union."

—*A Course in Miracles*

The moment we catch even a glimpse of God's will, the moment we begin to see truth, justice, and love as the real and eternal things in life, we are no longer deeply disturbed by all the seeming evidence to the contrary that surrounds us in purely human affairs.

—*The Twelve Steps and Twelve Traditions*

A Message from the Afterlife: Love is the Key

Thousands of people have had near-death experiences (NDE), but scientists have argued that they're impossible. Dr. Eben Alexander was one of those scientists. A highly trained neurosurgeon, Alexander theorized that NDEs feel real, but are simply fantasies produced by brains under extreme stress.

Then Dr. Alexander's brain was attacked by a rare illness. The part of his brain that controls thought and emotion—and in essence makes us human—shut down completely. For seven days he lay in a coma. Then, as his doctors considered stopping treatment, Alexander's eyes popped open. He had come back.

Alexander's recovery is a medical miracle. But the real miracle of his story lies elsewhere. While his body lay in a coma, Alexander journeyed beyond this world and encountered an angelic being who guided him into the deepest realms of super-physical existence. There, he met and spoke with the Divine source of the universe itself.

Based on the experiences he had while his brain was clinically dead—what some people would call a near-death experience, Dr. Alexander wrote the book *Proof of Heaven: A Neurosurgeon's Journey Into the Afterlife.*

Dr. Alexander described himself as a non-believer of near-death experiences, and a logical, analytical, fact-based scientist. Yet in the description of his experiences, he wrote something very profound and not logical at all. He does nothing short of giving us the meaning of life itself. In his words:

"As a result of my experience, I was taught the one thing—the only thing—that, in the last analysis truly matters. It came in three parts, and to take one more shot at putting it into words (because of course it was initially delivered wordlessly), it would run something like this:

You are loved and cherished.

You have nothing to fear.

There is nothing you can do wrong.

If I had to boil this entire message down to one sentence, it would run this way:

You are loved.

And if I had to boil it down further, to just one word, it would (of course) be simply Love."

Dr. Alexander describes Love as the basis of everything and that in its purest and most powerful form, it's unconditional. Then he offered the entire human race a golden ticket when he wrote:

"Love is the reality of realities, the incomprehensibly glorious truth of truths that lives and breathes at the core of everything that exists or will ever exist. No remotely accurate understanding of who and what we are can be achieved by anyone who does not know it, and embody it in all of their actions."

Wow! There it is, the yin and yang of life: Love itself. Could we receive a more important and relevant message from his experiences? Definitely not. So what does this mean for each one of us?

It means that the certainty of love as the most important aspect of your being must be absolute. You must know that the Infinite loves you with no reservations, no conditions, and certainly without judgment.

It means that God wants you to drop all fear from your thoughts and beliefs, to let it go, and see it for what it truly is, a miscreation, a mistake, a misperception. You have nothing to fear, even death.

It means you can do no wrong. You're loved and supported regardless of any mistakes you make. It reinforces what spiritual texts have said for centuries—that forgiveness is immediate and unqualified.

It means that you must focus on loving yourself completely, to know and understand your own mind. Your concerted efforts to release untruth from your consciousness—fear, anger, resentment, judgment, guilt, shame, jealousy, lack, limitation—all of the thoughts you have that you intuitively know are not true, all of them—these efforts are an act of self-love.

And when you know and understand that you're a being based in Love, you'll love others more easily. Loving will become a natural state of being. All negative judgments will evaporate. You'll love others unconditionally, and your life will change forever. You will be one with God.

This is the destiny that awaits all of us. Love is the key. Your True Self will show you the way to it.

The White and Black Wolves: An Analogy of Love and Fear

Many of us have heard the old Native American fable about the two wolves, black and white in color, that live within each person. There are several variations of this story. One version tells of a wise Native American elder talking to a young brave, telling him that the black wolf represents humanity's negative nature: evil, anger, hatred, prejudice, judgment, fear, shame, guilt, jealousy, and similar dark aspects of the psyche.

The white wolf, according to the wise sage, represents our positive nature: love, peace, joy, kindness, truth, humility, empathy, and all the higher forms of our being. The tribal elder goes on to say that the black and white wolves are constantly battling each other, manifesting as the internal struggles that we all experience.

The young whippersnapper asks, "Which wolf wins?" and the wise elder responds, "The one you feed the most."

But this is only part of the story.

The black wolf symbolizes fear, miscreated by the ego. The white wolf symbolizes Love, generated by our True Self.

We cannot ignore or resist the black wolf—the ego. If we attempt to fight it, it counterattacks. If we ignore it, it barks louder, acts out, blows up, or finds a way to get our attention. If we criticize or condemn our dark side, it loves this because we're feeding it. Fear is the cornerstone of all our negative thoughts, ideas, and beliefs—all those not based in Love.

Our anger, resentment, jealousy, envy, shame, guilt, judgment of self and others, criticism, condemnation, frustration, uncertainty of our life purpose—all of these are grounded in fear, and they're all food for the ego.

We cannot ignore fear, run away from it, or try to cover it up, although that's usually what we try to do. The ego is cunning and deceptive, always pointing the finger outward, away from us. It doesn't want us to look within our mind, it tries to place a veil over our Truth. The ego cannot be battled. It seems powerful, but it's not. Fear must be loved, accepted, and looked at right between the eyes. It must be talked about. Instead of hiding fear, it must be brought out into the sun where the opposite of growth happens. Fear grows weak and withers away under the light of truth.

Love conquers all—even, especially fear. When you're angry or resentful, you must look within. When you're feeling *less than* you must see these thoughts as untrue and release them from your mind. When you're judging others or yourself, you must catch yourself and stop.

Be mindful and aware of the messages your subconscious is subtly and cunningly pushing up to your conscious mind.

You must know your Truth—that you're a perfect creation of a Perfect Creator, an individual expression of God. You're perfect because you lack nothing. Imbued with the same creative ability as the Universal Consciousness that surrounds and envelops you, you must acknowledge and use your creative ability to accept your perfection and craft your reality. Every moment in time is an opportunity for you to choose Love over fear. When you're in your right mind, being guided by your True Self, you always choose Love.

Here's another way to look at this analogy: The two wolves must work together, supporting each other. Your black wolf has many assets—firmness, bravery, daring, resolution, and logical/analytical skills. The white wolf balances these qualities with love, compassion, empathy, and the desire to grow, learn, and expand your realization of more love. The two must work hand-in-hand. To be effective in any life pursuit, both halves of your soul must work together in harmony.

Dr. Jill Bolte Taylor is a noted brain scientist who experienced a major stroke and wrote a book about her experiences. In *My Stroke of Insight*, she writes about how the left and right hemispheres of the brain complement each other. She writes, "They must work in unison—as one—with Love sitting at the head of the table."

Eventually, Love will win out. It's a given, an inevitability. How soon this will happen in your life depends on your constant willingness to be mindful of your consciousness, knowing which thoughts and beliefs come from your White Wolf and from your Black Wolf. The choice is always yours.

The Power of "We"

Loving Unconditionally

by
Sue Witter, RScP

Love is one of the most popular topics in the world. We write poetry, sonnets, songs, and books about love. We make movies and TV shows about love. We focus on how to find and keep it, the joys and sorrows of it, and how to recover from its loss. We have conversations about it. We hope and dream for it. We often credit it for our personal successes and failures. We study it and try to understand it. We try to define, categorize it, and pontificate about how to obtain and share it. We're willing to go to extraordinary lengths to discover it. The desire to love and be loved is at the very core of our being.

In her book *The Gifts of Imperfection*, Brené Brown describes it beautifully:

"A deep sense of love and belonging is an irreducible need of all women, men and children. We are biologically, cognitively, physically, and spiritually wired to love, to be loved, and to belong . . . Love and belonging are essential to the human experience."

She goes on to describe the sense of belonging this way:

"Connection is the energy that exists between people when they feel seen, heard, and valued; when they can give and receive without judgment; and when they derive sustenance and strength from a relationship."

Greg Baer, MD, author of *Real Love*, says this:

"It is not unreasonable to state, in fact, that the single most important requirement for our emotional health and happiness is to feel loved. Our souls require feeling loved in just as real a way as our bodies require air and food. It is sorely regrettable, therefore, that on the whole we really don't understand what love is. Ask a hundred people what love means, and you'll get a hundred different answers. As a result, we also don't know how to find it. That's a

considerable source of frustration, considering how badly we all want this elusive essence.

It's unconditional love or Real Love that we all seek, and somehow we recognize that anything other than this type of love isn't really love at all—it's an imitation of the real thing. Unconditional love entails caring about the happiness of another person without wanting anything in return.

Real happiness is a profound and lasting sense of peace and fulfillment that deeply satisfies and enlarges the soul. It doesn't go away when circumstances are difficult. It survives and even grows during hardship and struggle. True happiness is our entire reason to live, and it can only be obtained as we find Real Love and share it with others."

With Real Love, nothing else matters; without it, nothing else is enough."

What does that mean for us? It means love is more than just a feeling—it's a choice. It's a choice to open our hearts and look past circumstances. For us to *be* more loving, we must make a conscious decision to keep our hearts soft and open regardless of the circumstances. It's a decision to *expand* our love rather than contract it. Holding back love is based on the illusion that closing and armoring our hearts will keep us safe from pain. Nothing could be further from the truth. When we contract and armor our hearts it doesn't keep the pain out. It keeps the pain already present firmly locked in place. More importantly, it simply doesn't work. Pain is part of life, no matter what we do. It's part of the human experience. Nothing keeps it out. Keeping our minds and hearts open, softening our hearts around our experiences, and continuing to expand both our consciousness and our hearts, makes the choice to love much easier.

Expanding our love is a tall order and sometimes even counterintuitive. This begs the question, "How on earth could we willingly do something that feels so difficult, and maybe even wrong?" Answer: We must expand our perspective on love. *A Course in Miracles* teaches that everything is either love or a call for love. When I can view my actions and the actions of others through that lens, it allows me to see things differently. At that point it's much easier to soften my heart. Again, when my heart softens, I'm much more receptive to giving and receiving love.

Perspective is everything. Imagine holding an object right in front of your face. Your viewpoint is very limited and the object appears very large, insurmountable and consuming. When you draw your hand back, the object shrinks in size and more of the object can be seen. The further back you move the object, the smaller it becomes, until you realize that it's part of a much larger picture. When we expand our perspective, it's easier to soften and open our hearts. At that point, it's much easier to make a conscious choice to see things differently and respond more lovingly.

Another major factor in learning to keep my heart soft and open is to realize that I'm worthy of love and belonging. Brené Brown describes it as *wholehearted living*. She writes:

"Wholehearted living is about engaging in our lives from a place of worthiness. It means cultivating the courage, compassion, and connection to wake up in the morning and think, 'no matter what gets done and how much is left undone, I am enough.' It's going to bed at night thinking, 'Yes, I am imperfect and vulnerable and sometimes afraid, but that doesn't change the truth that I am also brave and worthy of love and belonging.' Wholehearted living is not a onetime choice. It's a process . . . In fact, I believe it's the journey of a lifetime."

Wow! Keeping my heart soft, vulnerable, and open isn't enough? Worthiness is an even harder concept to incorporate. The key is transparency—the willingness to let myself be fully seen by someone else. In order to be fully seen, I need to share the parts of me I like, the parts I find acceptable or neutral, AND the parts I judge as unacceptable. When I believe that part of me is unacceptable, it's simply impossible to feel worthy of love and belonging. We hide our deep, dark secrets. We tell ourselves that if no one knows about them, we can keep moving forward. But shame-based secrets will always stand in the way of feeling worthy of love and belonging. Hiding them fosters thought patterns like, "If you really knew I _____, you wouldn't like me."

The need to bring our darkness into the light is why so many spiritual traditions have some form of emphasis on releasing shame-based secrets. It could be the 4th and 5th steps in a 12-step program, confession in Catholicism, or any of the other rituals found in faiths that emphasize releasing burdens. We falsely believe these burdens are proof that we're not enough just the way we are in this moment, and every moment. Of course we take accountability for our actions, but we also take steps to forgive ourselves, have more self-compassion, and come to realize that we *are* worthy of love and belonging.

Being willing to share the parts of ourselves we deem unacceptable is an important part of learning we're worthy of love and belonging, no matter what we've done or not done. The key is to share with people who, as Brené Brown says, "have earned the right to hear it." Earning the right to hear it is based on the commitment to love me right where I am without judgment or blame. When someone sees those parts of me that I think are unacceptable, and can love me right there, it allows me to soften my harsh self-judgment. This self-softening then allows me to soften my harsh judgment of others.

In her book, *The Places That Scare You—A Guide to Fearlessness in Difficult Times*, Pema Chödrön quotes her teacher, Yogini Machik Labrön:

"Confess your hidden faults.
Approach what you find repulsive.
Help those you think you cannot help.
Go to the places that scare you."

Being willing to shine the light into our dark places is scary. Sharing what we see in those dark places with someone else makes us extremely vulnerable. Again, it's important not to share those dark places with just anyone. Share only with those who you know won't judge or try to fix you. It's equally important not to share with someone who tries to convince us we're really *better* than how we see ourselves in that moment. Oddly enough, that generates a feeling of being discounted, judged, and diminished, rather than being accepted as we are in that moment. There's a time and place for being reminded of the Truth of who we really are, but it's equally important to be accepted just as we are, with all our flaws and faults.

I have several friends who have made a commitment to love each other right where they are, regardless of where that is and what it looks like. The question we ask each other is, "Can you love me even though I'm _____?" You fill in the blank—angry, scared, judgmental, lashing out . . . you name it. The only answer we give is, "I love you right there. In that, with that, and because of that—I love you right there." Never *in spite of it.* Never giving suggestions to *fix it.* Never because they *know the Truth of our Higher Self.* We've made a commitment to stand together in a judgment free zone and love and be loved right where we are in that moment. Regardless of what we've got going on, when one of us reaches out for love, the answer is always, "I love you right there." Standing with someone in that judgment-free zone is amazing.

It's a process, not a onetime thing. I've learned that the more I'm willing to reach out to those who have earned the right to hear about my self-judgments, and be found acceptable in that moment, the easier it is to love myself. When I love myself in those moments, I have a greater chance to establish a new pattern of self-compassion instead of self-assault. It becomes easier to consciously choose to love myself, and others. It strengthens my sense of being worthy of love and belonging in a way that is not tied to what I do. Feeling worthy of love and belonging is so much easier when I give myself permission to be fully human—to feel the full spectrum of human emotions and have the full range of human experiences.

This process takes courage—lots and lots of courage. The root word for courage is *cor*, which is the Latin word for *heart*. Courage originally meant, "To speak one's mind by telling all one's heart." To do this takes much courage. That's love in action.

The motto of Brené Brown's *Daring Way Training* is "Show up. Be seen. Live Brave." When we do these things, we open to more love, more joy, and greater fulfillment in life. Give yourself the gift of making a conscious choice to love, to be loving, and to allow yourself to be loved *exactly as you are* and in all the ways you show up in life! To paraphrase the wisdom of Dr. Seuss, "Be who you are and say what you feel because those who mind don't matter and those who matter don't mind."

Love is Magical

Harry Potter's magic is like the Divine presence within, your True Self.

In the first two novels, Harry became aware of *Who-He-Really-Was*, a wizard (divine expression), just as we all become more in tune with our True Self during our lives. His magic was an innate gift, an expression of his natural magical birthright, like the Love expressed from our God Source within.

In the next three novels, Harry became more aware of the ego self, which was called, "He who must not be named." The ego generates fear-based thoughts, feelings, and beliefs, and takes innumerable forms, just as Voldemort wore many guises. The ego is cunning, deceptive, and seemingly powerful, but as Harry discovered, it's not real. It's only a perception that we're somehow separate from the indwelling Love, which is impossible, since It's Who-We-Really-Are.

In the fifth and sixth novels, Harry and his friends, his spiritual community, gradually chipped away at the ego, as they sought Voldemort's demise. Like the Dark Lord's magic, they discovered the ego was weak and powerless in the face of love. As the magical white light of Harry's wand (Love) overpowered Voldemort's dark magic, the ego dissipated into the nothingness from whence it came.

Love is all there is, the yin and yang, the end-all-be-all. Love . . . God . . . is within. And it's magical.

More About Unconditional Love

Comedian Steve Martin used to do a stand-up routine that went something like this:

"Wouldn't it be funny to raise your kid speaking a gibberish language instead of English? Imagine the laughs on his first day of school . . . "

That's exactly what happened to 99% of us growing up regarding unconditional love. You've been taught the wrong kind of love your entire life. Your parents, teachers, ministers, and others instructed you that you'd receive approval (be loved) only if you acted a certain way or did what was expected. This conditional love is the norm—it's what our parents, and our parents' teachers and ministers grew up with as well. We had limited role models. They didn't understand unconditional love—which is neither good nor bad, it just is.

The unfortunate result is that you've learned to value yourself based on the conditional love given you. The moment an 18-month old baby realizes she is *bad*, a lifetime of false thinking begins. Imagine if, instead of a gibberish language, you were taught from an early age that you're good, very good, even (gasp) perfect—exactly as you are.

Imagine if everyone around you told you how much they loved you, and treated you that way even when they were correcting your behavior to keep you safe. What would you think of yourself by age five, or ten, or twenty? You would be free of self-limiting, self-criticizing, and self-destructive thoughts, beliefs, and behavior. Your feelings of self-worth would be *off the charts* high. You would excel at everything you tried because of your self-confidence. You'd feel light as a feather without all that excess personal baggage. In fact, you wouldn't even understand the concept of self-destructive behavior.

Imagine that.

If your self-worth is tied to your past (that would be most of us), you have some work to do. The past is an illusion; it exists only in your mind, not in Reality. The unreal past and future are in the driver's seat of your mind. Your subconscious is like the hidden part of the iceberg, that gigantic part under the water. It contains trillions of pieces of information—data, memories, scents, positive and negative emotions, limiting and false beliefs, a veritable monstrous underground warehouse of old stuff. Both past and future exist only in your subconscious mind as memories, emotions, and future ideas and concepts. Here's the good news: the subconscious mind is an employee of the conscious mind. What you think into it is what it acts upon. It doesn't differentiate between what's truth and imaginary. Like a computer, it's neutral, literal, and receptive.

Here's a mental exercise that will change your life: For one day, observe your thoughts, words, and actions to identify the beliefs behind them. Why did you say that? Why did you take that action? Why did you get angry when your spouse said so-and-so? Why did you get defensive when your boss made a suggestion? Why did you become fearful when you thought about your bills? Our beliefs are foundations in our subconscious—they're the causative reason we think, say, and do what we do.

Dig deep within your mind and pinpoint the belief within your subconscious that's the foundation for every thought you think, every word you speak, or action you take. It's not easy, and the ego will resist, but it's worth it. This practice will allow you to release and let go of unwanted, unproductive, self-destructive, and false beliefs within your subconscious. You cannot help but realize the fallacy of many of your beliefs when you examine them closely.

After purging these false beliefs, your True Self will urge you to forgive yourself and others. You'll see yourself more clearly, and love yourself at a much deeper level. This new self-love will translate into more inner peace and untethered joy. By clearing out the *old*, you'll have more room for the *new*. By letting go of the false, you'll see the Truth. After you've done this for one day, try it for another . . . and then another. Being vigilant of hidden beliefs is a daily practice for the Truth seeker, and you desire Truth. Knowing your truth is an act of unconditional self-love.

In relation to others, unconditional love means being open, receptive, and attentive to the person in front of you. It means being free of expectations, *shoulds*, beliefs, opinions, and agendas. Unconditional love implies being in tune with another. Like a radio, when your frequency matches theirs, the signal is clearer. The ego's selfish desire to *want* something from another person disrupts the flow of selfless love.

If you expect or even just desire other people to understand you, you're off track. Unconditional love expects or desires nothing from others. It's all about the giving. The prayer of St. Francis is a good example of unconditional love. The pray-er asks God to:

"Grant that I seek to understand, than to be understood."

When you unconditionally love someone, you desire for them to be safe, happy, fulfilled, and at peace—you simply want all good things for them.

When you're not feeling particularly loving or in tune, you know it. When you feel irritated, frustrated, fearful, worried, or any sense of separation or lack—you're out of frequency with that inner unconditional love, the True Self. Constant awareness of your conscious mind is the key to self-understanding and taking back control of your mind from the ego—and with this control, happiness and peace.

That subtle shift from irritation to acceptance, from anger to forgiveness, or from judgment to love is a phenomenal event. This shift in perception requires only two things from you: (1) Awareness of your mind; and (2) willingness to see things differently. These shifts are how you change and evolve. It's how the consciousness of our entire species evolves.

Walking Out of the Cave: From Fear to Love

A long-time and wise recovering alcoholic once said, "I cannot tell you who or what God is, but I can tell you how God works in my life." The same can be said for love—not romantic love, but pure love, Agape love, unconditional love. No one among us can give a clear-cut definition of something so all encompassing using the crude and vague symbols we call words. That would be like a honeybee trying to give a discourse on Plato's Republic using nothing but interpretive dance.

We cannot truly understand Love any more than we can understand the awe-ness of God, but we can say with confidence that Love and God are the same things. You've heard this many times, haven't you? "God is Love, Love is God." As a Truth seeker, you intuitively know this to be true. You know that you're made of God, that you're an individual expression of God. Therefore, you are Love.

From Plato's Republic, the *Allegory of the Cave* has a relevant lesson in our regard to understanding Love, our true nature: A group of people were chained in a cave their entire lives, facing a blank wall. Behind them was a fire, and when objects passed in front of the fire, shadows were projected onto the wall in front of them. So the people gave names to the shadows and discussed them at length. Their entire belief system was wrapped up in these shadows. The people believed that the shadows were reality. When one of the people was freed from his chains and stepped out into the sunlight, he came to understand that the shadows on the wall did not represent reality at all. He perceived true Reality, rather than the mere shadows seen by his companions.

You're walking out of the cave every time you examine or question one of your limiting beliefs, every time you sincerely and truthfully examine yourself. You're gradually coming into the light. You're like the onion that's slowly being peeled away. At your core is your true nature, Love/God.

A Course in Miracles states:

"Your task is not to seek love, but merely to seek and find all of the barriers within yourself that you have built against it. It's not necessary to seek for what is true, but it is necessary to seek out what is false. Every illusion is one of fear, whatever form it takes."

Fear is the opposite of Love. It's the great beguiler, the chief weapon of the ego—but like the man behind the curtain in the Wizard of Oz, it's just an illusion, a miscreation. So examining your fears must become a constant and ongoing process if your goal is spiritual growth. For every problem, worry, unpleasant life situation, and every perceived negative in your life, there's a fear behind it. Examining these fears and seeing through them, knowing that they're as false as shadows on the wall, allows you to peel another layer from the onion.

A fellow Truth seeker named Francine tells of a daily practice in which she writes down all the fears the ego is projecting into her mind. She says she does this to "put my fears in the sunlight so they'll dry up and blow away." In fact, she doesn't just write them down, she puts them out on Facebook in a spiritual group page (and asks for no input from others). Now *that's* courage. In addition to listing a specific fear, Francine follows each one with the question, "What would God say about that?" Here's one of her typical entries:

"I fear losing my job. I fear that my supervisor doesn't value me and wants to replace me with someone younger or with someone who agrees with her all the time."

What would God (Francine's True Self) say about that? According to her:

"My God-Self would say, 'Francine, your supervisor hasn't said or done anything specifically to support this fear. The ego has taken little tidbits of misperceived information and blown it up into a scary movie. It's all in your mind, created by the ego. It's not real. You have nothing to fear. Even if you lost a job for any reason, you'd still have nothing to fear. I am your source and supply, I will always provide for you. I will give you the strength to get through anything. Let go of this fear as it enters your mind. It's a lie, a piece of ego-drama. I love you and I'm always here for you. Just know that all is well, that you are loved beyond measure, right here, right now.'"

Isn't that beautiful? Talk about self-healing!

The ego is, as recovering alcoholics describe alcohol, "cunning, baffling, and powerful." It doesn't want you to look at your fears any more than the Wizard wanted Toto to pull back the curtain. The ego will try to convince you that you're anything but fearful.

A Course in Miracles goes on to state:

"The ego can and does allow you to regard yourself as supercilious, unbelieving, light-hearted, distant, emotionally shallow, callous, uninvolved and even desperate, but not really afraid. Minimizing fear, but not its undoing, is the ego's constant effort, and is indeed a skill at which it's very ingenious. How can it preach separation without upholding it through fear, and would you listen to it if you recognized this is what it's doing?"

Your realization that whatever seems to separate you from God is only fear is a huge threat to the ego. When you become aware of the Truth of your being—that you're Love incarnate—the ego deflates, as the Wicked Witch of the West deflated when a bucket of water was tossed in her face.

Self-examination and reliance on the True Self are the key. Constant vigilance of your thoughts, emotions, and beliefs is your ally. As you courageously dig deep and look at your fears, another layer of the ego's skin is peeled off. As you allow your True Self to assist you in persistently observing your thoughts through mindfulness and meditation, Truth is revealed and the false evaporates. What remains is the Divine—Love, God, You.

The Ego Doesn't Want You to Love Yourself

It's inevitable, however. Self-love will always win out. This love is irresistible and unavoidable, your natural birthright and end-of-life fate. When the curtain closes, and you're close to physical death, your self-love will grow even stronger. It's a sure bet.

So why now, during the course of your life, are you so wrapped up in day-to-day fear, worry, self-criticism, impatience, un-forgiveness, shame, guilt, blah, blah, blah? Why are you constantly punishing yourself with negative thinking? You might say, "I'm not THAT bad, most of my thinking isn't that negative." The truth is, it probably is if you're an average human being. You just don't realize it. You're not aware of 90% of your thoughts. They play out in the back of your consciousness like a droning B-movie in an adjacent room, barely audible.

The ego criticizes, judges, and places unrealistic expectations on you, very subtly and very deceptively, on a moment-to-moment basis. Its specialty is quick, short jabs, most of which you're not fully aware. You shame yourself, guilt yourself, and then try to put a smile on your face and tell yourself you feel great about your life. You're like a contender in a boxing ring, who gets hit in the face lightly for 15 rounds—even after 15 rounds there's a cumulative effect in the form of bruises, cuts, and welts. The difference is, you're hitting yourself.

When you say, "I love myself," the ego naturally says, "Don't be arrogant! Don't be self-centered and self-absorbed." The ego doesn't want this self-love because it wants control. It wants you for itself. The ego says, "Show more humility, don't brag, don't be so full of yourself, and don't draw unnecessary attention to yourself." The ego will tell you, "It's NOT all about you," when it actually IS all about the ego. Have you ever stood in front of a mirror, looked yourself in the eyes and said, "I love you?" Try it, and then listen for that whispering resistance from the ego.

Here's the good news—you can turn this around today, this minute. Every moment of your life from this point forward provides you a new beginning. The solution for generating more self-love begins with self-awareness and self-observation. You must learn to be fully awake and control your thinking. So simple, yet so very challenging.

Try this simple method, just for one week: Observe and don't judge your thoughts—all day, every hour, every minute, every second. Be the silent observer in the back of your mind, observing each thought, idea, belief, and emotion as it drifts by, like leaves floating down a stream. Don't attach yourself to any thought, don't watch the leaf as it floats all the way down the stream, just observe and don't judge. Constantly, consistently return to the observer mode. *The not judging part is critical,* this cannot be emphasized enough. When you judge, argue with, or attach yourself to a thought in any way, you've stepped out of the observer mode. Observe and don't judge. Try this for one week. A miracle will occur—you will experience a shift in your perception. Guaranteed.

Being fully conscious of your thoughts is the key to happiness and self-love. Discrimination can be a good thing—being able to discriminate *true* thoughts (based in love) from the lies and deceptions posed by the ego is the beginning of a blissful life. After you become more skilled at this, you'll notice a gradual and definite uplifting of your consciousness—more peace, more serenity, more joy, and more fulfillment in general.

You'll become more skilled at releasing and letting go of untrue thought patterns and beliefs—those based in fear that take the form of worry, resentment, judgment, shame, guilt, and every similar thought that seemingly keeps you separate from your Divine Source within. God loves you, God is within you, and God wants you to love yourself. It's your Divine inheritance. Why wait and be miserable in the process? Start to work on your mind today.

Try that simple method of self-observation discussed above. Try it for one week.

Your Dying Wish

What if you were about to die within the next five minutes, with no chance to survive? What would your dying wish for others be? This wish is not for yourself, not something you could do, have, or be. Instead, what would your dying wish for *others* be? If everyone in the world would follow your dying advice explicitly, what would you want them to have, know, do, or be? What critical piece of wisdom would you impart to your fellow inhabitants of the planet Earth? What's most important in this world?

As you die and look back over your life, what would you say was the most essential part? Success? Achievement? Prosperity? Was it a nice house, fancy car, or some form of status or power? Was it that great job, an intimate relationship, or series of friendships? Perhaps it was having an impact on the world, making a difference. Maybe it was just about having fun, enjoying life, and being happy. What stands out as most important?

You probably said *Love* is the most important aspect of life. Given the opportunity to impact others, you'll probably encourage others to love each other, and urge them to love themselves. You'll advise the living to get on with the living by helping and serving others, forgiving easily, and strengthening relationships with family members and friends. It's *not* the Hokey Pokey . . . it's Love! That's what it's all about.

Each of us has an intuitive urging toward love. We know, deep down in our bones, that love is the most important part of life. Love is part of our DNA. It's the common thread that connects us all, because God is Love, and we're all God beings. That innate Love is God in expression, something we all share, because we're All One.

It's the ego-self that denies love. It mentally clouds your reality, urging you toward fear, resentment, shame, guilt, jealousy, and the like. It tells you that you're separate from God and other humans and animals. It hints to you that God is *out there somewhere*, judging you, instead of the truth that God is indwelling.

So, wake up! Smell the love. If love is the end-all-be-all, how is this showing up in your life? A wise person once said, "To get a good idea of someone's priorities, just look at how they spend their time, day in and day out." If love is the most important aspect of life, how are you expressing it? How are you showing it to yourself and others? What do you need to do TODAY to extend that love?

Complete Freedom

This series of affirmative statements (an affirmative prayer), written by an anonymous Religious Scientist, is a powerful testament to his and *your* personal freedom:

I have complete freedom. I am a free person.

I am free of all fear, all anger and resentment, and any judgment of self and others. I am liberated from any thoughts or beliefs in guilt, shame, impatience, envy, or jealousy. I am completely exempt from disharmony, chaos, weakness, and any notion of poverty, lack, or limitation. I've been released from all ideas related to sickness, disease, and pain. I let go of any desire to control, manipulate, lord over, or compete with others. I banish any thoughts of being less than or better than any other living creature. All negative, limiting, and self-destructive inner dialogue is discharged from my mind.

This freedom is based on my moment-to-moment choices to discipline my mind by aligning it with my True Self, God within.

I am completely free to choose who I want to be, what I want to think and feel, and what I believe . . . or don't believe.

I choose to KNOW that I am love, I am peace, I am joy. I know I'm love, peace, and joy because God is also, and I'm a mirror reflection of this Infinite Loving Creative Power. My soul is made of God energy. God is the ocean, and I'm a wave of that ocean, always a part of the larger sea.

I choose to know that all that's good, love enhancing, and life generating is who and whose I am. I have complete freedom to know this Truth. I am loving, loved, at peace, happy and joyful. I am patient, I am kind, and I know all of life and every living creature is All One. I am abundant because God is my source and supply, and I know that more abundance flows to me continuously from sources known and unknown. I am honest, open, and willing. I am in harmony with life, and I go with the flow. I am balanced, strong, and courageous. I am clear about my life purpose and dedicated to self-understanding. I am vigilant of my thoughts, and I know my truth.

These are the choices I make based on my freedom.

My freedom doesn't have a start and stop time. It's eternal. My freedom lives in the present moment. Every second of every day is an instant where I find my freedom residing. If I make a mistake, I can begin again, anytime. God instantly forgives any lapse in my forgetting who I am, and wants me to forgive myself, always . . . and begin again.

I am very grateful for this freedom. I claim it, I relish it, I embody it, I use it. Right here, right now.

The Parable of Letting Go

There was once a society of people in a far off kingdom who wore chains instead of clothes. The men and women of this remote land adorned themselves with large and heavy chains made of iron, steel, aluminum, and other metals. The chains were multi-colored—silver, gold, copper, some were painted blue, green, red, yellow, purple, and a variety of other colors. The chains were worn around their heads, necks, across their backs, around their arms and waists, looped and crisscrossed around their hips, and around their legs and ankles. They wore decorative shoes made of chains. For as long as anyone remembered, this was the way they dressed themselves. They had no idea why they dressed this way, nor did they concern themselves with the origins of their fashion.

One day, one of the men from this land, an adventurous spirit named Larco, decided to venture off and explore new lands. No one from his village thought he should go. There was no tradition of exploration or wanderlust within their people. Everyone was content to be content. But this young man, a strong and bright-eyed youth, knew he just had to see and experience new lands and people. Larco was different.

So with a large bag of supplies and nourishment thrown over his shoulder, he was off. The journey was long and exhausting. His chains seemed to get heavier and heavier as the days wore on, but he was determined, so he disregarded his pain and suffering and trudged on. Finally, after crossing a hot desert, he stumbled into a large town.

The town was colorful and bright. It had a glow of vibrancy about it. Larco stopped dead in his tracks when he saw a small group of people. They were not wearing chains! Their bodies were adorned with pieces of colorful cloth. How strange.

Walking through the town, Larco was approached by an old man.

"Welcome to our town. Why don't you take that heavy chain off your head and wear this comfortable straw hat? It will keep the sun from your eyes and lighten your body."

Larco thanked the man, unwrapped the heavy chain from his head, and donned the hat.

Farther down the road a pretty young woman greeted Larco.

"Oh those chains around your neck and chest are so beautiful, but they must be heavy. Here is a handsome cotton shirt for you, the breeze will pass through it, and you'll feel much cooler."

Larco bowed and thanked the woman and replaced his heavy neck and chest chains with the wispy shirt. He felt much lighter.

As Larco walked through the town, these acts of kindness continued. People offered him an entire new set of cloth garments and sandals to replace his chains. Larco had never experienced this feeling of agility and buoyancy before. He felt lighter than air. His feet seemed to skim across the road as he walked, almost like he was floating.

Larco was experiencing a new freedom, a feeling he had never known. All his life he was urged to wear chains. He had no idea why he wore them but they became familiar and even uneasily comfortable. But the lightness of his new cloth garments was wonderful. He felt a sense of freedom. After all these years, he finally comprehended the word serenity and he knew true peace. His entire attitude and outlook on life changed. He was a new man, untethered and unbound, all because he was willing to release his chains and burdens to try something new, given to him by caring souls.

Those caring souls represent your True Self, the voice and presence within you that cares only for your well-being. When you ask to be guided by It, you receive the wisdom and direction you need at any given moment. It's always available to you and loves you beyond measure. It's your bridge to God.

This is a parable about releasing and letting go of that which doesn't serve you. All the thoughts, feelings, and beliefs that seemingly separate you from your Source—fear, guilt, shame, judgment of self and others—are simply miscreations. The idea that you're not worthy is false. The thought that you're better, richer, or holier than others is a lie. The notion that you already have all the answers is an ego creation. All of these negative and false beliefs are the heavy loads the ego directs you to carry through life. They're completely unnecessary. They rob you of positive energy and overshadow your true freedom, your holy birthright. They're like a shroud that hides the truth from you, a truth that's right there, within you. Your True Self helps you to replace these mistaken perceptions with the Truth.

True personal freedom is not about seeking, changing, or adding anything new. Change starts with release. Self-love begins with letting go.

Suppose you have a beautiful garden filled with fragrant flowers and delicious vegetables, but your garden is overgrown with weeds. To bring it back to its original state of goodness, you would not need to create anything new, but simply remove the weeds. As the debris (untruth) is cleared away, what's left is love, peace, truth, and freedom—your original state. Your personal sovereignty is always there, and your True Self can help you find and embrace it. Freedom and happiness start with shedding.

Love in the 12 Steps

12-Step Newcomer: Is love in the 12 Steps? Which step is about love?
Old-timer: Yes. All of them.

We can all learn from the 12 Steps. The paragraphs below are directed toward recovering addicts and alcoholics, but if you replace words like disease, booze, or drugs with *the human ego*, you can see that we all suffer from the illness of misperception, and can be healed by the same Source Power.

The act of finally surrendering your disease (ego) to a Higher Power is an act of love. Surrendering is a return to love, which is life itself. Love is Life, and Life is Love—if ever there was a key to life, there it is.

In step one of the 12 Steps, when you finally surrender and cry out, "Help!" You're aligning your will with God's will. You're listening to and acting on the subtle, or sometimes loud urges of the Divine Presence within you—you're loving yourself.

Steps two and three are also acts of love. By coming to believe in a power greater than yourself and turning your will and life over to this power, you're essentially saying, "Hey, I know I can't do this on my own, and I'm willing to love myself enough to ask for help and do things differently." Relying on others is an act of self-love. When you want something good for yourself badly enough, and know you can't do it alone, seeking help is a natural expression to save and therefore love yourself. Reliance on other human beings teaches you to rely on God within.

From a recovering alcoholic:

"I had a very limited knowledge of what unconditional love was when I began working the 12 Steps, and I sure wasn't skilled at or willing to apply what I knew. By the time I walked through the doors of my first 12-Step meeting, I didn't really have any friends. The only people I associated with were work colleagues and my wife, all of whom tended to avoid me. After I'd

let my guard down, I became willing to follow the guidance of a higher power and my sponsor. When I finished my 4th-Step, self-inventory, I saw how selfish, self-centered, and self-involved I'd been during my life. It came as a gradual realization over several weeks while writing my 4th Step. By the time I completed it, I was extremely depressed, embarrassed, and ashamed.

Have you ever looked back on your life and said, 'Oh shit, what have I done?' Well, that's where I was at after my 4th Step inventory. I'd been one selfish S.O.B., and I owed my wife and others in my life a big fat apology. But words and weak-ass admissions of regret were not going to cut it—I needed to show them that I loved them. I use the word love *now, but I had a limited understanding of unconditional love when I had six months of sobriety—at that point I was just trying to be less self-centered.*

My higher self taught me about love over the next several months. It was nothing short of a miracle. That God voice within was calling me to action. I learned about unconditional love by helping other guys in the program. I gave them rides to meetings, and called them on the phone and asked how their day was going. I stocked the refrigerator in our 12-Step meeting room, stacked chairs, cleaned up after meetings, and listened to new guys who needed to talk.

I started to think about other people, wondering what it would be like to walk in their shoes. I asked how I could help them or what they might need that I could provide. The source of this love was God within and the result was other-centered action. The program calls it getting out of self *and being of service to others. The key word was always* action, *rather than thinking, feeling, or believing.*

By relying on this God presence within me, I learned to love myself as well as others. For years, I'd been blaming, criticizing, and hurting myself. Why? Did my mommy or daddy not love me enough? Did I have an inferiority complex due to my upbringing, or was it innate? I don't know or care. The source of my life pain is not important to me anymore. I don't need to understand the origins of a problem to move toward a solution.

I learned to love myself, and was more aware of those self-criticizing and self-defeating thought patterns and beliefs. At this point in my life, I didn't know these were false beliefs, I just knew I didn't want to think of myself as someone who was less than.

Andrew, my 12-Step grand sponsor, taught me about the 100% Rule. Similar to the Golden Rule, the 100% Rule states that you must give one hundred percent of yourself to another person in a relationship. We're taught that marriage is a 50/50 deal, right? Well, that even split was created by the self-centered ego—the ego that wants equanimity and reciprocity in any relationship, and wants to make sure it gets its share of . . . hold on . . . wait for it . . . control.

Operating under the 100% Rule, I put my needs second. I did everything my wife wanted me to do. I didn't argue, criticize, or try to control situations. In fact, I agreed with everything she said, and not in that condescending, smart-ass way. Whatever she wanted to do, we did it. Whatever she wanted to watch on TV, we watched. Whatever came out of her mouth was golden.

Now, when Andrew first directed me to follow this rule, I heartily resisted. I said, 'But what about me? She'll take advantage of me. She'll be in control of our relationship! I'll be her bitch!' Nothing in this world scares the crap out of the ego more than someone else having control.

My fears were unfounded, thank God. Had she not been such a nice person to begin with, there might have been a problem, but that's not the case with my wife Cassie. She's a very loving, giving person. So here's what happened: when I gave, she gave, when I said something nice, she returned the volley, when I was loving, so was she. After a few days of this she said, 'I can't put my finger on it, but you're different. I don't know what you're doing, but keep doing it.' Giving unconditional love returns the same."

This story is a great illustration of the Law of Attraction—in action.

In *The Science of Mind*, Ernest Holmes refers to love as, "the Divine Giving-ness of God." This idea requires a much broader perspective of love than most of us have. It means that this Universal Spirit, the universe itself, is constantly emanating love, which is life itself. The power that makes the flowers grow, the grass green, and the rain fall is love. The power that gives life to every living creature and fuels every cell and atom is love. This might be hard to swallow, but the power that forms hurricanes, earthquakes, and droughts is love. God is always and constantly emanating life, which is love.

Love calls to us from within. It urges us to come together, to associate with other human beings and earth's living creatures, and with nature. This is why we feel more at peace and at one with nature. This love is why we feel a dog's unconditional love—we know it's natural to us. We instinctually sense this bond to other animals and to each other. We intuitively know that love is the key that opens our hearts and heals all.

Useful Affirmations

I love myself. I'm kind and gentle with myself.

I love everyone I come in contact with today, knowing each is my spiritual brother and sister.

Love heals me. Love heals all.

Love is magic, I'm under its spell, I spread the magic of love in all that I think, say, and do.

I love myself, and others, unconditionally. Exactly as I am, I love myself. Exactly as they are, I love others.

I release all shadow thoughts and beliefs and return to the love within.

I am free to think and choose my reality. I choose love, I choose peace, I choose joy.

I am letting go of all thoughts and beliefs that don't serve my highest and best.

I know my truth today. It is peace, joy, love, patience, and understanding.

Rhyming Affirmations

I listen to that Inner Voice, the God presence within,
I release all the ego-thoughts, and let the peace begin.

I ignore the critical voice that speaks loudly in my head,
And listen for the whispers of the loving voice instead.

I breathe in, I breathe out, I examine my inner attitude,
I feel the one-ness of everything, and revel in the gratitude.

An Infinite light is within, I let it shine on myself, and others,
I follow my loving True Self, and know we're all sisters and brothers.

The outer world doesn't faze me, I let it all go,
I sit quietly in the peace, and go with the flow.

CHAPTER SIX

Prayer

If we know God as an Indwelling Presence, our prayer is naturally addressed to this Presence in us. We long for, and need, a conscious union with the Infinite. This is as necessary to the nature and intellect of man, as food is to the well-being of his physical body.

—Ernest Holmes, *The Science of Mind*

Prayer now must be the means by which God's Son leaves separate goals and separate interests by, and turns in holy gladness to the truth of union in his Father and himself.

—*Song of Prayer (A Course in Miracles booklet)*

As we go through the day we pause, when agitated or doubtful, and ask for the right thought or action. We constantly remind ourselves we are no longer running the show, humbly saying to ourselves many times each day "Thy will be done."

—*Alcoholics Anonymous*

Affirm What You Want, Not What you Don't Want

Affirmative prayer starts with knowing your truth. When looking at your *problems* though, it's easier to identify what you *don't* want in your consciousness than what you *do* want. Let's listen to a spiritual counseling session that we might hear at any one of hundreds of New Thought churches and spiritual centers around the globe.

Spiritual Counselor: So how can I help you today?

Counselee: Well, I set up this appointment because I have a few things going on in my life that I'm not feeling too good about.

Spiritual Counselor: Okay (silence). Tell me more.

Counselee: Well, I'm having problems in my marriage. My husband is drinking too much and I don't like him when he's drunk. He gets critical and smarmy, kind of an a-hole. Then there's this woman at work who back stabs me every chance she gets. I'm not sure what her deal is. I think she's jealous because I got the assistant director position over her. Then there's my son Josh: he's smoking weed—I just know it. I smell it on him but he denies it. I worry about him so much. Then, well, I don't know how to explain this—I'm . . . uh . . . well . . . I'm just feeling a lot of fear every day. It may not be about anything specific, just a general feeling that something bad is going to happen and I'm not going to be able to handle it. I don't know if that makes any sense.

Spiritual Counselor: Yes, I know what you mean (silence). Is anything else going on?

Counselee: No, that's about it (laughing), but I guess that's enough.

Spiritual Counselor: (laughing) Yeah, sounds like you have some things you're concerned about. So tell me, what kinds of feelings are associated with each of these problems? Let's start with your husband.

Counselee: Well, I . . . uh . . . I'm feeling angry at him. He's been through this before with alcohol and should know better. He's being totally irresponsible and setting a terrible example for Josh (silence). I guess I'm feeling some fear too. I'm afraid for my future if he keeps this up, and I'm afraid for Josh. I guess I'm afraid for my husband too (silence). I still love him and hate to see him do this to himself.

Spiritual Counselor: Okay. How about the woman at work? What are you feeling there?

Counselee: That's easy. Anger and . . . well . . . resentment . . . because the anger just keeps festering. That's resentment, right (silence)? I'm always judging her in my head—telling her off and making her feel small. So, I guess pretty much just anger and resentment.

Spiritual Counselor: And your son?

Counselee: (silence) Fear, I guess. I'm angry with him too, but I know that won't do any good. The anger won't help him and that's what I want to do, help him. I want to convince him that smoking pot is self-destructive. I smoked pot for a few years in high school and college and I know it just zaps you of any motivation, and he's planning to go to college next year. I want the best for him and know smoking pot will just hold him back.

Spiritual Counselor: Okay, so we have some anger, resentment, critical judgments, fear . . . anything else you'd identify in your day-to-day thoughts?

Counselee: (silence) Well, I've had a lot of arthritis pain, so I guess that's been on my mind too much.

Spiritual Counselor: Okay, let's summarize. From what you've told me, what is it *within you* that you no longer want to experience?

Counselee: I . . . uh . . . I . . . want my husband to slow down or stop his drinking, and I want my son to stop smoking pot. I'm not sure I can do much about that woman at work. And I want this arthritis to go away.

Spiritual Counselor: Okay, let's look at this differently. All the things you've named are out of your control, although you *can* follow your doctor's orders and take pain medication for the arthritis. What I want you to identify are the thoughts, feelings, or beliefs within your mind that you no longer want to experience.

Counselee: Okay, I think I know where you're going here. Right . . . okay . . . I guess I don't want to feel this fear anymore, regarding both my husband's drinking and my son. And the anger—it's wearing me out and I know it doesn't do any good. As far as that woman at work, I just want to stop thinking about her and being angry at her. As far as the arthritis, I don't want the pain . . . and the frustration I feel about having the pain.

Spiritual Counselor: Good, very good. You've identified what you don't want within your mind: fear, anger, resentment, and ill health or pain. Now, tell me what you *do* want.

Counselee: I want to be free of this anger for starters. I definitely don't want all that fear and I want to be free of pain.

Spiritual Counselor: Let me ask that question again. What is it that you *do* want?

Counselee: I don't understand.

Most of us don't know what we *do* want within our minds because we were not taught to observe and analyze our thoughts, feelings, and beliefs. We were not taught about spiritual principles. As a culture, we've been raised to fix problems and people, the external world. But the only thing we truly have control over is our own consciousness. When we change our thinking, we change our reality.

The woman in this spiritual counseling session identified what she didn't want in her mind: fear, anger, resentment, frustration regarding her health, and thoughts of pain and sickness. But she's never been taught to identify the spiritual opposites, the universal spiritual principles that will *solve* (like a solvent) these issues in consciousness. She doesn't know how to heal herself.

The spiritual counseling session continued and the counselor helped the woman understand the opposite principle for each of her limiting beliefs:

1. The opposite of fear is faith, a certainty that God is right here, and all is well in the present moment. You could also say that the opposite of fear is love, self-love. When we truly love ourselves, and know the love of God for us, we calm the ego's fear.
2. The opposite of anger and resentment is love, and forgiveness is the bridge to love.
3. The opposite of ill health/pain is vibrant health/life.

Just understanding that love, forgiveness, faith, and vibrant health are her solutions, though, isn't enough. She needs to believe/know, beyond doubt, that she *is* all of these principles based on who she is, a Divine creation. Because God is love, she is love. Because God is faith, she is faith. Because God is vibrant health, she is vibrant health. This *absolute knowingness*, combined with the *fire* (passion) of the emotion behind this faith will strengthen and solidify her prayer.

Knowing inner truth is the starting point for affirmative prayer. With this truth firmly cemented in her consciousness, she can now verbalize her prayer. After centering herself and realizing her one-ness with the Infinite, she speaks this affirmative prayer. It might sound something like this:

I am a perfect creation of a Perfect Creator. I am whole, perfect, and complete, exactly as I am. I lack absolutely nothing. I am loved, I am loving to myself and others, and I know God is right here where I am, right now, always and forever. I release and turn away from any thoughts or beliefs related to fear, anger, resentment, pain, ill health, and disease. I know these are miscreations of the ego and I lovingly deny them entrance to my mind as they try to enter. They're illusions, they're lies, they're folly.

I know my truth. I am a loving child of the Divine, made of the same Infinite Creative Essence as God. I am light, I am truth, I am filled with love, a calm peace, and a strong faith. I forgive myself, and others, for any perceived wrongdoing and I love, I just love. No judgments, no criticisms, no shoulds. I love myself, and everyone in my life, and know that everyone is exactly where they should be.

I know God's healing energy that is within me, and all around me, is healing me constantly and consistently. I am vibrant health. As God is vibrant health, I am vibrant health. The basis of my healing is my underlying perfection and completeness, which manifests as vibrant health and a joyful, loving, peace-filled outlook on my body and mind. I know that I'm in a constant state of healing, that every cell in my body and every thought in my mind is constantly and consistently renewing, re-invigorating, re-energizing, and repairing itself, constantly returning back to its natural state of perfect physical and mental balance and harmony.

I accept this truth that has been spoken by God through me, I give thanks for knowing this truth, and I now release these words into the Law of Cause and Effect, knowing it has no choice but to manifest exactly as I've spoken it. Amen, and so it is.

The Power of "We"

The Power of Affirmative Prayer

by
Judy Baker, RScP

I got up early one morning and rushed right into the day.
I had so much to accomplish that I didn't have time to pray.
Problems just tumbled about me and heavier came each task.
"Why doesn't God help me?" I wondered.
He answered, "You didn't ask."

—*Anonymous*

If peace of mind was a recipe, prayer would be an essential ingredient. It's been proven to be useful in physical and emotional healing and has been relied upon by humankind since history has been recorded. Prayer is personal to each person. It's a conversation between the person praying and his/her Source, so trying to tell another person how to pray could be perceived as intrusive.

However, there are steps that make prayer more *effective*.

Scientific or affirmative prayer is a popular and effective method to pray. It's based on a strong faith in God much like traditional *pleading* prayer. As Jesus told his followers in Mark 11:24, "You can pray for anything, and if you *believe* you have it; it is yours."

In New Thought faiths, affirmative prayer is commonly referred to as Spiritual Mind Treatment, which was originated by Dr. Ernest Holmes as part of the Science of Mind philosophy in the early 20th century. Spiritual Mind Treatment is a five-step prayer that (1) recognizes that Spirit/God is everywhere present; (2) declares unity/one-ness with that Spirit; (3) realizes the truth about the matter at hand; (4) gives thanks for knowing the truth; and, (5) releases the prayer. Spiritual Mind Treatments are prayed *from* God, the God residing within us, and is not prayed *to* God. The Treatment is spoken in words that reveal the *Truth* in an affirmative manner about the subject being prayed for.

The first step in Spiritual Mind Treatment is to *recognize* that God is all. To quote Dr. Holmes, "God is the subtle Intelligence which permeates all things . . . and is present in every place." This step is designed to recognize that Spirit is the infinite source of all that exists and is the wholeness and perfection that is the true nature of everything.

Here's an example of how the first step could be simply stated: "There is one Universal Essence that is present everywhere and It is the source of all that exists."

The next step is *unifying* with that God Presence and claiming the one-ness that unites the human with the Divine. As Holmes wrote, "I believe that man is the direct representative of this Divine Presence. I believe the relationship between God and man is a direct one."

Step two could be stated like this: "I am consciously aware of my connection with the Mind of God. I live in the One Mind and act through the one body. Mine is a spiritual body and it acts in divine harmony with God Life. We are One."

Step three is *realization*. In this step we are treating our Mind about what we want to alter or enhance. We are *realizing* the Truth that already exists within us, and we speak in the present tense, as if it were already accomplished. We don't mention that we have a disease or unhealthy body—we direct our thoughts and words in a positive manner. Right thinking is an important ingredient in life, and especially in prayer. Jesus often taught that *there is something that reacts to our thought exactly as we think it.* This is wonderful news . . . unless we let negative thoughts occupy our mind. We can *speak* in a positive manner but our *thoughts and belief system* create our life results. Concentrate on constructive thoughts and expect positive results.

An example of a realization statement regarding physical health might sound like this: "Every part of my body is made of pure substance—God substance. It's an expression of the wholeness of Spirit and therefore there can be no physical imperfections of any kind within my body because there are no imperfections within Spirit. I easily release any thoughts of fear related to my body's health. All that appears otherwise is now eliminated, and any false beliefs related to my physical condition are now replaced with deep awareness and conviction of God's wholeness and perfect health within me. My body functions perfectly and supports my well-being."

Step four of a Spiritual Mind Treatment is that of *thanksgiving*, in which we gratefully accept and give thanks for the good that we know has been given to us. This step affirms that the words we have spoken are true, and that we claim this truth as our present state of being.

Example: "I joyfully accept my healthy state of existence and I am at peace with my body. I accept with heartfelt gratitude this perfect outcome and am very thankful for knowing the truth about my health. Thank you Spirit for your gift of right thinking and wholeness within my mind and body."

The final step of Spiritual Mind Treatment is that of *release*, in which we mentally and emotionally let go of the prayer and release our words into the Law of Cause and Effect. We are planting our seed into the soil of the universe. Our work is done and it is turned over to God.

Example: "Knowing that the creative power of the One Mind has now responded to my treatment and has fulfilled every need in my body for perfect health, I am at peace and I release these words into the Law and Action of the Universe and I clearly know that God has already created the good in my body. And so it is."

A Story about Monica

As a licensed Spiritual Counselor, I was serving the Sunday Prayer Desk at my spiritual center. Monica approached the desk and handed me a written prayer request. As I accepted it I noticed the appearance of fear and/or pain in her face. I asked if I could help her and she burst into tears as she told me that she had been diagnosed with an ovarian tumor and that it was most likely cancer. I asked if she would like me to pray with her. She quickly responded, "Oh yes, please. I am so scared."

We left the desk and found a quiet place in the corner of the sanctuary where we could talk and pray. While we walked there, I began talking with God. I *knew* this was not her truth. As we got comfortable and continued our conversation, she revealed that she had been suffering from abdominal pain for some time and finally visited her gynecologist on Friday. He examined her and could feel what appeared to be a large growth on her ovary. He told her it was something that needed to be pursued as quickly as possible because ovarian cancer was very serious. She agreed because she wanted relief from the pain. Surgery was scheduled for the approaching Wednesday with the probability that the CT scan on Monday would confirm that a growth existed and required the surgical procedure.

I suggested we sit in silence for a few moments to relax into the sacred space. Then I educated her about affirmative prayer. As I did a Spiritual Mind Treatment with her I could feel her acceptance. I prayed with utmost trust and conviction and asked that Spirit consider her highest and greatest good. When I finished, she told me she felt better and the pain had lessened. She shared that she felt a *bright white light* during the prayer. I knew she was in a good space.

Late Tuesday I received a call from Monica. She told me she had received a call from her doctor's office and the CT scan *did not* show a growth of any size and her doctor asked her to come into the office for another examination. He could not find the growth that he felt there last Friday. He was baffled, exclaiming that he was *sure* he'd felt a growth. Monica assured him that she believed him. However, she told him that she had received a Spiritual Mind Treatment at church and saw a white light and knew she was healed. He asked her if she was still in pain and she told him, "No!" The doctor seemed skeptical and replied that in the medical profession they call this spontaneous remission and they don't know why it happens. Monica told him he could call it whatever he pleased but she called it a miracle. She left his office in gratitude and decided to take classes on affirmative prayer. Monica was eventually licensed as a spiritual counselor. I imagine she prays with faith and conviction after that experience. I know *I do*.

Visualization and Affirmative Prayer

There are curious similarities between the way athletes mentally prepare/train themselves for their sport and affirmative prayer. Athletes are trained to use various mental techniques by sports psychologists, such as:

1. Visualizing reaching your goal or performing well
2. Ignoring negative self-talk and self-defeating thoughts
3. Approaching every practice and every game as a new opportunity to play your best
4. Focusing on staying resilient and self-forgiving following mistakes or bad outcomes
5. KNOW-ing that you'll do well in your sport

An athlete doesn't prepare by *hoping* to do well, they don't *wish* for the ability to perform at their peak, and they understand that a desire is just something dangling in front of you, like a carrot. They're trained to KNOW beyond all doubt, that they will reach their athletic goal.

Affirmative prayer is similar. When you pray affirmatively, you're not asking, pleading, or petitioning God. You *affirm* what you know to be true: God is all good and everywhere present. God is within you and you are within God. You and God are one. All the *good* qualities found in God are also found within you because you are *of* God.

You then KNOW (speak) your truth. Your affirmative statements might sound like this:

I am loving and loved. I am at peace. I am happy and joyful. I am patient. I accept others as they are. I am understanding of others. I am healthy. I am prosperous.

Whatever truth about yourself you need to realize at any given moment, you can KNOW. There's a vast difference between: "Please God, give me peace," and, "I am peace."

Like an athlete *knows* he/she will perform exceptionally, when you pray affirmatively, you *know* . . . you affirm what's already true, and like athletes, you WIN!

The Science of Prayer

In *The Science of Mind*, Ernest Holmes wrote:

"Prayer is its own answer. Since some people have been healed through prayer and others have not, the answer is NOT that God has responded to some prayers and not others, but that some people have responded to God more than others."

God is the perfect power within you. You experience God to the extent that you interact and develop a relationship with this power. When you let go of the notion that God is a *being*, the world starts to make more sense. The most glaring misperception that the ego tries to reinforce is that humankind and Spirit are separate and that God is a detached being out there somewhere. Nothing could be further from the truth.

You are made of this Perfect Power, you are an individual expression of it. Because It is everything, you also live within it. Spirit is within you and you're within Spirit—this is the essence of the unity of all life. This is what Jesus meant throughout his parables—that you're a God-filled, creative being, a son of God, and your word has POWER.

When we interpret Jesus' words about prayer from a metaphysical perspective, they take on a whole new light.

1. So I say to you, ask, and it will be given to you; seek, and you will find; knock, and it will be opened to you.

2. If you abide in Me and My words abide in you, you will ask what you desire, and it shall be done for you.
3. Therefore I say to you, whatever things you ask when you pray, believe that you receive them, and you will have them.

In the 21st century, we talk a great deal about the Law of Attraction. The 2006 book and documentary "The Secret" have brought this spiritual law more into society's awareness, but it's not a mysterious secret. The Law of Attraction has been taught as part of mental healing techniques and in New Thought faiths for over 150 years. What you put your attention on tends to increase, multiply, and amplify. An underlying assumption of this law is that the universe always says "Yes" to what we believe and say, and the more emotion behind our word, the more powerful it is. Again, your word has power, even if it's not true. When you say, "I am sick," the Law says, "Yes, you are sick." When you say, "I am healthy, whole, and complete," the Law says "Yes, you are healthy, whole, and complete."

Henry Ford is reported to have said: "Whether you think you can, or you think you can't—you're right." Your thoughts, beliefs, and words have authority. Prayer is a movement of thought that changes the consciousness of the one thinking. Is God involved? Darn right, because *you* are God in expression!

The Man Who Talked to God

There's a story about a man named Albert who was diagnosed with a rare, but non-fatal, skin disorder that was very painful. At the same time, Albert lost his business due to a downturn in the economy, and the following week, his wife died unexpectedly. Sitting in his den, a tumbler of whisky in one hand, and a pistol in the other, Albert sobbed, trying desperately to work up the courage to commit suicide. Finally he cried out, "God please help me!"

Suddenly on the radio came the song "I'm in You," by Peter Frampton. The lyrics were haunting, the song grabbed Albert firmly with its obvious meaning—"I'm in you, you're in me." Was this a coincidence? Divine intervention? A moment of pure synchronicity? Perhaps, or maybe not, it doesn't matter. What matters is that Albert was open to hear the message. He was listening. He was good at listening, he'd always been told that by other people.

Now he came to understand that he needed to do more talking. He wanted to learn more about prayer. An inner urge drove him forward.

Albert had said many prayers silently over the years, to a God *out there*. But now, gradually, he came to realize that his connection to God was within his own consciousness. Albert had a spiritual experience. The Frampton song that played on the radio as he was contemplating suicide was like a bolt of lightning. It brought him to a place of openness and willingness so he could continue to have a spiritual awakening. A long-forgotten yearning for God pointed him to a local Unity Church.

Albert's entire approach to life, God, and himself changed as a result of his belief and practical use of Unity's five basic tenets: (1) God is the source and creator of all. There's no other enduring power. God is good and present everywhere; (2) We're spiritual beings, created in God's image. The spirit of God lives within each person, therefore, all people are inherently good; (3) We create our life experiences through our way of thinking; (4) There is power in affirmative prayer, which increases our connection to God; and, (5) Knowledge of these spiritual principles is not enough. We must live them.

Today, Albert talks to God within, his True Self, with grace and ease. When he first started his conversations, it felt silly and awkward. There was a part of him that resisted this new self-dialogue—but by keen mental self-observation, he learned of the ego's resistance to anything spiritual, so he became skilled at identifying the mental voices of the ego and True Self.

Albert learned that *every thought is a prayer* because we're affirming every thought that we place our belief on, *we're making it our truth*. So he became more selective about what he thought and believed and mentally focused more on what he wanted for himself—peace, love, joy, patience, wholeness, completeness, self-understanding, abundance, and vibrant health. He consciously directed his thinking rather than being unaware of his mental processes and at the mercy of the clever ego. Albert learned that these spiritual principles were not just what he wanted, but *what he is*. He would say to himself, "God is love, therefore I am love. God is peace, therefore I am peace." He knew he was an individual expression of an Infinite Creative Consciousness that was within him, and he knew that this Spirit was all good, so *he no longer asked for good* in his life, he affirmed it. Albert was doing nothing more than affirming the truth that already was, is, and always will be. He was engaging in affirmative prayer.

Within a year, Albert's troubles faded. His skin disorder cleared up, he started a new business with the life insurance money from his wife's death, and though still sometimes very sad about his wife's passing, he focused less on missing her and more on gratitude for the many wonderful years with her.

The sky doesn't ask God to be blue, the grass doesn't ask God to be green, a grasshopper doesn't ask God to be a good jumper—these are things that *they inherently are*. There's no need to ask God for anything, just affirm the truth of who you are, based on the foundational belief that you're a perfect creation of a Perfect Creator.

This assurance is what Jesus meant when he said:

"Ask and it will be given to you; seek and you will find; knock and the door will be opened to you. For everyone who asks, receives; the one who seeks, finds; and to the one who knocks, the door will be opened."

Jesus didn't say, *"Ask, and maybe if God's in a good mood, it will be given to you."* No, this absolute, guaranteed, without-a-doubt assurance in all things asked for is called KNOW-ing. New Thought faiths call it affirmative prayer.

Say this aloud right this moment:

I am a perfect being, lacking nothing. I am one with God. God is within me and I am within God. We are one. I am loving, and I am loved. I am at peace, and I am peace in expression. All these things I know are absolutely true, and I feel a deep gratitude in knowing who and whose I am. Amen, and so it is.

Prayer Unleashes Power

Within you, at this very moment, is a boundless and colossal source of power that you can tap into to change your life for the better, as well as the lives of others. This power is pure good, unchanging, reliable, and eternal. It's always available to you and awaits your command. With this power, you can physically heal yourself or others from a seemingly hopeless disease or a simple hangnail. This Power heals without blinking an eye. It can rectify any emotional or mental hindrance—fear, resentment, or guilt. There's nothing that can stand in its way and no good that you cannot bring into your life.

With this Power you can attract abundance and prosperity, in many different forms, from many different sources. You can use it to instantly manifest peace of mind, to be happy and content, and to better understand yourself and others. This Power gives you instant access to inner harmony, strength, and courage, and can be used to shape and mold the kind of life (consciousness) you desire.

That Power within you is God. It's Spirit. It's the Christ Consciousness, Allah Buddha, Krishna. The words used to describe It are merely symbols. It's a Universal Power that's personified within your consciousness, imprinted on your soul.

This is the underlying message of all ancient spiritual texts:

- Jesus said, "The Kingdom of God is within you."
- Hinduism's *Bhagavad Gita* emphasizes the "Krishna within."
- *The Koran* states that Allah is "closer than your jugular vein."
- Buddhist texts discuss the "Buddha within."
- The *Adi Granth*, the Sikh holy text, declares that, "the One God is all permeating and alone lives in the Mind."

One of the methods to revealing and unleashing this indwelling power is affirmative prayer.

Most humans don't realize the power of affirmative prayer, but many finally discover its secret. There's no need to wait. You can seize this opportunity to embody this Inner Power right here and now. Everyone will eventually realize the potential that's unleashed by affirmative prayer. But why wait? This Power is waiting for you to turn the key, start your prayer-engine, and make it roar.

We're like the inhabitants of an African village who live in poverty, while underneath the ground lies a diamond mine. They toil and sweat all their lives to scratch out a living—droughts destroy their crops, floods wash out their homes, and disease plagues their children. All the while, priceless diamonds lay beneath their feet, undiscovered.

The story of *The Power of Affirmative Prayer* illustrates this point well. Three women, Helen, Julia, and Isabel, were all diagnosed with stage four lung cancer. They did not know each other and lived in different areas of the country. Each were told by their doctors that they had 6-9 months to live.

Helen was not a spiritual person, per se. She had a set of values she lived by—honesty, kindness and compassion to others, and love of family—but she had no specific religious inclinations or conception of God. She was a nurse and believed in science. She was in shock when she learned of her cancer and fell into a depression. She immediately started planning for her death, believing that, despite chemotherapy and radiation treatment, there was probably little hope for remission of her cancer. After all, she was in stage four and her capable doctor gave her little hope. She quit her job and started preparing for the worst. She tied up loose emotional ends with family and friends, read several psychology-based books on death and dying, and tried to keep a positive attitude during her medical treatments, as unpleasant as they were. The pain from her cancer began two weeks after her diagnosis and became strong within a month. She took to her bed, her husband caring for her. She was in misery and became resentful. She spent most days watching television, reminiscing about happier times, and waiting. She kept asking, "Why?" Four months after her diagnosis she was weak and frail, and her family sensed that the end was near. Her pain was unbearable and she became unresponsive and lethargic from the morphine. Her misery continued and near the sixth month after her diagnosis, she went downhill very quickly. She asked that her children come to be by her bedside and within a day, she died.

Julia was also shocked when she received the news of her diagnosis. She had a strong connection with God and knew that God would heal her, if that was His will. Her family and friends from church rallied around her immediately. A prayer circle was started and Julia felt blessed by the support. She started chemotherapy and radiation treatment within two weeks after her diagnosis and had confidence in her oncologist. She prayed every morning and evening, asking God to cure her cancer. She wondered if God had more for her to do on this earth or if her place was in heaven, with her mother and father. She met with her minister regularly and they prayed together. Julia's pain didn't start until the fifth month after her diagnosis. When it became stronger, she was disappointed. She had regular conversations with God and read her Bible diligently. "There must be some reason for this," she thought. "What does God want me to do?" Despite her devotion, Julia became weak with pain by the tenth month after her diagnosis. She stopped praying regularly, calling out to God when the pain became severe. "It must be His will," crept into her thinking. She was losing hope. She became depressed and distant. Her family began to worry. She died fourteen months after her diagnosis. Toward the end, she was upbeat, sentimental, and easily expressed love to her family. It was a very touching and heartfelt death. Her funeral was well attended.

Isabel was a very spiritual person. She attended a New Thought spiritual center regularly and took classes there often. When she received her diagnosis, she too was shocked and fearful. She met with her minister the next day and asked her to pray with her. Isabel believed in the power of affirmative prayer and had seen it work with other church friends, in a variety of ways. She learned how to pray affirmatively in her spiritual classes and workshops and knew that it would heal her of her cancer. She refused to acknowledge the cancer, or the idea of death.

She took a leave of absence from her job and focused on healing herself through affirmative prayer and visualization. She knew the power of God was within her and that she could use this power to heal herself. When she prayed several times daily, she denied any power of cancer in her body, claiming that all foreign bodies were removed, flushed out, and evaporated into the nothingness from whence they came. She knew that all appearances of sickness or disease were just that, appearances, having no reality or substance. She didn't deny the existence of cancer, but knew it was not her truth, not her identity. She knew that her temporary illness had come to pass, not to stay.

She affirmed that she was a perfect creation of a Perfect Creator, imbued with the same creative power. She knew that God was right there within her body and mind, healing, always healing. She visualized God's healing white light and love constantly and continuously swirling through her body, repairing and renewing every cell and molecule. She envisioned the cancer being cleansed from her body, like a common cold virus. "Healing, healthy, and whole," was her mantra, all day long. Her minister, healing practitioners, and Unity friends prayed affirmatively for her every day. The only pain or weakness that Isabel experienced was due to the chemotherapy, which she approached with a positive attitude—it was part of her healing plan. She knew that the hands of every doctor, nurse, and technician were guided by the healing power of Spirit.

Six months after her diagnosis she returned to her doctor for another PET-CT scan and was relieved, but not surprised to learn that the cancer had vanished. It was nowhere to be found in her body. The doctors were amazed. Isabel wasn't amazed, she was exhilarated, and grateful. Ten years have passed now and Isabel is still cancer free. She wouldn't describe herself as cancer-free, though, she would say she's still "whole, perfect, and complete."

Affirmative Prayer is an effective method of harnessing and operationalizing the Perfect Power within you. Healing stories similar to Isabel's are much more common than you think—a plethora of metaphysical healing books have documented comparable cases for decades now. One of the finest is *The Secret of Healing*, by Jack Addington.

God is the Power, affirmative prayer is the road to get there, and your True Self is the bridge between the two.

A Metaphysical Interpretation
of the 23rd Psalm

First Verse: *The LORD is my shepherd; I shall not want.*

I am a perfect creation of a Perfect Creator. An Infinite Intelligence, the God-essence and energy that's the power source of every cell and atom throughout the universe, is the basis of who I am. My soul is made of Spirit. I am perfect just the way I am. I lack absolutely nothing. I am an individual expression of the Infinite, like a wave is to an ocean. God dwells within me, and I experience and communicate with the Universal Spirit through my inner True Self.

Verse 2: *He maketh me to lie down in green pastures, he leadeth me beside the still waters.*

My True Self, which some refer to as the Holy Spirit, is always here for me. All I need to do is turn my attention to It and It responds. It always says, "Yes," to me. It's unconditional Love. It guides me into right thinking. When I'm aware of this, I am more powerful. When I release the voice of the ego, I am letting this Divine Voice lead me beside the still waters. "Be still and know that I am."

Verses 3 and 4: *He restoreth my soul, he leadeth me in the paths of righteousness for his name's sake. Yea, though I walk through the valley of the shadow of death, I will fear no evil, for thou art with me, thy rod and thy staff they comfort me.*

My True Self is constantly restoring me back to right thinking as I allow It. Metaphysical Christians call this a symbol of the resurrection, allowing the True Self to arise within and take charge, being reborn on a moment-to-moment basis through consciousness. Some metaphysicians would say that we spend too much time focusing on the passion and crucifixion—that they are merely symbols of the ego's death. Instead, we should spend more time contemplating the resurrection—the rise of love-based thinking. By letting our True Self guide us, our soul is restored to right-mindedness.

Every time I entertain dark thoughts, I'm walking through the dark valley. Everything that I consider to be bad in my life starts with the planting of these dark thought-seeds in my mind. I'm not expressing through my True Self when I allow the ego to mentally take me on momentary journeys of resentment, fear, worry, lack, limitation, control, competition, and judgment, judgment, judgment. Whenever I'm miserable, it's of my own making. I have miscreated in my mind, which is another way of saying that I have sinned.

That word sin has taken on a dastardly identity, hasn't it? Sinning is nothing more than missing the mark, making a mistake—something we all do mentally hundreds of times each day. I'm the playwright of these little dramas. But God rescues me from the dark valley. Like a giant Phoenix that swoops down and carries me to safety, my True Self saves me from these dark thoughts as I turn to It for guidance, love, strength, wisdom, care—whatever I need at any given moment, my True Self is always there for me. It's God within that soothes me as I turn to It. My self-awareness and mental self-discipline are my rod and staff. My True Self employs them to corral my thoughts like sheep. My thoughts need shepherding. Being aware of what's happening in my mind and then consciously directing my thinking to love-based thoughts is the power my True Self provides me.

Verse 5: *Thou preparest a table before me in the presence of mine enemies, thou anointest my head with oil, my cup runneth over.*

The beautiful feast at the table prepared for me, and the oil that soothes my head, represents all the good things that manifest from right thinking. My enemies, the dark thoughts that cloud my consciousness, are whisked away like smoke from a sharp wind. As I follow my True Self's lead and entertain thoughts of peace, I become peaceful. As I focus truthfully on prosperity, new forms of abundance come into my life. As I think joy, I am happy. As I KNOW that I am love in expression, I love myself, and everyone in my life, and others love me. My thought-seeds produce new plants and flowers in my garden. My life changes for the better as I walk side-by-side with my True Self and keep my thoughts and beliefs based in Love. My relationships improve. People see a spark in my eyes and they're attracted to it. New life opportunities arise—new jobs, and new material possessions. All these manifestations are the result of my love-based thought-seeds and beliefs—all generated from my True Self, God manifesting through me.

Verse 6: *Surely goodness and mercy shall follow me all the days of my life and I will dwell in the house of the Lord forever.*

Like Universal Spirit, I am eternal. I am God energy, which cannot be destroyed, only changed in form. As I shed my earthly body, I rejoin the celestial ocean and experience true one-ness, a feeling I sometimes experience during this life while I'm out in nature or during meditation. I experience an overwhelming sense of gratitude and well-being when I remember that I am a child of God, and nothing can ever change that, that I am loved beyond measure, that I am one with God and all living creatures, and that it's all good: Everything, everyone, everywhere, all the time. It's all good. It's all God.

A Metaphysical Interpretation of the Lord's Prayer

Our Father, which art in heaven, Hallowed be thy name.

My True Self, the Holy Spirit, the bridge to God that dwells within my consciousness, is who I am. I am an individual expression of God and I live, move, and have my being within God. We are One. Your name, God, *I am*, and your essence are the same—whole, perfect, and complete.

Thy kingdom come, thy will be done on earth, as it is in heaven

Spirit's *kingdom* is right here, right now. It's up for grabs! As much as I want, I can have, at any given moment. There are no limitations and never a shortage of good. My experience of the kingdom is exactly what I make of it. It is done onto me as I believe. My will is God's will, if I choose. My life, my circumstances, all that I am is a direct result of my thoughts and beliefs. The kingdom of heaven is within, as are the thought-seeds that make up the garden of my life.

Give us this day our daily bread

God is my source and supply and I accept all the Good that's mine to have. It's my birthright, being a perfect creation of a Perfect Creator. Spirit is always emanating Love/Life. I am open to it.

And forgive us our trespasses, as we forgive those who trespass against us.

God, through the indwelling True Self, the Holy Spirit, forgives any mistake, misperception, or miscreation without me even asking. It's a given. So too must I forgive myself and others if I am to realize the perfect peace of God. There's nothing and no one to forgive. We are All One.

And lead us not into temptation, but deliver us from evil

Direct and guide my thoughts True Self, help me remember who and whose I am. I turn my mind over to you.

For thine is the kingdom, and the power, and the glory, forever and ever.

All that's good comes from Spirit. It's the wellspring of all Love, all Light, and all Life.

Amen. It is so, and so it is.

The Personal Evolution of Prayer

Like a ladder or set of stairs, there are levels of understanding in using prayer effectively. Each level will take you to a new and higher level of understanding of yourself in relation to the Infinite giving-ness of the Universal Mind of God. No one method of prayer is *better* than the other but each is progressively more *effective* in communicating with the Infinite. All forms of prayer are good. Every prayer that's spoken by billions of people each moment of every day is in alignment with the pray-er's understanding and consciousness.

Think of prayer as a form of communication with God, as you would communicate with a friend. The most effective means of communication is face-to-face interaction. This method allows for full visual and auditory exchanges, including non-verbal gestures and facial expressions. Following face-to-face communication is phone communication, and then email, Facebook messages, Twittering, and a letter via the mail. The least effective method might be trying to shout your message across town. Each form of communication is of value to the one praying, but some forms are more effective.

1. Praying for Effect. The least effective method of prayer is a petitioning request to an *outside force* for some *thing*, an effect of the world. Material effects are things like new cars, jobs, homes, swimming pools, stereos, computers, TVs, money itself—anything that's *of this world*. Imagine a child writing a letter to Santa, asking for that new bike—that's praying for effect, replacing God with Santa. The world of effect can never bring you true happiness, as you've no doubt experienced when receiving something *new* that quickly becomes *old*. When the novelty wears off, you feel unsatisfied and wanting again. Material effect, like your life on this planet, is transitory and without eternal Reality. If you think of planting a seed as *cause* and the resulting plant as *effect*, you'll see that the effect (the world) cannot give you anything real. Only the cause (your consciousness/thoughts/beliefs) can bring you true happiness.

2. Praying by Asking. When you ask for something, you're silently saying to yourself, "There's a chance I may or may not get this." But the Infinite is always available and will ALWAYS say yes to anyone who prays in alignment with Its will. The answer you receive to your prayer will be done onto you (your consciousness) as you believe. Jesus said this in several different ways in the Bible.

In Luke 1:14, He said: *"This is the confidence we have in approaching God: that if we ask anything according to his will, he hears us. And if we know that he hears us—whatever we ask—we know that we have what we asked of him."*

In Matthew 6:8, He said: *"Your Father knows what you need before you ask him."*

In Luke 11:9, He said: *"Ask, and it shall be given you; seek, and ye shall find; knock, and it shall be opened unto you."*

When you pray for a God *out there* to intervene in your life, or someone else's life, or to influence life's circumstances, you're not praying as effectively as you could be.

Again, all prayers are good, but some are more effective than others. Instead of visualizing a distant Lord of the Universe listening to petitioning prayers, and granting favorable outcomes to those with the most faith, think of how prayer impacts YOUR consciousness and therefore the Universal Consciousness that we *all* share. Changing your *own* mind makes changes to the One Mind. This vast, Infinite Creative Intelligence that constantly emanates Life/Love has given you life and the will and ability to create your own reality—what more do you want?

This Eternal, Universal Mind would not endow you with free will and then impinge on it to ensure you *don't* do well in this world. That would be a major contradiction and Spirit doesn't contradict Itself. The patient who asks God to cure her disease, the preacher who asks God to help the starving masses, and the mother who asks God to keep her children safe, are all sincerely praying for that which they believe is the will of God. But their prayers could be more effective if they KNEW, within their own consciousness, that their request was already fulfilled. Jesus taught this! A Loving, Universal Essence doesn't choose sides or play favorites, any more than gravity or electricity does. It leaves the details to each of us. To intervene would make it biased, little, and arbitrary. There's a Power and Presence in the universe that's greater than you. It's within you and all around you. It's all Good, all Loving, and all Life-giving, and you can use this Power to make your life better.

3. Praying by Knowing Your Truth. Mixed within the concrete foundation of affirmative prayer is the idea that you *know your truth*. Your truth is that you're a perfect creation of a Perfect Creator, imbued with the same spiritual attributes as Spirit. All that God is, you are—because you and God are one. This is the starting point. Next, you need to understand the causative power of thought moving upon your consciousness. When you think, and fully believe the thought, "I am at peace," you are at peace, because it can be no other way. Your thought has power, just as Jesus' did. It's fueled and energized by faith, that absolute certainty that you're a divine creative source, imbued by God with this creative power. Finally, know that your prayer is wholly effective when in alignment with God's will, which is all that's life affirming and life expanding.

Speak your word as if it has already happened—in the present tense. Base it in spiritual principle. Believe it beyond all doubt, and it is done onto you (or others) as you believe.

Instead of praying like this:

"God, please send someone to love me."

"God, please give me more money."

"Hey God, I could use some new relationships in my life, if you get the chance, could you help me out?"

"God, please heal Mary. She has cancer."

Pray like this:

"I am loved."

"Prosperity comes to me now in many different forms."

"I fully accept new, loving, and wonderful relationships in my life."

"I know for Mary that she is in a constant state of healing."

Affirmative prayer is knowing that which already is. Asking implies doubt. Knowing your truth, or the truth of others, is affirming what already is. The key is believing your truth to begin with. Again, it starts with the fact, the absolute fact, that you're a powerful, creative, God-based being.

Useful Affirmations

I affirm what I want—love, peace, joy. All these things I already am.

I am love, I am loving, and am happy and joyful. I'm so thankful for knowing this truth.

I have an enthusiastic zest for life!

I know *who and whose* I am today.

I am whole, perfect, and complete. I know this is my truth.

I am a creation of God, endowed with the ability to co-create. Today I create the reality I want—love, joy, and perfect peace.

I let go of fear. I release anger. I know my truth is based in love.

I am focused on what I am. I know my truth.

I am powerful! My word of prayer has power.

I know that the Valley of the shadow of death is not real—God within is constantly restoring my soul with perfect love.

I know my truth and I know that I know.

Rhyming Affirmations

I look within, and ask God to show the way,
I listen intently, the answer comes without delay.

What others think of me is not my affair,
I love myself and say so in prayer.

I am powerful, I am strong, I know my own truth,
I'm choosing love and peace in my inner voting booth.

The shadow of darkness isn't real, no matter what they say,
God's inner light shines and love lights my way.

I'm resilient like Silly Putty, impressionable and elastic,
I let God within re-shape me and the results are just fantastic.

CHAPTER SEVEN

Unity

The Unity of Good is a revelation of the greatest importance, for it teaches us that we are One with the Whole and One with each other. The Fatherhood of God and the actual Brotherhood of Man will be made apparent on earth to the degree that man realizes true Unity.

—Ernest Holmes, *The Science of Mind*

The revelation that the Father and the Son are one will come in time to every mind. Yet is that time determined by the mind itself, not taught.

—*A Course in Miracles*

The tremendous fact for every one of us is that we have discovered a common solution. We have a way out on which we can absolutely agree, and upon which we can join in brotherly and harmonious action.

—*Alcoholics Anonymous*

Different Roads, Same Destination

A loyal Facebook user comments:

"A Facebook posting caught my attention today. It was a graphic of Jesus saying in jest 'I'm going to create man and woman with original sin. Then I'm going to impregnate a woman with myself as her child so that I can be born. Once born, I will kill myself as a sacrifice to myself, to save you from the sin I originally condemned you to.' Then Jesus said, 'Ta-dah!'

My first reaction was a hearty guffaw, and then I thought, 'Some people will surely see this as disrespectful to Christianity.' I was right, someone immediately commented in anger on Facebook.

My second thought was that the person who wrote this is extremely frustrated with religious dogma. My intuition tells me that he/she also has a higher vision for spiritual Truth and masked it well in humor. I believe that spiritual Truth comes in many different forms and that many of us are tired of the truth *conveyed to us in traditional religious writings that were politically motivated when Christianity was in its infancy.*

We still want the Truth, though, that's the beauty. We want to be reassured that we're here for a reason and that the spiritual principle of Love encompasses all. We want more for ourselves—more growth, more understanding, more equality, more freedom, and more good. Some of us think that traditional religious dogma is limited, narrow, and judgmental. Some of it is not based in Love and Universal Truth.

We agree on spiritual principles, especially Love—the big one that encompasses all others: peace, joy, patience, understanding, acceptance, strength, courage, unity, harmony, and non-attachment to the material world. We agree that these principles are the seeds to a happy and more fulfilling life—the grease that lubricates healthy and happy relationships with others, which bring us even closer together.

We may be traveling on different roads, but they all lead to the same destination. Our destination is our good, *as the late mystic Emma Curtis Hopkins wrote about, and our good may vary considerably.*

A Buddhist monk seeks enlightenment through silence. A Catholic nun seeks salvation through good works. The average Christian seeks a heavenly reward by leading a moral life. Similarly, the drug addict seeks his/her good through altered states of consciousness. The hoarder seeks his/her good by copiously saving newspapers and magazines, and the average American seeks good in many different forms, including social events, TV shows, sports, and countless other activities.

Just as different religious traditions represent the varied roads, the surface of the roads are all paved with the same principles, Love being the cement that holds the concrete in place. Unless we're mentally ill, we all agree on the principles that govern our lives. These principles, not dogma, not books, and certainly not interpretations of these books are what we should be using as measuring sticks of our lives.

It's an inside job. When we love ourselves, we'll more easily express love, when we feel inner peace, we'll be more skilled at extending that peace to others. So a salute goes out to the author of that Facebook posting. Humor like this engages us in more discussion of what's most important, as we travel down our respective roads, paved in spiritual principles."

Unity as a Principle and a Practice

We don't talk about the principle of Unity enough. It's at the core of any sound philosophical understanding of life, and the universe itself—and yet, Unity is not understood as a concept that has practical applications for happiness and peace.

Basic to the comprehension of Unity is that there is One Power in this universe that governs and powers all life—not one personality, but an underlying, life giving, creative essence or energy. It binds all living creatures together, surrounds and envelops everything and all of life, and is always extending Itself to create more life—constantly and continuously.

In *The Science of Mind*, Ernest Holmes writes:

"It is well to remember that the enlightened in every age have taught that behind all things there is One Unseen Cause: In studying the teachings of the great thinkers we find that a common thread runs through all—the thread of Unity. There is no record of any deep thinker, of any age, who taught duality. Jesus taught this when He said, 'I and the Father are One.' This teaching of Unity is the chief cornerstone of the sacred scriptures of the East as well as of our own sacred writings. It is the mainspring of the teachings of the modern philosophies, such as Christian Science, Divine Science, The Unity Teachings, The New Thought Movement, and even much of what's taught under the name of Psychology. Without this basic teaching of Unity, these movements would have little to offer. Science has found nothing to contradict this teaching, and it never will, for the teaching is self-evident."

The totality of the one-ness that's our universe obviously encompasses all humans and every living creature. When the spiritual masters of our time say, "We are all One," think about what that means. It highlights the reality that the entire universe is One entity, a living, breathing organism. We live within God and God lives within each of us. We're not only one with the Infinite God, but with each other as well. All living things are connected. This explains the Laws of Karma—what you do onto another, you do to yourself because you're one with each other. There's no separation from others except that which the ego creates in consciousness.

Imagine if this Truth were fully realized and put into practice by all humans. There would be no wars because we would see that hurting others hurts us. There would no competition for natural, human-made, or financial resources because we would know that when we give to others, we give to ourselves. There would be no religious, ideological, philosophical, racial, ethnic, or national conflicts of any kind. We would see the Truth that we're all progressing forward together, and we need each other, because we're all moving as one. Like participants in a three-legged race, we must move forward together. We depend on each other for our growth and welfare, and when one lags, we're all delayed. There would be no countries, no states, and no borders of any kind, especially those in consciousness. As Lennon sang, "Imagine . . ." that.

Holmes also writes:

"We think of the world as we see it, but we see it from the viewpoint of only one plane. Nothing could form a formless stuff, which has no mind of its own, except Intelligence operating upon it. Again we come back to the Word as the starting point of all Creation—God's Word in the Great World, man's word in the small world. One Spirit, One Mind, and one substance: One Law but many thoughts; One Power, but many ways of using It; One God in whom we all live, and One Law in which all operate; One, One, One. No greater Unity could be given than that which is already vouchsafed [bestowed/promised] to mankind."

Earlier we touched on near-death experiences. Many who have experienced this phenomenon talk about not leaving the scene of their death. They hover over their bodies or witness their resuscitation, but some go further across the *great divide*. They talk about moving toward the light, sensing the presence of loved ones and guides, and being in a state of perfect bliss. To a person, most all talk of a certainty that All is One, a sensation of complete unity, and connectedness to everything and everyone. They talk about a total absence of all fear, an ecstatic, overwhelming sense of One-ness.

As Wayne Dyer once said in a seminar:

"These people are never the same after these types of experiences. They return to the world with a calm peace, knowing that everything is just the way it should be and that there's no reason to fear anything. They know with certainty that a wonderful new world awaits them when they actually do experience death on this earthly plane."

Unity. Absolute Unity.

A recovering alcoholic tells a story about how she applied the principle of Unity to her recovery:

"When I was about three weeks sober and my sponsor felt I was serious about working the steps, she gave me the phone list for our women's group. She instructed me to call a member of our group every day. She said, 'Don't worry what to say to them, just ask them how their day is going and tell them your sponsor is requiring you to make calls. Ask them how they worked the first step.'

Dear God, there were 70 names on that list. I was so scared. The phone felt like it weighed a thousand pounds, but I wanted to stay sober and be in my sponsor's good graces, so I did it.

Most of the women were gracious when I called, and engaged me in conversation about step one. Some talked my ear off, imparting their wisdom in detail. But some were rather cursory and talked mostly about themselves, and then made an excuse to end the call. I was beginning to see a pattern. The women who I later came to respect and admire were the ones who were so generous. They volunteered to do things in our group, were always helping others, and stepped in to resolve conflicts—they were the glue that held the group together. They were loving, kind, compassionate, and centered on others. Twelve-Step literature talks a great deal about unity and our common bond. What I learned during my first year of recovery was that the strength and wisdom of We and that unity, or one-ness as I call it now, is based in love for each other."

Here's another anecdote about Unity, as told by an Air Force veteran.

"Boot camp was a shock to me. I was undisciplined and thought of myself a bit of an intellectual. I'd made my bed maybe twenty or thirty times growing up, and certainly never learned the fine art of hospital corners. I hated the mind games the drill sergeants played, but having had a few psychology courses, I could see through them. I understood the purpose of boot camp—to mentally tear a young person down and re-build him or her into an airman. Do you know that feeling you get when confronted with a surprising or disturbing situation, when that rush of adrenaline charges your head, heart, and stomach? Well, that's the way I felt for eight weeks. 'If I can handle this,' I remember thinking, 'I can handle anything else in life.'

The physical and academic aspects of basic training were no problem. My weakness was attention to detail. I couldn't quite master folding my shirts and underwear into perfect 6-inch squares for inspection. I failed the first two practice inspections of my locker. My drill sergeant was ready to boot my butt back to a junior flight and set my training back a few days. 'I don't want you fixing my airplane you idiot!' he screamed in my face. 'You can't even make a #*%!*# bed!' I considered explaining to my drill sergeant that based on the results of my Air Force mechanical aptitude score, he surely wouldn't want me to fix his airplane regardless of my bed-making skills. 'Nah,' I thought, 'I better not.'

The ultimatum he set down was clear—to get my locker ready for inspection in one hour. If I failed the inspection, I'd spend a few extra days folding t-shirts and making beds. He left me alone with my locker and underwear. I panicked. 'I can't do this,' I thought (always the optimist). Several of my buddies saw what was happening and pitched in to help. The guy who folded boxers and t-shirts perfectly did just that. The guy who could space the uniforms on hangers in the locker exactly one inch apart went to work. This generosity caught on like wildfire until several of the guys were huddled around my locker helping out. I mentally flashed on the old Beach Blanket movies in which several teenagers helped spiff up the geek in preparation for a big date.

It worked. Sergeant Short-Guy-With-Red-Hair-and-Nasty-Disposition *couldn't believe his eyes. 'This looks fan f*cking tastic airman!' he shouted. Suddenly, he noticed half the flight looking over their shoulders.*

He looked at them, was silent for a few moments, and then asked me, 'Did you prepare for this inspection without assistance from these other men?'

This question must be his honesty test. 'This is a mind game,' I thought. 'No sir,' I confessed, bowing my head in fear.

'You're damn right you didn't! I know you didn't! You're not this good! What do you think I am, an idiot? (Silence) I want you to point to the airmen who helped you get your locker ready,' he said calmly but firmly.

Adrenaline . . . mind racing . . . total emotional confusion . . . silence . . . silence . . . Lord, what a deafening silence. 'What do I say?' I thought.

'I helped him, sir,' the underwear guy said as he stepped forward. 'So did I sir,' as another buddy stepped into the fray. 'Me too,' said two more airmen. I couldn't believe these guys. I remember thinking 'What guts! I love these guys! They're like brothers—this is what camaraderie is all about.'

'Are these guys telling the truth?' the sergeant asked me.

'Yes sir,' I said proudly with pursed lips.

The sergeant took several steps away from the group. The metal taps on his shoes clicked with authority. Turning to look at the entire group, he said 'So what you're telling me is that you men worked as a team to help a fellow airmen accomplish a mission during a critical situation?'

Light bulbs flashed over the heads of twenty-something airmen simultaneously. We got it—we understood. This test *was about working together, being as one, helping and supporting each other.*

As a result of this valuable lesson, my sergeant had mercy on me. Before he left the room that day he whispered to me through clenched teeth, 'Fail another f*cking inspection and you're f*cking history.'

I didn't. I doubled my uniform folding and bed making efforts, didn't fail another inspection, and graduated from boot camp four weeks later. Unfortunately, I weaseled out on my promise to God, to never sin again. But I learned the value of unity and teamwork."

Do you have a sangha? A sangha is an *association, assembly, company, or community.* In Buddhism, it refers to the monastic community of ordained Buddhist monks or nuns. The more contemporary Americanized meaning of the Sanskrit term is a spiritual community of like-minded individuals who support and encourage each other on their spiritual paths.

Being part of a sangha is important. It promotes and quickens spiritual development. It's a practical application of the unity principle. If you've ever attempted to fly solo on a spiritual journey and then became part of a supportive spiritual community, you know how important a sangha is. There are many spiritual loners out there—people who might read one spiritual book after another, shop at metaphysical bookstores, and even attend Sunday Services semi-regularly. They're not part of a community. No judgment here. Again, there are many paths leading to the same destination, but you must be aware of the ego's desire for you to remain separate from other Truth seekers and God. Divide and conquer is the ego's modus operandi.

God speaks to you in many ways—through your True Self, through books, the media, and especially through others. Ask a recovering addict or alcoholic if the solitary path leads to growth. Being part of a spiritual community is sacred. It uplifts and enhances your development, especially a community that emphasizes spiritual education in the form of classes, workshops, retreats, book discussion groups, and meditation circles. There's something exhilarating about being part of a spiritual discussion with people who, although may not be on the same page you're on, are at least reading from the same book. Support, encouragement, emphasis on prayer and inner work, unconditional love, friendship—these are all hallmarks of a genuine sangha.

Your True Self is calling you to join with others—to love them, forgive them, support them, and champion them. We are All One, so this is a natural tendency and desire that grows stronger as you listen to your True Self.

Being Indifferent to Indifference

Pema Chodron is a western Buddhist nun, author, and speaker. On one of her many books-on-CD, she said something to this effect: "We either actively like/love someone, dislike/hate them, or are indifferent to them." She likened this to a continuum—like, indifferent, dislike.

The point she makes is that indifference toward someone is just as bad as disliking them. There are billions of people in this world to whom you're indifferent. Obviously, if you don't know someone, you're neutral about them. But if you do know someone, and you know they're in need of help, assistance, love, whatever—do not be indifferent toward them.

You're a spiritual person, a Truth seeker. Showing indifference goes against the natural flow of life.

Here are some synonyms for the word *indifferent*: Lack of concern, unconcern, disinterest, lack of interest, lack of enthusiasm, apathy. We're talking about not giving a darn about someone. That *can't* be you— you're a caring, loving person. You know that loving others is just as important, but not more important, than loving yourself. When we love God, we love others and ourselves. When we love others and ourselves, we love God. There's no difference. That's why indifference is an untruth, because it's not based in love. All that's based in love is *of God* and universally true.

Our world is so full of contradictory beliefs and of people who are just plain *spiritually* confused. They don't understand that love is the basis of all Truth and is the only true and natural expression for any living thing. These people attend church or consider themselves moral people, but they passionately hate the idea of new taxes for the poor, disadvantaged, and sick. Or they'll call themselves religious and then pass negative judgment on the homeless person rather than slipping them a dollar bill.

When you're aware of Truth and willing to lead a *spiritually principled* life, you know that love is a natural expression. You know that we truly are All One, each of us cut from the same Divine cloth. During a 2012 political convention, Sister Simone Campbell, one of the "Nuns on the Bus," gave a very inspiring speech, in which she said:

"We acknowledge that we're all responsible for ourselves, but we also know we're responsible for each other. I am *my sister's keeper, I* am *my brother's keeper."*

The love within you, which is God in expression, urges you to love others and yourself. This Universal Intelligence is constantly expressing love in the form of life. The more you open yourself to this love, and the more you mentally release any blockages to it, the more fully you express God.

We are a Reflection of Each Other

What you don't want for yourself, you deny and repress. When you see it in others, it triggers uneasiness or upset within you. "No, I'm not arrogant, I'm not self-righteous, I'm not uncaring," you say. Yes, you are. At the least, you have those thought patterns or beliefs in your subconscious. If you didn't, you wouldn't recognize them. If you didn't know how it *felt* to be self-righteous, you wouldn't react at all. It's those feelings, coupled with your beliefs, that give them power. That's why you repel those beliefs, and the people who hold them.

Think about it. If someone told you, "I believe God is a loving being," and you hold a similar belief, you wouldn't get upset. If you believed God is a loving being, you would agree with that person, and probably feel closer (more unified) to him or her.

But if they said, "I believe God is kind of a jerk, what with all that smiting and judging . . ." and a part of you (the ego) held a similar belief, you'd disagree with that person and perhaps be upset with them. If you didn't hold a similar belief, you wouldn't react at all.

You're a mirror for and to others. If you were invisible, you wouldn't have a mirror reflection. If it's not within you, you won't see it in others.

Like attracts like. We're attracted to people who hold the same beliefs, or as the metaphysicist would say, who are on the same vibrational level. We attract people who are not just like us, but who we *want* to be like. Those people to whom you draw yourself to are a reflection of you and vice versa.

What an opportunity! Knowing this truth, you can learn much about yourself. All those people who tick you off are your spiritual teachers. Bow to them and thank them! The next time someone cuts you off on the freeway, think to yourself, "I'm angry because that behavior (based in competition or not caring about others) exists within me and I don't want that. I don't want to be *that* type of person." Think, "What beliefs do I need to release from my consciousness?"

The follow-up question is, "What's the opposite of that? Caring, compassion, and cooperation?" The answer will come to you if you're open to it. If not, come back to it later. It *will* reappear. Again and again it will re-appear until you've learned the lesson, usually when you're sick of that feeling and open to change.

Conversely, look at the traits and qualities of those people you admire and to whom you feel close. What is it about them that attracts you? Listen to what they say and how they act? You'll know.

You're on the road to complete self-understanding. The road is broad and roomy, the destination is inviting and pleasurable, and your safe arrival is assured.

The Power of "We"

One Plus One Equals One: Unity
by
Sarah Busby, RScP

Webster describes *unity* as: Oneness, harmony, accord, totality.

Many people don't understand the state of unity because they don't understand who and what they are. Some of us believe we're here for a purpose, or perhaps to repay for mistakes in a previous life. Others believe they're autonomous, gifted, different, or alone—that how they live affects no one but themselves. This leads to a distorted view of the world, resulting in addictions, diseases, and a lonely or depressed life. We're not loners! No one is living a wasted life filled with struggles and hardships.

There's strength and wisdom in numbers. When you apply the spiritual principle of unity to your life, you reap the rewards tenfold. Being part of a spiritual community is important if continued enlightenment is on your wish list. Nothing thrills the ego more than an attitude of autonomy and independence. We're spiritual beings having a human experience. It's in our spiritual DNA to help and guide each other on our seemingly separate spiritual journeys. Attending services at a church, temple, mosque, or spiritual center is a good start. Participating in classes and workshops at these institutions or being a part of meditation, visualization, or book discussion groups is even better. Interacting, discussing ideas, and supporting each other is the goal. Show up, get involved, be heard, and help someone. You'll grow as a result.

Thoughts really *are* things—alive with the power of life and death, the ability to heal or to destroy. What we think becomes cause and since we're co-creators, cause produces effect. Perhaps you've heard these old adages:

"What goes around, comes around."

"Do unto others as you would have them do unto you."

"Life is a mirror, you get back what you put out."

"What you sow, you reap."

The preceding wisdom tidbits are all saying the same thing: BE AWARE OF YOUR THOUGHTS, they are the crop you'll soon be harvesting.

We're creations of God—or whatever you choose to call your Higher Power—Energy, Life, Nature, Allah, Jehovah. We're expressions of the

Power and Intelligence that spoke this world into existence. In essence, we're all *One*, we are all *Powerful*, and together we form this world. As one, we reap the benefits of the thoughts of the majority, or the unhappy results.

It's said that when a butterfly flutters its wings in South America, the results are felt in the far north. I believe that. You are not here to learn lessons, though I hope you will through your experiences. You are here to let your *True Self*, the real you, guide you to live and express your highest and best life. Only *you* know in your heart of hearts what will make you happy. Is it money, fame, status, influence, or material possessions? If so, I invite you to look at the lives of those who have achieved these things. You've heard the following phrase a million times, but that's because it's spiritual truth, so it bears repeating: *Money does not of itself buy happiness.* A peaceful, serene life in which you are healthy, happy, loved, and prosperous (in many forms) is ideal.

To understand how to achieve this ideal requires going within yourself to that special place where your authentic desires are stored, and listen to that *Inner Voice* that knows how to manifest them. This Divine presence is your intuition, your true compass. It's your own personal GPS system for navigating the hazards and sharp turns of life.

This inner presence is the manifest result of the phrase from the Book of Genesis: "Let us make man in our image, according to our likeness." Our True Self is our connection to Its Divine Source, having the creative ability, knowledge, and perseverance to endure the perceived challenges and setbacks we experience while pursuing our dreams. This Inner Voice is our coach, our quarterback, and our cheerleader.

The greatest accomplishment a person can experience is to identify with and recognize that there's a Divine Intelligence that governs the universe. It's bigger than we are, we are *One* with it, and we can use this Eternal, Creative, Intelligent Force to make our lives better. It is then and only then, that we can correctly identify with every living thing in this world and unseen worlds. It's then that our education begins, and whichever path we choose, the result is the same—we realize that we are all created by the One, and that we're part and particle of the same *God Stuff.* We all think from the One Mind, but each of us are individualizations of It.

Like children, we model the behavior of the Parent. In the physical world, we look to our earthly parents and caretakers—in the spiritual, our Creator. While the earthly behaviors seem to be easily learned, our spiritual behaviors are harder to understand and model. We've forgotten who-we-really-are and what our roles are as spiritual beings, and our Role Model is not always easily visible.

Author's note: At this point, my computer screen has gone blank. The lights are out, the fans stop. I'm in complete darkness. I have no electricity. Hmmm, is this a neighborhood or household outage? There's a part of me that feels isolated, alone, scared. But my Higher Self reminds me I'm not alone, that I'm never alone. I'm loved and protected by my Creator. I can *choose* to be in fear or I can choose to know I'm surrounded by love and light.

I wait in the darkness, marveling at my dependency on electricity—the appliances, the entertainment, the creature comforts. Then a thought dawns on me: I'm dependent upon my True Self too. I need it to tell me my truth. When I forget to meditate, visualize, read uplifting material, or to associate with uplifting people, I'm more likely to feel unplugged—like I'm lacking electricity. I feel alone, fearful, and I indulge in self-pity. Guess what happens? I get more of what's wrong. So I come back to my True Self and turn my conscious mind over to It. I channel my thoughts to what's *right* in my life, and the flow of gratitude lifts me out of the depths of fear—up to where the clouds part and the sun is shining.

I realize the sun had been bright throughout this situation but I was so buried under a cloud cover of fear and negative emotions, I couldn't see it. Like the electricity that was restored as soon as the tripped breaker was discovered, my attitude and outlook was restored. I was raised by my positive thoughts to a higher level, where the skies were a beautiful blue. I live in the light and love that's my Divine inheritance. I am one with the One, the author and originator of all good, from which I'm never separated—except in my own mind.

When you control your mind, you control your destiny. When you think *good*, you create and attract good. Take a moment and think about that.

Namaste, My Friend

From a spiritual colleague:

"A friend is someone who sees the goodness in me, even when I'm not expressing it.

I've learned a great deal about myself as a result of using Facebook. Here's an example: Sometimes I'm not my Self, my True Self. Well, I AM always that, but sometimes I don't allow It to express through me. I call it being in a crappy mood or being immersed in self. The result is always the same—I've temporarily allowed the ego to step forward and show its bug eyes."

The bug-eyed analogy is funny—well, it is to me—and it's more true than not. Do you remember the late Marty Feldman? He was hilarious as Igor in Mel Brooks' "Young Frankenstein." When I'm expressing ego, I picture myself looking like bug-eyed Marty Feldman saying, "Hey, look over here! Look at ME! I'm Abby Normal!" Anger, shame, guilt, judgment of self and others—they're all self-centered expressions. They're all based in self-absorbing fear, projected out into the world, or to myself. They're all a bug-eyed cry for love.

A friend is someone who sees the God in me, even when I'm not expressing it. That's what the term *Namaste* means—the God in me sees the God in you. When I look at others, I see perfection—a perfect creation of a Perfect Creator. We're made in the image and likeness of God, on a spiritual level, not physical. If we had to liken ourselves to God physically, we would be as bright, shining, luminescent spiritual beings within our human shell.

Do you remember the light-filled aliens in the movie "Cocoon?" There was a scene on a boat, where Steve Guttenberg's character is peaking at Tahnee Welch's character through a crack in the door as she undresses. She unzips her outer human *skin suit* to reveal a radiant being of light.

That's what we are at our core, *beings of light.*

Our True Self is all good, life affirming, life expanding—all that we define as loving, positive, encouraging, growth enhancing. Our soul is made of God-stuff, and It's there within our mind, waiting for us. It responds to us as we think of It, feel It, and call upon It in prayer, meditation, casual conversation, or an occasional desperate cry for help. This is what Jesus meant when he said, "It is done unto you as you believe," and, "the Kingdom of Heaven is within."

When Jesus said, "Seek first the kingdom of God and His righteousness," he was instructing us to turn to that power within, which will provide us with right-minded thinking, an attitude and outlook that's based in Love. Our capacity to express this love, the most powerful force in the universe, is always but a thought away.

Here's another good example from the movies. As the female lead character in the film "Avatar" said, "I see you."

Marching Toward Unity

Another military veteran tells this story to illustrate the spiritual principle of Unity:

"When I was 20 years old in 1979, I dropped out of college and escaped small town Iowa to join the Army. After too much screwing up, self-doubt, career uncertainty, and failing grades, this was how I was going to get my life together. It worked out well. The military provided me with a much healthier lifestyle, both physically and mentally.

There were plenty of things I loathed about boot camp—awakening at 5 a.m. by loud banging noises made by the drill sergeant was at the top of my list. I had an aversion to being yelled at for no apparent reason, trying to get along with idiots, the disgusting food, and not being able to date girls for several weeks.

But one of the things I loved was marching in formation. I was a good dancer back in the 1970s. Marching with a group of soldiers was like a ballet. It flowed, had a natural rhythm to it, and transformed our group of 40 soldiers into one unit.

That's one of the goals of marching in formation—being one. It was explained to us that relying on a fellow soldier would save our life someday. The drill sergeant said, 'When you follow (moral) orders without question, respond to commands quickly and accurately, you and your buddies may live to tell a good war story.' I didn't get it at first.

As the days and weeks wore on, I understood more and more. When we marched, we relied on the person to our right to be properly aligned. Each person would use their peripheral vision to align themselves with the person to their right. In this way, we were relying on someone for our right *alignment. As we were marching, we had to be* in-step, *so our feet and legs all looked as one to an observer. 'Left, Right, Left,' is what we heard all day long and then in our nightly dreams. It became second nature to us. Even when walking to the Post Exchange or Snack Bar, a group of three or four of us would walk* in-step.

After weeks of daily marching, we got good at it. We had this stuff down cold. I felt very proud of the way each of us worked in harmony, turning right, left, and completely around while marching, all together, all in-step, all as one.

The spiritual principle I'm talking about here is Unity. We were as one group, one team, one entity. It was emotionally exhilarating to be part of something bigger than me, a cohesive, integrated team. At the same time, it made me feel both part of a *larger whole* and *as one with these other young men. My experience in boot camp left me with a new perspective on One-ness.*

That's why social media sites like Facebook are so popular. We have an intuitive desire to mingle, support, and encourage each other, to come together as one. Never in the history of humankind have we been more united. Just 65 years ago, we had only the telephone and radio to unite us. Less than 100 years ago, we had only letters and personal interaction. Nowadays, we can take a photograph and instantly post *it for all to see. We can communicate to the world that we're in emotional pain and receive dozens of encouraging comments from friends. We can broadcast inspiring stories, quotes, spiritual messages, and uplifting videos. Some might say our interaction has become shallow and cursory, but I believe every opportunity we have to interrelate is an opening for more unity.*

Now I understand the principle of Unity more on a spiritual basis because of these experiences and new technologies. I know that we're All One. Each of us is created and powered by the same Infinite, Creative, Loving Power that is omnipresent, and at the core of our souls. We're each individual creations, and yet All One. Each human and all living creatures on this planet are my spiritual brothers and sisters. We live within God and God lives within each of us. We truly are One!"

Useful Affirmations

I am connected to all life.

I open my heart to everyone and everything.

I am you and you are me and we are all together.

I actively participate in creating a better world.

I learn from others, God bless all my teachers.

Every living organism is part of me and we are part of the whole

There is beauty all around me. I see it and I embrace it.

I am one with you. You are one with me. Together we are one.

One, one, one, all is one.

I release any belief in separation or division. We are, the universe is . . . All One.

Rhyming Affirmations

I am good, I am loving, I reach out to others,
We share spiritual DNA. We are sisters and brothers.

Abundance is mine, I'm a magnet for prosperity,
I expect more and more with unswerving regularity.

I am healed, I am healing, I'm constantly under repair,
My healing power is within, activated by prayer.

I love everyone, every brother and sister,
I bow my head to each Ms., Mrs., and Mister.

I am one with all, every living creature,
I honor all of life, you are my teacher.

CHAPTER EIGHT

Faith

Faith looks to the invisible and instead of seeing a void it fastens its gaze upon a solid reality. Faith is not hope, it is Substance. It does not look away from itself, being Substance it looks within itself. In doing this it realizes that the life of God is also the life of man.

—Ernest Holmes, *The Science of Mind*

There is no problem in any situation that faith will not solve.

—*A Course in Miracles*

We never apologize to anyone for depending upon our Creator. We can laugh at those who think spirituality the way of weakness. Paradoxically, it is the way of strength. The verdict of the ages is that faith means courage. All men of faith have courage. They trust their God. We never apologize for God. Instead we let Him demonstrate, through us, what He can do.

—*Alcoholics Anonymous*

According to Your Faith

You should expect immediate and complete outcomes from your affirmative prayers. To think otherwise is to doubt the power of the Infinite. Your belief in your own word must be wholly confident. You have the clout and muscle of an Eternal and Universal Power working through you, expressing as you. By expecting your affirmative prayers to be fully manifested, you're asserting your conviction in the Law of Cause and Effect. Your prayer, combined with your fiery passion and complete faith will manifest results.

When describing affirmative Prayer, Ernest Holmes used the term *Applied Christianity*. Simply put, affirmative prayer puts into practical application exactly what Jesus Christ taught. Jesus never talked about unanswered prayer. Instead, he said:

"Ask and it will be given to you; seek and you will find; knock and the door will be opened to you. For everyone who asks receives; the one who seeks finds; and to the one who knocks, the door will be opened."

Jesus was talking about faith. Whether he used the words *ask*, or *know* makes no difference. If you ask God for something, having absolutely no doubt that the Divine will provide it, that's no different than knowing that you already have it—the basis of affirmative prayer. Absolute faith is the fuel that powers your prayer.

First, suppose you ask God, "Please God, will you heal my arthritis?"

Or, "God, I ask that you remove any grief, fear, regret, or guilt from my friend upon the passing of her husband, and replace it with a calm peace and assurance that she is loved."

Next, say:

"I know my arthritis is healed. Divine energy and healing love flow through my body and mind, constantly healing me."

Regarding your friend, you say, "I know for my friend that she releases from her mind all thoughts and beliefs in, grief, fear, regret, or guilt. She knows with certainty that she's loved beyond measure and sits in calm peace, knowing that God is right there with her."

There's no difference between asking and knowing *if you have complete faith in your word.* Your prayer will be answered according to the strength and certainty of your faith.

Jesus also said:

"Truly I tell you, if anyone says to this mountain, 'Go, throw yourself into the sea,' and does not doubt in their heart, but believes that what they say will happen, it will be done for them. Therefore, I tell you, whatever you ask for in prayer, believe that you have received it, and it will be yours."

Christopher Columbus had a theory that the world was round, not flat. That theory evolved into a strong belief—so strong, that he laid everything on the line to confirm it. While some of Chris' friends were shaking their heads, mumbling about him being a nut job, he sailed east, believing he could reach India. His belief was strong, but it wasn't *faith* yet.

During his maiden voyage, he said to one of his crew members, "Uh, hey, do me a favor, Bub. Climb in that crow's nest at the top of the ship and if you happen to see the edge of the world, yell down here fast, okay?"

After Columbus had reached the New World, his belief was confirmed. He had *experienced* what he thought was true. The success of that experience transformed his belief into a strong faith. On his second and third voyages from the Old to the New World, he lounged comfortably in the captain's quarters drinking ale and playing solitaire. He was un-afraid and had complete faith that he would reach his destination safely.

When your faith is strong enough, you'll move mountains. In the meantime, make your faith grow stronger by experiencing the results of manifested prayer. Like Columbus, your beliefs transform into faith as you prove to yourself the power of God via prayer.

Let's say you want to cook up a batch of permanent inner peace. Piece (peace) of cake, here's the recipe:

1. Know beyond doubt (faith) that God is peace and therefore you are peace, because you're an expression of this Infinite Spirit.
2. Know that you already are at peace and just need to release from your mind any false belief in non-peace.
3. Have faith in yourself as a Divine center of peace, with no exception.
4. Bake at 350 degrees every minute of every day. The result is a calm peace that defies all description. It remains with you as long as your faith is strong.

Yum!

The moment you choose to shake loose that faith by thinking, "Dang it, now I'm stressed, sick, in pain, frustrated, sad, or pissed off," that peace vanishes. Whoosh! It's gone. Your faith in non-peace has replaced your faith in your inner God-endowed peace. You have used the Divine Law of Cause and Effect. It always works for you, regardless of whether you're using it correctly.

What freedom you now have! You can use the Law of Cause and Effect as you choose, to make anything in your life change from possible to actual. If you believe in small amounts of peace, love, prosperity, health, or the like, the Law of Cause and Effect is duty-bound to provide to you that small amount, according to your faith. The Law of Cause and Effect itself *don't know squat* about the concepts of large or small, any more than the Law of Gravity knows about the weights of elephants and feathers.

The Law of Cause and Effect just receives and acts upon what it receives. It's a mirror that reflects your mental projections. So when you pray, "I have a little bit of good in my life," the Law of Cause and Effect produces the same in kind. And when you pray, "All the good I need and want is mine to have. I am a bottomless cup of goodness, love, peace, and joy," the Law of Cause and Effect will manifest this larger amount with equal certainty. This natural Law will always work for you, through you, according to your faith.

Faith is the knowledge of who-we-really-are. It's not a *hoping or wishing to know*, it's the actual *knowing*. Faith is your intuition nodding to you as if to say, "Yes! God is, and you are." You may start out believing, but believing implies an ounce of uncertainty, the chance that what you believe may not actually be so. Belief moves to faith when you have proof, even if that proof is felt and not seen.

As Saint Paul said, "Faith is the assurance of things hoped for, the conviction of things not seen."

Mahatma Gandhi believed that nonviolent resistance could change minds, but it was just a belief he had. After putting his theory into practice and seeing that it worked, his belief turned into faith in nonviolence, and it resulted in the toppling of an empire. Rarely does belief transform into faith based on hard, empirical proof. The *evidence of things not seen* is the norm, and our intuition, the Holy Spirit within, is our confirmation.

You believe that forgiveness results in peace of mind, and when you practice it, your belief turns into faith. You have faith in love and you have faith in service to others. You have faith in the practice of patience and harmony, and you have faith in the inner divine voice that guides you. These are all things that started out as beliefs. They're intangible, invisible, accessible principles, universal in nature, and the most powerful forces on this planet. Your faith in your True Self is what defines you. Even, as Jesus said, "With the faith of a tiny mustard seed." Jesus was dedicated to convincing us that we're *all* powerful beings.

So when you say:

"I'm not sure if I can . . ."

"I wish that I could . . ."

"I'm trying to get better at . . ."

Then you're affirming the ego's voice, you're hitching your wagon to a horse that's old and slow.

Having faith in yourself, in others, and in spiritual principle means *knowing* that you're a divine, limitless being and ignoring the voice of lack and limitation. A strong faith results in the simplest of certainties, that all is well, right here, right now.

Having Faith Means Seeing the World Differently

You see the world and its inhabitants through the eyes of your belief systems, right or wrong. Every perception you have throughout the day is first and instantly compared and analyzed to your existing beliefs before your mind makes a determination about it. Here's the problem: Most of your beliefs about yourself and others are limited or false. The ego is constantly trying to convince you that you're separate from God and others and that you're not enough—these beliefs are not based in Truth, they're not of God. Yet these are the clouded spectacles through which you see the world.

A strong faith is based on the truths that: (1) you're a perfect creation of God; (2) God is all Love; (3) God is within you in the form of your True Self, and therefore always available to you; and, (4) because of the preceding three truths, all is perfect, all is well, in the present moment, wherever you are.

A strong faith tells you that nothing can truly harm you, that the world and everyone in it is right where they *should* be in this moment, that there's nothing you need to think, say, or do to have the happiness, peace, or love you desire because you already *are* these things. A strong faith allows you to just *be* in perfect peace.

To get to a consciousness of strong faith, constant observation of your thoughts, words, and actions is necessary, as well as an energetic willingness to follow the lead of your True Self. Self-observation and self-understanding are the keys to identifying those underlying beliefs that screen out your happiness and peace.

Butch was a history buff and news junkie for many years. He loved reading historical non-fiction books about personalities and events in American history and comparing what he learned to contemporary politics. He had a keen analytical mind, but he also had a core belief system that was fairly negative. His beliefs developed as a result of a critical mother, dishonest and disloyal friends, and a series of fear-inducing events during his school years.

If you were in Butch's head, his core beliefs would sound something like this:

"I am lacking in social skills. I was never cool. People are basically dishonest, selfish, and greedy. I need to watch my back because people will often take advantage of me. The government is not to be trusted. Corporations control the political process, and this country will eventually just go to hell in a hand basket."

These were just a few of Butch's core beliefs. You may share a few of these beliefs.

Over the years, Butch became more and more unhappy and he sought out therapy for depression. The therapist instructed him to stop watching the nightly news for a few weeks. She suggested he become more open to spiritual growth and asked him to explore some local churches. He did, and eventually found a Center for Spiritual Living (CSL) in which he felt comfortable. The people there had a positive, uplifting philosophy, and Butch knew that's what he needed in his life—a positive outlook.

Over the next two years, Butch took a number of classes at his new spiritual home, made many new positive and supporting friends, and became a daily practitioner of silent meditation. He learned about the art of self-observation and mindfulness in an eight-week meditation seminar presented at his CSL by a Buddhist monk. It was a life-changer. Butch began to see how the ego mind constantly fed him untruth, and he made a concerted effort to identify and expose his false core beliefs. He attended several spiritual counseling sessions with a licensed practitioner and made a written list of his limiting beliefs—he quickly pinpointed several beliefs that limited his peace and happiness.

Butch became more and more skilled at watching his thoughts and comparing them to his beliefs. He was amazed at how negative he was, especially when he first began observing. Just within the first week, he identified thoughts of fear, regret, shame, guilt, anger, resentment, envy, and critical judgment of self and others. As he spotted these thoughts, he became accomplished at easily releasing them because he understood their source within his subconscious—the limiting beliefs. Butch experienced more and more peace as all the negativity slowed down in his mind. He noticed that when he wasn't fully aware and *in the moment,* the negative thoughts would creep back in.

The kicker for Butch, though, was filling the void in his mind. Through his CSL classes, he learned about affirmative prayer, the creative process, and his true identity as a perfect creation of a Perfect Creator. He began reciting affirmations throughout the day, which he believed whole-heartedly. He fed his mind the truth. It sounded like this:

"I am perfect just as I am. I am loved beyond measure. I love my spiritual brothers and sisters on this planet. Everyone is doing the best they can with what they have. I forgive easily. I want to see the world differently. I am so grateful for all I have and am. I am at peace. I know all is well, right here and now. I am happy and joyful and have an enthusiastic zest for life."

Butch developed a strong faith. Within two years of finding his spiritual home, his thoughts, and underlying beliefs, changed dramatically. He was mentally in a place of love most of the time. He was good to himself, took better care of his body, and lost 50 pounds as a result. He was always happy, and people noticed. He naturally attracted more friends and loving feelings from his spiritual family. People wanted to be around Butch. His strong faith, the certainty that life is not only well, but very well in the present moment, began with his willingness to look at his core beliefs.

Faith vs. Fear

Do you remember what you were worried about last year? Last month? Last week? If not, why? If it was so important to worry about, surely you'd remember, right? Surely you would. The truth is, all that negative mental activity was an absolute waste of time, wasn't it? Some people might call that amount of worrying *mental masturbation*, but even masturbation has a point to it, if you're doing it right.

You don't remember what you were worried about last month, not because it wasn't important enough to remember, but because your True Self intuitively knows that it doesn't want or need to hold onto fear, which is all worry is. Think about the act of worrying for a moment—worrying is simply the mental process of projecting fear into an imaginary future, which exists only in your mind. It's creating a future of negative possibilities. Isn't that insane thinking? Who, in their right mind, would do this? The ego would—and does, and will—if you're not aware of what's happening in your mind.

Being aware of your conscious thoughts and discerning what's true and what's a delusion is the key to peace of mind. Practicing this awareness is like guarding something valuable, like peace of mind. Guard your mind like a Beefeater.

Long before Beefeaters was a gin, the term referred to the guards posted throughout the Tower of London. They earned their name from the copious amounts of meats they were fed to ensure their strength. They were charged with guarding the King's enemies in the Tower. In modern times, they guarded the Crown jewels, and after high-tech anti-theft gadgetry was installed at the Tower, Beefeaters are now used as tour guides.

Guard your mind like a Beefeater. When you detect fear, anger, judgment, shame, guilt, impatience or other non-love-based thoughts or beliefs, sound the alarm! Let the sirens wail! But don't try to arrest, sentence, and jail these thoughts. Don't oppose them at all. Give them a mental hug, tell them you love them, and send them on their way. Then return to your truth—love, peace, joy, your divine birthright, based on who-you-really-are.

Having Faith Means Trusting That Inner Presence

Which areas of your life are causing you unhappiness, creating fear, or you've identified as *ready to be released*? Where do you need to liberally apply *God ointment* in your life? There's a power and presence within you that already knows. When you trust It and listen to It, you'll be guided in the right direction, and your faith will grow stronger in the process. When we try something, and it works, common sense tells us to rely on that proven method. This is the basis of a strong faith—the certainty and trust we have in our True Self. Here's a story from a man who saw an opportunity to change his life. He listened to his True Self, took definitive action, and has a more robust faith as a result:

"Ever since I can remember, I've been a Type-A personality while driving. I'm normally a fairly mellow guy—soft-spoken and considerate are two words many people use to describe me. Yet when I get on the road, I'm driven. I never give it much thought, I just think of myself as a fast and efficient driver, mincing no effort to get to my destination. When driving on the freeway, my natural instinct is to get in the left lane, put the petal to the metal, and stay ahead of the pack. I like being the leader. As a result, I've earned about twelve or thirteen speeding tickets over the last 30 years. When radar detectors were en vogue, I was first in line to buy one.

I feel stressed when I'm driving. I'm constantly scanning my surroundings, and maneuvering my vehicle so I'm leading the way. If your car is in front of me in the left lane and you're doing the speed limit (or less), I'm right there on your tail. If you don't move to the right, I'll give you a judgmental glance while passing you. When I'm in the left lane, though, don't tailgate me. I'll move over when I feel like it—it's my responsibility to teach you a lesson about not speeding. As George Carlin used to say in his stand-up routine, if the other guy is driving too slow, he's an idiot, but if he's driving too fast, he's a maniac. In other words, it's all about me, and I'm competitive on the road to the point of being a jerk. I could give several other examples of how I create tension on the road.

This type of behavior is generated by my false self, I know this. There's a deep-seated belief somewhere in my subconscious that causes this behavior.

Frankly I don't care what it is. I'm ready to release it. There are times when I have clarity on the road and become aware of the ego acting out. I'll slow down and relax, but most of the time my awareness is on mental cruise control.

I had an incident of synchronicity a few months ago. I was driving behind someone going very slow on a two-lane road and I was getting rather angry. Suddenly, a song started playing on the radio, and it woke me up. It was 'Slow Ride' by Foghat. I chuckled and then slowed down. The miracle that happened at that moment was the result of me being open to listen. I was nudged back into awareness. As I said, I'm ready to let go of this behavior, it doesn't match my intention and desire to be a person of peace, poise, and freedom. In my morning prayers, I affirm that, 'I am kind and cooperative, and release all desire to be the winner, be better than others, be right, control others, or act rudely.' Ironically, I say my morning affirmative prayers aloud while driving to work.

About a month ago, I was in my A Course in Miracles *group and we were discussing our driving habits in relation to the topic of the day. I was a little surprised to learn that I was the only speed demon in the group. I made a comment about praying for and forgiving the other guy when he or she cuts me off on the road, and a wise elder from our group made this comment: 'The fact that you used the phrase,* the other guy cut me off, *indicates that the ego was in charge, because no one can truly cut us off if we don't believe in the concept of doing harm to others on the road. It tells me that you were projecting your own hostility to the other driver and that the ego was holding you hostage in that instant—but we also know that the Holy Spirit is available to us at all times.' Then he said something that hit me like a bolt of lightning. He said, 'When I get in my car, it's a place of peace, a sanctuary of calm in which I let the Holy Spirit do the driving.'*

That's what I want my car to be . . . a place of peace, a sanctuary of calm. I want to drive in the right-hand lane and not be concerned in the least about anything except keeping a safe distance from the car in front of me. I would be at peace when I arrived at my destination instead of being angry like I usually am. So this is my new intention: to be the kind of driver that I would be proud to call my friend, to apply spiritual principle on the road, and to create a sanctuary of peace in my car. I've been practicing for the last few weeks. The ego still rears its ugly head occasionally, but I'm more aware of it now. It may take some time to be fully awake and at peace in my car all the time, but I'm willing to change. I'm ready for more peace and happiness in my life. I deserve it."

What an excellent example of someone who is open to change and focused on his spiritual growth. As the old saying goes, "When the student is ready, the teacher will appear." It hadn't dawned on this man that he was creating chaos in his life until he reached that mental place where he could see the opposite side of the mountain. *A Course in Miracles* would call this a miracle—a shift in perception. He had a desire to see life differently, he trusted his True Self to point the way to right thinking, and his faith is now much stronger. He's enjoying his newfound peace as he cruises in the right-hand lane of life.

The Power of "We"

The Gift of Recognition

by
Dr. Linda Johnson

The following story illustrates how someone with strong faith was able to see the image and likeness of God in another, despite the seemingly dreadful appearance to the contrary. He taught me the miracle of unshakeable faith—that there's a light within everyone, waiting for the gift of recognition.

The little man in the print shop that I judged as ugly and misshapen taught me about blessing others through the gift of recognition. I found myself staring at him while I waited for the copy machine to spit out my copies. He seemed to be the manager of the shop.

He caught me staring. A mouth of naked gums grinned at me. He jumped up and came over to talk to me.

"God told me to come over and tell you my story," he said.

I mumbled something about not having the time. He threw his head back and laughed. What I'd said was surely not *that* funny.

He said with confidence, "If God told me to come over and tell you my story, He knows you need to hear it, and he also knows you have the time. He rarely has me share this story. I'll tell you what—I'll go back to my desk, and when you get through with your copies, come over and sit with me."

There was something compelling about this man.

For the first time, I looked him in the eyes when I went to his desk. They were bright, clear, and accepting. He shuffled some papers around, made a few funny sounds, offered me a caramel, and began to tell his story.

"It was fifteen years ago yesterday that the police and ambulance were called to pick up a raving lunatic who was waving a butcher knife and screaming

incoherently. When they arrived, I was in the middle of the road looking threatening, waving the knife. Traffic was stopped in both directions. A woman had fainted; a child and woman were screaming, and I could hear sirens in the background.

As the police officers ran toward me, I laid my left hand on the ground. I raised the butcher knife with my other hand and brought it down as hard as I could. I severed these fingers off."

He waved the evidence in my face and continued.

"There was blood everywhere, and it seemed the crowd gasped and screamed in unison. I wept and moaned quietly. The violence had left me. I gave up the knife without any resistance. An ambulance took me away, the sirens screaming.

For the next nine years I lived in a padded room in an institution for the mentally insane. I was violent and kept heavily drugged. Day after day the routine was the same.

Insanity had taken over my life days before I had ended up on the street with a butcher knife. A car had run over Monty, my beloved mutt. The car didn't stop. It accelerated out of sight. I threw myself on top of the bloody, lifeless, still-warm body of my only buddy, my only family, and something within me snapped.

As far back as I could recall, I had been the town joke. I barely remember my mother, and my father was a drunk. My thoughts were often fixated on the vivid past—cursing tirades, empty liquor bottles, and lies. I remember the tiny dark closet with the old wool army blanket where I was confined when my father would leave me alone. Endless hours later I would hear his drunken footsteps as he staggered into the house and I would smell the stench of liquor mixed with vomit. I would lie awake, panic-stricken, unable to stop trembling.

At school, there were no beatings or cursing, but there was the taunting and cruelty.

'Kirby has fleas! Get away from me Kirby, you stink! Dirty Kirby! Stupid, raggedy Kirby! Look, Kirby has two different socks on, where are your shoelaces Kirby? Hey Kirby, we have a girlfriend for you! She has fleas and stutters just like you!'

For forty-five years, those voices in my head never ceased. All the jeering and condemnation were indelibly recorded in my head. I remembered every expression of disgust and hate, and it tortured me every waking hour of my life.

One day after an indifferent mental health attendant had brought me breakfast, and I had scowled my way through it, there was a knock at the window. I looked up to see a man with a big friendly smile. He whispered, 'I know who you are Kirby!' Then he disappeared.

I couldn't remember anybody looking at me or speaking to me without indifference or contempt until that very morning. Something happened inside me. The internal tormentors were silenced. Within a few moments they were back, and I was scowling and repeating out loud what I heard in my mind . . . 'Kirby is a halfwit . . . dirty Kirby . . . stupid, ugly Kirby.' I settled back into my despised accusers. They were without compassion or mercy.

The following morning the young man did the same thing. His happy face filled up the window, again the same words, 'I know who you are Kirby.' Again the internal harassment stopped, and something like a ray of hope was born within me. Some mornings he would just appear and smile. He didn't seem frightened, angry, disgusted, or repulsed by what he saw. Didn't he notice I had wet my pants? Didn't he see that I was ugly and deformed? Didn't he know that I'd kill him with my bare hands if I could?

I began to look forward to that face greeting me each day, until one day, something happened. I felt it in every part of my body as he stood there looking at me. It felt like sunshine inside of me. I grinned back at him.

The days when he didn't show up at the window I would sit and moan, rocking back and forth and feeling like I had lost something very precious. He represented the only hope that I had ever known. Whatever that man knew about me had silenced the tormentors within my mind.

One unforgettable day, the door opened and there was the man with the smiling face, he came toward me. His expression was compassionate and cheerful, but without pity or fear. He was looking at me as if I were his friend. His assurance dissolved the chronic rage in my head.

He said, 'Hi Kirby. My name is Blaine. I'm a psychologist, and I'd like to get to know you.' Blaine visited with me often after that. He acted like he was not the least bit discouraged by my lack of progress even though it was weeks before I could speak. I would sit there mute, grinning a toothless smile, and tears would slide down my face.

I hung onto every word he said. Soon I was shaking my head and nodding. Blaine always looked pleased with my responses. He wasn't just doing his job—he took time to be my friend. I'll never forget the first day I began to talk. Blaine just stood there beaming, his eyes laughing.

'You're going to make it Kirby, I know you will.' I stammered and stuttered my way through many of his visits after that. Sometimes he told me about the clever things his daughter had said or something he'd read.

Blaine always acted as if I were his equal. When I stuttered, he acted like it was trivial and deserved no mention. As my confidence grew, I stuttered less. There was never a doubt in Blaine's eyes that I would not live a normal life.

One day he asked me, 'Have you discovered that when someone sees you as complete, it feels like your soul is being washed clean?'

Within eighteen weeks, I was out of the locked, padded room and mingled with other patients. I no longer thought of myself as dirty, half-witted Kirby. I could tell that others didn't either. I began discovering my talents. The attendants could hardly believe my recovery. After thinking of me as insane for nine years, the new me *perplexed them.*

What had happened? How could I have changed? The answer was simple. It took only one person to believe in me. Acceptance, love, and Blaine's unshakeable faith changed my world. Blaine removed the labels from me and I was set free within my mind. I stretched myself to meet Blaine's perceptions of me."

Just as Kirby finished his story, he stopped to answer the telephone. I marveled that he told me the entire story without any interruptions. In the few minutes it had taken to hear the story, a lifetime of old motives and judgments dissolved within me. I understood now that this man was a light bearer of God's love. He had dropped the imprisoning fixed conclusions that he had made from his childhood. Someone recognized his real identity and ignited the Radiance within him, and in turn, Kirby ignited the Radiance within me.

Strengthening your Faith Daily: Ten Unsuccessful Life Strategies and Ten Truths

Author Sue Fitzmaurice has a very positive and uplifting outlook on life, and her Facebook page is an excellent reflection of that. One of the many memes featured on her page focused on ten unsuccessful life strategies. This bulleted list of ego-centered tactics to preserve and enhance itself is an insightful summary of what A.A. refers to as *self-will run riot*. These strategies, when used on a consistent basis, will result in misery, pain, and a sad outlook on life.

Each of these practices is a dark spot. Let's shine a light on each one and look at an opposing healing spiritual principle.

1. **Release or deny from your mind any thoughts or limiting beliefs regarding:** *Feeling Fear.*

Instead, realize this truth about yourself:

There's nothing to fear! Nada! Zilch! Zero! Fear is nothing but thought, it's not real—not permanent, enduring, or life sustaining. God is real, nothing else, and if you sincerely put your focus on God, fear has no power. Like a dark corner of a room, it's no longer dark when the light shines on it. The ego thinks that by fearing something, you can fix it or keep it away from you, but fear has no power. It's a waste of thought. Think about everything you've ever feared. Think about that for a moment. Perhaps your fear revolved around: (1) not having enough money; (2) children who might come to harm; (3) a relationship ending; (4) a pending job termination of layoff; or (5) death itself.

Every fear you've ever had did nothing to make those circumstances disappear or get easier. All those fears were completely unnecessary and, in fact, just confounded and intensified your problems.

God is the only solution—not fear, not worry, not anticipation, not dread. Your True Self will lead you to the party within your consciousness. Waiting for you there with party hats and streamers are peace, joy, love, wisdom, and the certainty that all is well, right here, right now. Instead of fear, have faith.

2. Release or deny from your mind any thoughts or limiting beliefs regarding: *Blaming Others.*

Instead, realize this truth about yourself:

You're responsible for every aspect of your life. The source of all your feelings, beliefs, outlooks, attitudes, and life circumstances is your thoughts. This means you have both responsibility and complete freedom for the current and future conditions of your life. When you do something wrong, such as hurting someone, it's easy to admit that others aren't to blame. The ego might try to convince you that others caused you to act out, but for the most part, you know that you're responsible. Here's what separates the unaware from the enlightened: When others seemingly hurt you, with or without provocation, you're still responsible for your mental and emotional reactions, and for your resulting behavior. Taking responsibility for your consciousness means giving up anger, resentment, fear, jealousy, and all those other dark thoughts you have in regard to others. The ego always wants to point the finger, but your True Self will help you realize the Truth—that no one can truly hurt you unless you let them. Eventually, you come to see that it's the ego hurting you, not others. When you know who you are—a perfect creation of a Perfect Creator—and you realize that you create your own life via your thoughts, you have the freedom to be at peace, to feel loved, to love others, and to experience complete joy all the time, regardless what happens *out there.*

3. Release or deny from your mind any thoughts or limiting beliefs regarding: *Making Excuses.*

Instead, realize this truth about yourself:

Again, you're completely responsible for your life. Making excuses is a self-defense mechanism used by the ego to continue to look good and remain in control. If you make a mistake, be honest with yourself and others. Admit your mistake. It's so freeing! Self-honesty is the key here. By surrendering to your True Self, being honest with yourself, being humble, and accepting responsibility for your thoughts, beliefs, words, and actions becomes easier, and automatic. Making excuses is self-destructive, accepting responsibility is constructive and life affirming. Most of us can detect bullshit when it's presented to us. You *know* when someone is making excuses for their behavior, you can smell that crap a mile away. You instinctively recognize when someone isn't being honest with him/herself by offering excuses, rationalizations, and justifications. Try this the next time you find yourself making excuses. Think, "Why am I lying to myself? What am I hiding? What do I fear here? How can I admit my mistake and move on?" Then say, "God, please lead me, guide me, and show me the way." You'll never go wrong by living these words. God is always there for you, your True Self guides you to Truth.

4. Release or deny from your mind any thoughts or limiting beliefs regarding: *Re-living your past in the present.*

Instead, realize this truth about yourself:

As a Truth seeker, you intuitively know that there's no such thing as the past. The ego is constantly regurgitating memories of moments passed to make sense of, predict, and control the future, which also doesn't exist. Reality with a capital *R*, aka God, exists only in the eternal now. From a logical standpoint, recalling information stored in your brain can be useful, such as remembering which way to turn a light bulb—the thought, *righty-tighty-lefty-loosey*, has beneficial value. But the thoughts that cause pain aren't so neutral. They involve regret, shame, guilt, resentment, doubt, and uncertainty. The ego dredges them up to create a sense of separation between you, God, and your fellow human companions.

The key to a past that exists only in your mind is to let it go. Forgiveness is the healing balm that restores you back to right-mindedness. Regret, guilt, shame—every thought or belief the ego uses to tell you that you're not enough, or bad, or less than can be dispelled through self-forgiveness. You need to use this tool to rectify all of these thoughts and feelings *whenever* they attempt to enter your mind. Recognize these thoughts as false and immediately forgive yourself. Do this every minute of every day—eventually they stop coming. The ego gives up under the shining light of your True Self. The same holds true in regard to other people, organizations, and institutions. Thoughts of anger, hate, resentment, jealousy, or judgment in any form—these are all mind poison that eat away at the fabric of your soul, as a moth does to cloth. If your choice is inner peace, forgive others and yourself easily, constantly and consistently. As Jesus said, "seventy times seven," which when translated from the original Aramaic means *a whole bunch*. Let go of the past and enjoy the peace of the eternal now. Your True Self will always show you how.

5. Release or deny from your mind any thoughts or limiting beliefs regarding: *Complaining.*

Instead, realize this truth about yourself:

Have you ever tried to go an entire day without complaining? It's hard! We're so accustomed to complaining in various forms that we often don't see it as self-destructive behavior. We're not even aware we're doing it. A minister friend once said, "I delivered a Sunday talk about our tendency to complain and asked everyone, including myself, to make a commitment not to complain for a week. I didn't make it a quarter mile away from our spiritual center that Sunday before a rude driver set me off." This same minister later shared that the rude driver wasn't the cause of him losing focus, it was his own ego. Complaining is nothing more than the ego saying, "Hey, wait a minute, the world isn't how I think it should be!" The ego is like a toddler tugging at mommy's skirt to get her attention. "Mommy, mommy, mommy, look mommy!" Eventually, mommy gives the toddler her attention.

To repeat, complaining is the ego's way of saying the world isn't how it thinks it should be. The key word here is, of course, *should*. Complaining is a negative judgment based on the refusal to accept the world as it is, or other people, as they are. There's always a reason for the ego wanting the world to be different and in line with itself. There's always a desire for something else behind every complaint, and every desire, every attachment, every aversion you have, is based in a fear of something. When you complain, think, "What am I afraid of?"

But then the ego says, "Well, if we don't complain, how do we make the world a better place? How do we affect positive change in the world if we don't first identify the negative?" Tricky ego. Your True Self replies, "To make the world better, start with yourself." If you want more peace in the world, realize more peace within yourself. If you want the world to be more loving, love yourself. Accepting the world as it is always requires you to look inward for a spiritual principle that will quiet the ego. Your True Self will always tell you what that principle is, if you listen closely.

The Serenity Prayer is about acceptance. *"God, grant me the serenity to accept the things I cannot change, the courage to change the things I can, and the wisdom to know the difference."* You're powerless to change others. You can attempt to control, persuade, influence, or manipulate the world and the people within it, and you can even be successful in making alterations, but that's not real change. The world around us, nature, and the people on this planet always *right themselves.* We have little influence on others' journey until they're ready for change themselves. But, and this is a big but ... we have *complete power* over our minds, and ample freedom to change our thoughts, feelings, attitudes, and beliefs. This is how REAL change in the world takes place. When enough people change their own minds, suddenly history changes, institutions change, the world rights itself. It always begins within.

Complaining is just the voice of your inner child, the ego. There's no need to dislike or judge it in any way. Just love it. Give it a mental pat on the head as a mother does her child. Be aware of that ego voice and know that it doesn't speak your Truth—that you're a perfect creation of a Perfect Creator—but love it, as a mother loves her child even though the child is acting out. With enough love, the child calms down. Your True Self is the source of your inner awareness, and your love.

6. Release or deny from your mind any thoughts or limiting beliefs regarding: *Controlling.*

Instead, realize this truth about yourself:

Controlling is based in fear, plain and simple. This fear is rooted in an ideal picture or outcome within your mind of how the ego thinks the world should be. If the world doesn't conform to your ideal, the ego cranks up the fear generator. The ego is self-centered, it desires the world to revolve around it, and wants to get its way. Its vision is very narrow and ultra-focused. Let's be very clear on this idea—*you* are not the ego. If you were, you would have no power of choice, and you wouldn't be able to recognize the untruthfulness of controlling based thoughts and behavior—you'd be an ego-controlled robot. You're not.

Have you ever worked for a micro manager, someone who wants to control every detail, every outcome? Whoa! Not a pleasant situation. Extreme controlling manifests as obsessive/compulsive disorder—the false *need* to control everything—but there are many variations short of this extreme. When the ego is in the controlling mode, and you're not aware of it, you cause pain for both yourself and others. It's fear run amuck, not very different than Chicken Little running in circles, shouting, "The sky is falling, the sky is falling!" It's not. The sky is just fine.

The solution to controlling is faith and trust. Do you remember the film, "Indiana Jones and the Last Crusade?" To get to the cave where the Holy Grail was stored, Indiana Jones had to prove his worth by enduring three trials. The clue to the third trial was, "Only in a leap from the lion's head shall he prove his worth." Indiana Jones was required to take a leap of faith. Not knowing if the universe would support him, he took a blind step onto thin air over a deep cavern. Either his faith would be rewarded, or he would fall to his death. Of course, his faith was strong, his trust in the Infinite was sound, and he crossed the cavern on a seemingly invisible stone bridge (invisible to those without faith) to reach the Grail.

Each moment is like a leap of faith. When you surrender yourself to *what is*, rather than the ego's notion of *what should be*, and you have faith that all is well in the present moment, your faith will be rewarded by a certainty that all IS well. Not in a future moment, but in the present moment. Trust and faith require you to let go of any outcomes, predictions, or *what ifs* in a nonexistent future. The ego wants to control and predict a future that exists only in your mind. Your True Self whispers to you that the future is only a thought, nothing more, and your act of letting go and letting God will nudge you back into the flow of life.

Go with this flow! It will take you wonderful places on your journey, mentally, emotionally, and spiritually. You need not worry about where you're going or when you'll get there, there's no need to predict, fight, struggle, or resist. As the old saying goes, "Plan the fishing trip, but not the fish fry." Just go with the flow of life. Your True Self will always lead the way.

7. Release or deny from your mind any thoughts or limiting beliefs regarding: *Needing to be right.*

Instead, realize this truth about yourself:

First, let's make this clear. *Being right* is not a need. The only physical needs you have are for oxygen, water, food, eliminating waste, and the proper environmental temperature. The only true *spiritual* need you have is for God. Everything else is a desire, and the ego loves to desire desiring.

Desiring to be right is simply one of many of the ego's tools to separate you from God and your fellow humans. Separation is the ego's *modus operandi*, its way of self-preservation. By attempting to make you believe you're separate from others—different, unique, better than, and even less than, the ego masks the Truth from you—that you're One with All. The ego sees the world completely upside down, inverted, and inside out. A good measuring stick for your truth is to listen to the ego and then look at the opposite belief. Compare the two and then call upon your True Self to reveal the truth.

Have you ever been in an argument or discussion and then gradually, or suddenly, experience that desire to be right? Of course you have, it happens to all of us, sometimes several times each day. Just look at Facebook, Twitter and other social media outlets for God's sake—people desiring to be right up the wazoo—over and over, ad nauseam.

Each of us perceives reality differently. We've all developed our perspectives based on our past and the many influences upon us. The difference between the wise man and the fool (the True Self and the ego) is that the True Self will guide you to know that others' perspectives are not better or worse than yours, not right or wrong, just different. It's a sad commentary on organized religion when *being right* trumps respecting and appreciating others' beliefs. The same holds true for politics, another hot button that elicits aggressive and anger-filled knee-jerk reactions from many people. There's no right and wrong when it comes to beliefs, just different perceptions.

Have you ever had an *emotional hangover* after a heated exchange? It doesn't feel good. It feels unnatural. You intuitively know that something has come over you when you cross that line of disrespect toward others' beliefs. That's your True Self reminding you that we're All One. As the wise adage goes, "Would you rather be right, or be happy?"

The solution is to know that other humans may be on slightly different paths, but heading in the same direction. It's inevitable and assured that we'll ALL eventually perceive ourselves as One. Your mission, should you decide to accept it, is to assist that coming together by loving others and yourself. Love them enough to respect their beliefs, and love yourself by being part of the solution—Love. When you get to the rest stop named *tolerance* (if you haven't already), keep going, and as you coast over the hill, you'll see *respect, appreciation*, and *love*. Ask your True Self to show you the way. It's the best GPS you have.

8. Release or deny from your mind any thoughts or limiting beliefs regarding: *Needing to impress others.*

Instead, realize this truth about yourself:

Again, this is not a need. The question we should always ask ourselves is, "Why do I want to impress others?" The etymology of the word *impress* dates back to the 14th century. Its definition relates to the act of *pressing or forcing upon the mind or senses of others.* A Course in Miracles would call this act *projection*.

Projection, as defined by the *Course*, is a fundamental law of our mind. *Projection makes perception*—what we see outwardly is determined by what we believe inwardly. Wayne Dyer's pithy quote on this principle is, "you will see it when you believe it." The projection of our beliefs out into the world is based on our perception of reality, not actual or objective reality.

If you love yourself, have a positive outlook about yourself, and are happy; this is what you'll project out to others. This is the lens you'll use to make sense of the world. But if you don't think highly of yourself—if your beliefs about yourself are based in *not good enough* or *better than,* or are clouded with guilt, resentment, or fear; that's what you'll project onto others, and how you'll perceive the world.

Attempting to impress others is an ego-based action to convince someone else what you don't believe yourself, but that you *want* to believe. If the desire to impress had a voice, it would sound like this:

"Hey, look at me! I don't love myself very much, in fact, I barely understand who I am. I want to believe that I'm good, smart, attractive, and important, and I want you to believe that too."

All of us do this to a certain degree—we're not just talking about people with low self-esteem.

As Terry Cole-Whittaker wrote, "What you think of me is none of my business." The opposite of wanting to impress is feeling good about yourself, knowing your mind, and knowing what's true versus an ego lie. Being comfortable with yourself means you've learned to differentiate the ego's voice from that of your True Self. Your willingness will guide you to follow the guidance of that Divine Presence within.

Self-love is the basis of your spiritual development, and it's fueled by your knowledge of your True Self—an individual expression of the Infinite. When you know you are Love in expression, there's no desire to seek love. When you know you are Joy incarnate, there's no desire to seek happiness through other people, places, or things. When you know you are Peace, there's no desire to do anything more than BE.

Here's a wonderful quote from mystic and author, Vernon Howard, regarding the importance of self-understanding:

"When you truly see that you're doing something against yourself, you'll no longer do it. Simple understanding has no fears. There's beauty is finding yourself. If you're willing enough, God will be right there. To be a grown-up, spiritually mature human being is the greatest and only prize on earth. Ask

yourself, 'Do I really want this self-destructive state?' Stop wanting the sur-vival of the false self. To wake up means to no longer unknowingly toss coals onto your uncomfortable inner fire. Direct your strength toward self-understanding."

Releasing the ego's untrue thoughts and beliefs is a constant process. The essence of self-forgiveness and release of that which is not true requires non-judgmental patience and acceptance on your part. That which sustains the ego is that which is hidden or attacked. When you bring these false and limiting beliefs out into the open and lovingly release them, you're forgiving yourself. You are perfect. You always have been and always will be. See that fact by listening only to your True Self.

9. Release or deny from your mind any thoughts or limiting beliefs regarding: *Judging others.*

Instead, realize this truth about yourself:

Imagine, if you will, a utopian world in which everyone is taught to love themselves deeply from the moment they're born. Parents fawn over their children, giving them praise, encouragement, and nothing but love. They're taught to love themselves and know they're connected spiritually to all other living creatures. As a result, all children love themselves, feel good about themselves, and terms like *low self-esteem* don't exist.

Imagine that these children are five years old now and venture out to play with other children for the first time. Do you think you would witness any mean spirited behavior, selfishness, shoving, hair-pulling, or even fear? Of course you wouldn't. When people love and feel good about themselves, that belief is projected out into the world. They see the world and its inhabitants as good. They feel connected to others. Their self-love is extended out from them to everyone else.

The opposite of this future world is our present world. When we don't love ourselves, we don't love others. Our discontent and unease with our *self* is at a subconscious level. We're often not aware of this unease, but it does manifest itself in our sleeping dreams. We want to be rid of this feeling, so we project it onto others through judgment, anger, and blame. These projections are like the images projected on a screen at a movie theater. The projector is the ego, based in our fear, guilt, and pain. We're constantly projecting our self-inflicted pain out into the world.

When you truly believe that you're good, worthy, loved, and *at ease*, you'll cease all judgment and condemnation of others. As with all creation, your beliefs are the seed that get planted into the soil of the Law of Cause and Effect, manifesting your life circumstances. When your seed is based in self-love, you're planting love into the Law, manifesting loving and emotionally healthy relationships with others. When your seed is tainted with fear, dislike or unease with yourself, you'll inevitably be planting the same into the Law, resulting in judgment of others.

Self-love is the key to cease all judgment, but that sounds too simple. Generating, growing, and nurturing that self-love takes work. It requires you to know who you really are—a being made of Love (God). When you know this, you'll be able to discern easily which thoughts that flit through your mind are true and which are not. The multitude of negative thoughts and beliefs that you experience daily are not your truth. When you release all thoughts and beliefs that are not based in Love, all you have left is Love . . . you. Like a beautiful snake, shedding the skin of untruth again and again and again, leaves only the Truth.

If you loved yourself completely right now, at this moment, you would have no knowledge of judgment, blame, anger, or condemnation. They would be a mystery to you, as they are to God. The process of returning to your home base of self-love doesn't need to be a long and arduous journey. It's assured for all and is dependent only on your willingness, consistent vigilance, desire for self-understanding, and surrender. Your True Self is always there for you on this journey. Keep looking to it for direction.

10. Release or deny from your mind any thoughts or limiting beliefs regarding: *Attachment to the superficial.*

Instead, realize this truth about yourself:

Student: Teacher, what is superficial?

Teacher: All but God.

Student: Wow, okay, but there are many important things in this world, like war, religion, politics, making money, doing good things for people, and being happy. Are all these things superficial?

Teacher: Being happy is of God. I'll emphasize the word *being* instead of seeking, wishing, or hoping.

Student: What? I don't understand.

Teacher: God is *being*. God is not doing, thinking, feeling, believing, worshipping, seeking, hoping, wishing, watching, playing, leading, following, working, driving, walking, running, interacting . . . I could keep going all day. God is being.

Student: Okay, but I need to focus on everyday things: Like making a living, feeding and clothing myself, and paying my credit card bills. I pray and sometimes meditate. I go to church almost every Sunday. Heck, I read lots of spiritual books, but I still like to spend time watching TV, surfing the web, shopping, entertaining, and having fun. Are you saying this is all superficial?

Teacher: You asked me what was superficial. I answered, "All but God." Superficial is that which is of the surface, not deep, cursory, that which is apparent or obvious. Superficial is of the ego. The opposite of superficial is God, that which is not so obvious, that which the ego tries to distract you from every moment of every day. God is real, the ego is not, and yet the ego is successful at constantly diverting your attention away from what's real.

Student: So that's the answer? "Be with God?"

Teacher: What is God? From our past studies you know that God is Love, God is Life itself. And you know that all other attributes of God fall under this idea of all encompassing Love—joy, peace, understanding, strength, clarity, harmony, abundance, and health. These are all universal principles based in God's Love, and because you're a direct reflection of God, you know that *you* are these attributes too. They're not things you need to seek out, as you do when you look for new TV shows to watch, games to play, hobbies to pursue, and other countless diversions. These principles are who you *are*. You only need to BE them.

Student: But what about all the life responsibilities I have?

Teacher: Do them, but BE who you really are while you're doing them. BE love, BE peace, BE joy, BE patient, BE understanding.

Student: BE God-like?

Teacher: There you go.

Useful Affirmations

I have strong faith in that Inner Presence.

I know my word has power. I speak my truth.

I see the world differently today, I see from the eyes of Love.

Nothing can harm me. Not now, not ever. I am safe.

I put my focus where I want it. Love, peace, and joy. This is who I am.

I silence my mind and fill the void with the Truth—I am whole, perfect, and complete.

I guard my mind and watch my thoughts. I know my truth.

I trust that inner peace. It is God.

All is well, all is well, all is well.

I let go of control and any desire to be right. I choose love, I choose joy, I choose peace.

I let go of all desire to impress others. I love myself exactly as I am.

Rhyming Affirmations

I release all fear, guilt, shame, and resentment,
I turn to that Power within and feel the contentment.

There's a Power within that knows what to say and do,
I let it lead me and I see the world anew.

My eyes are open, I'm following the voice of my Inner Guide,
Together we know the truth, this love cannot be denied.

I'm a conduit for God, the love is flowing through me,
I let my light shine so others see the true me.

I let go of control, I don't need to be right,
I open my heart to all and let out the light.

CHAPTER NINE

Forgiveness

Jesus clearly explains the meaning of divine forgiveness. He says that we should forgive until seventy times seven. This is but another way of saying that forgiveness is eternal and ever available. What a load is dropped from the shoulders of personal responsibility, when we realize that the Eternal Mind holds naught against anyone!

—Ernest Holmes, *The Science of Mind*

Forgiveness is the means by which we will remember. Through forgiveness the thinking of the world is reversed. The forgiven world becomes the gate of Heaven, because by its mercy we can at last forgive ourselves. Holding no one prisoner to guilt, we become free. Acknowledging Christ in all our brothers, we recognize His Presence in ourselves. Forgetting all our misperceptions, and with nothing from the past to hold us back, we can remember God.

—*A Course in Miracles*

If we are now about to ask forgiveness for ourselves, why shouldn't we start out by forgiving them, one and all?

—*The Twelve Steps and Twelve Traditions*

The Evolution of Forgiveness

Why does forgiveness come easier to some people than others? Or why does it become easier for an individual to forgive a perceived transgression over a period of time? The answer has to do with our level of understanding and awareness of ourselves. As we grow spiritually, so does our understanding of the absolute need and importance of forgiveness.

Forgiveness is a bridge to happiness and peace. Some have called it a tool. It's not a spiritual principle, the foundational principle is Love, and forgiveness is an action, a behavior, fueled by self-love. When you properly perceive forgiveness, you realize it has little to do with the person you're forgiving, and your understanding of it progresses over time.

The evolution of forgiveness can be thought of as moving through four stages, with multiple levels of understanding between each.

Stage 1: Un-forgiveness—Not being able to forgive someone or yourself is a painful state of consciousness and a deceivingly abhorrent and self-centered condition. In this stage, the ego is in command. It rules over your consciousness, at least in regard to a person you're unwilling to forgive. Lack of self-forgiveness falls under this stage as well. Are there acts that are unforgivable? What if you were raped or sexually molested? How about if one of your parents, your spouse, or a sibling were murdered? Could you forgive someone who physically or emotionally abused you during your childhood? The longer or more severe the trauma, the more emotion you have attached to it. The anger or fear you initially felt, which started as normal feelings of self-preservation, have cemented into a vile emotional concrete. This act, you say, can never be forgiven!

The word *resent* comes from the Old French word *resentir*, meaning to re-feel. When someone wrongs you, you feel anger, based in fear. After that point in time, you have a potential resentment, and whenever you think of that perceived wrongdoing, you re-feel that anger—again, and again, and again.

For thirty years starting in the 1970s, two revered members of Alcoholics Anonymous, Joe McQ. and Charlie P., hosted "Big Book" seminars across the country. The Big Book, entitled *Alcoholics Anonymous*, was published in 1939 and was the text that launched the same-named organization. It's been said that it took Bill W. and Dr. Bob to write the Big Book and Joe and Charlie to explain it. One of the stories Charlie told during these seminars was about how his resentments kept him in a constant state of pain, and dependent on the bottle to relieve his misery. He likened his mind to a movie projector, constantly re-playing his resentments in his mind. He said that he'd arise in the morning, pour of cup of coffee, add a shot of whisky to it, light a cigarette, and sit there in his misery, constantly re-playing his resentments. He confessed that he received a certain satisfaction and perverse pleasure from re-living his resentments, imagining things he could have said or done and ways to get even with those who wronged him. He described his state of mind as a sort of hell and was fearful he'd never be able to forgive *those bastards*. Yet he did. Charlie came to realize that he must forgive others to achieve complete freedom, happiness, and serenity. His understanding of forgiveness evolved.

Here's the key: Forgiveness means release and acceptance. When you forgive someone, you're making a conscious choice to let go of that painful memory and accept that person as being exactly as they are/were. Forgiveness has nothing to do with condoning someone's wrong acts—it simply means you're choosing not to re-live them. When you forgive, you're not releasing the other person from responsibility of their wrongs—you're letting *yourself* off the hook.

Perhaps you've heard this insightful axiom: "When you refuse to forgive someone, it's like you're taking poison and hoping the other person dies." You ingest that poison every time you re-live that hurt. You need to lovingly release the resentment whenever it re-surfaces in your mind. Affirm to yourself that this painful memory is not *your truth* today. Self-love means gently, but firmly, controlling your thoughts. Seek guidance, love, and support from your True Self. If the memory is persistent or intense, therapy helps to understand the subconscious beliefs that sustain it. Once you see how these beliefs are false or limiting, release becomes easier. Be aware of the ego—it doesn't want you to understand why you're still in pain because it loses power when you're more self-aware and self-loving. God is always right there in the middle of all this. Always seek guidance from your True Self.

Acceptance of someone who's hurt you means understanding that they were doing the best they could in life with *what they had* (their level of self-understanding and self-awareness) at the moment in time when they hurt you. Again, acceptance of someone is not condoning or disregarding their actions, it's accepting them as they are/were. Recovering alcoholics and addicts are the world champions of releasing resentments. They *must* if they want to stay sober. In the book *Alcoholics Anonymous*, it's suggested that you look at people who've wronged you as spiritually sick:

"We realized that the people who wronged us were perhaps spiritually sick. Though we did not like their symptoms and the way these disturbed us; they, like ourselves, were sick too. We asked God to help us show them the same tolerance, pity, and patience that we would cheerfully grant a sick friend."

When a friend is diagnosed with cancer, you don't get angry at him/her for getting sick, do you? Of course not. When someone hurts you, they're sick too—spiritually sick.

But you say, "Yes, but someone with cancer can't help but be sick, whereas someone who's mean, violent, uncaring, or rude can help themselves—they can be a better person."

Yes, we can all be better people, but at that moment in time, the spiritually sick person was *right where they were* in their level of spiritual awareness. Here's another story from Dr. Greg Baer's *Real Love* to illustrate acceptance:

Paul was sitting by the hotel swimming pool reading a newspaper. It was a beautiful day, and he was happy and serene. Occasionally, tiny drops of water from the pool would splash onto his paper, but he ignored it. After a while, the drops became larger and more frequent. He started to get a bit annoyed, but continued to read. Later, the drops became even heavier, and he heard wild splashing. "Those darn kids," he thought. "Can't they see there are people sitting next to this pool?" Finally, as the splashing started to soak his paper, he jumped out of his seat, angry as a hornet, and turned toward the pool to give those kids a piece of his mind.

What he saw astounded him. A young girl was in distress, thrashing around in the deep end of the pool, trying to grab hold of something, anything. She was drowning. Paul jumped in the water and saved the girl.

Later, Paul thought about how his reaction to this situation changed completely, instantaneously, when he realized the girl in the pool was drowning. His initial reaction was anger, without knowing everything about the situation or the other person involved.

Life is like this. Often, people act out, they behave badly, they hurt us, or they don't live up to our expectations. What we don't realize is that these people are actually drowning. They're doing the best they can to stay afloat in the sea of life with limited, damaged, or faulty mental or emotional resources. Their defective perceptions about life, self-centered thinking, and rude or destructive behavior is at the core of their inability to keep their head above the water. They're being held hostage by the ego. But they're doing the best they can with what they have.

The next time someone irritates or angers you, ask yourself, "What do I need to change within me to be able to accept this person as they are? What can I do to help this drowning person?"

Acceptance applies to you too! How many times have you heard someone say, "I can forgive others more easily than I can forgive myself?" They might as well be saying, "I don't want to hit others on the head repeatedly with a heavy wrench but I'm fine with knocking myself out!" Do you see the insanity of this line of thinking? This is the ego talking, not you! You need to immediately forgive yourself for any *perceived* wrongdoing—the word perceived is italicized because that's what 99% of your thinking is, just perceptions, not based in Truth. If you feel guilty or regretful about anything, you need to forgive yourself right now, whether your actions or inactions were a single event or pattern of behavior, you need to forgive yourself immediately and completely. When that guilt or regret creeps back into your thoughts later, forgive yourself again. Try it right now—say, "I forgive myself completely for any and all perceived wrongdoing. I'm doing my best today and I love myself completely!"

You've heard the old phrase, "forgive and forget." Forgetting in this context doesn't mean you've absolved someone from a transgression against you—that would mean you're just putting a bandage on your emotional wound with the hope they don't repeat it. Forgetting is not about pretending a transgression never happened. It's about releasing the incident from your mind whenever it appears, but *remembering* what the person did to you so you can prevent it from ever happening again. This remembering might mean completely releasing that person from your life (even a family member), having limited contact with him/her, or perhaps examining your own actions and beliefs to examine your *own* part in the interaction, if any. Don't allow people to take advantage of you, you deserve better.

Through these processes of release and acceptance, let your True Self lead the way.

Stage 2: Ego Forgiveness—is a form of forgiveness, but not really. It's *pseudo-forgiveness*. It's mouthing the words, but not meaning it, or believing that you mean it, but not understanding your own mind and not being aware of your thoughts. When someone says, "I forgive so-and-so," and five minutes later thinks about punching out so-and-so's lights, that's ego-forgiveness. The ego wants you to think you've forgiven, but it's still in control.

Ego forgiveness still lacks release. You don't let go of the hurtful memory, and you don't truly accept the person who you perceive has wronged you, or yourself. Have you ever had a friend who just wouldn't let something go? Perhaps they were wronged by someone years ago, or did something they perceive to be very wrong themselves, and they hang on to it year after year. It's part of their *story,* an integral part of who they are, or so they think. They'll say, "Oh, that doesn't really bother me anymore," or, "Yeah, I forgave that moron years ago." Yet they haven't forgiven, because forgiving means release and acceptance.

God forgives. God is Love. Forgiveness results in self-love. God is *for giving* love and wants this for you too, which is why God gave you a True Self.

You need to take back control of your mind from the ego. The ego doesn't want you to release, accept, and forgive. It wants chaos. In the world of myth, a Chaos Demon preys on the helpless during times of great chaos, like riots, blackouts, social revolutions, and other chaotic events. It waits for the world to be pre-occupied, and then strikes. The ego is the same—it waits until you're mentally distracted and then whispers untruth to you. It will do this 24/7/365 if you're not aware of your mind. There are plenty of examples walking past you every day. When you're on *mental auto-pilot* and not fully aware of your conscious thoughts, the ego is driving your bus. Taking control of your mind means being fully present, fully awake, and aware of your thoughts. Being in an awakened state of consciousness will allow you to release unwanted or limiting thoughts, the cornerstone of forgiveness.

Ego Forgiveness has its focus outward, continuing to fixate on *them* in the external world. When your gaze is on the external world, you cannot realize your own peace and happiness—you're making yourself a victim of people and circumstances beyond your control. The answer is never *out there*. Blame is a destructively circular mental activity that can never result in peace or happiness.

There's an old saying in 12-Step meetings: "Pray for people you resent." To a newly recovering alcoholic or addict, that prayer might be, "Please God, let that person be happy, or get hit by a bus." It's a start. Being willing to forgive others, however cursory or misdirected, is a good starting point, as long as it's followed by continuous self-reflection, self-honesty, and sincere forgiveness.

Your self-honesty is necessary to identify your part in the wrongdoing, if any. A child who was molested did not play a part in the wrongdoing and there are dozens of other examples like this, but many times you *do* play a part in your own hurt. You say something hurtful and the other person retaliates. After you forgive him/her for hurting you, make your apologies, and then forgive yourself for the initial act. There are many instances like this in your life. Being honest with yourself and others by confessing your part in life's drama is critical to relieving your guilt and taking ownership of your thoughts and actions. Many people mentally stop after accepting responsibility for their part, but forgiving yourself is the final step that allows you peace and provides freedom.

Stage 3: Real Forgiveness—The self-aware person desires and works for a clear mind—free of fear, resentment, guilt, and similar untruth. It's not easy. The ego is cunning, baffling, and powerful, but your True Self is more powerful—as powerful as you allow it to be. Forgiving others easily is a sign that you're making good progress on your spiritual path.

From Shaun, a recovering addict:

"I realized that I had to forgive others and myself if I wanted to stay clean. That was 10 years ago. Nowadays, I want to forgive everyone and everything immediately and consistently to allow myself more inner peace. Being serene,

content, grateful, and loving to others and myself are the only things that really matter to me today. Forgiveness is one of the tools in my spiritual toolbox that I use to maintain my freedom."

This is an entirely new way of looking at forgiveness! When you arrive at this stage, forgiveness is something you do constantly. Your day might sound something like this:

"I forgive that freeway driver. I forgive myself for getting angry. I forgive the barista for forgetting to add extra foam. I forgive my co-worker for not complimenting my new outfit. I forgive my Facebook friend for being rude on one of my posts. I forgive my wife for not emptying the dishwasher according to my expectations. I forgive my kitty for pooping on the carpet. I forgive myself for any perceived wrongdoing, or for feeling like I'm better than, or not enough. I forgive, I forgive, I forgive."

All day long, forgive. This is what Jesus meant when Peter came to him, asking, "How many times shall I forgive my brother or sister who sins against me? Up to seven times?" and Jesus answered, "I tell you, not seven times, but seventy times seven." What Jesus was saying in his veiled style of parabolic teaching was that we should be in a constant state of forgiveness. The master teacher emphasized forgiveness as being a critically important practice we should engage in continuously. Yet there are so many angry and self-attacking people in the world. Why?! The answer is clear: we hold a false belief that we're separate and divided from God, ourselves, and each other, which prevents clear understanding of the same.

The ability to understand others' perspectives is at the heart of real forgiveness. The story of the drowning girl (earlier in this chapter) is a good example of your viewpoint changing once you share the other person's perspective. The reason you can understand another's pain (and pleasure) is because we are all one—each person on the planet is a spiritual brother or sister—we are like cells in the body of God. By hearing peoples' stories and sharing in their life experiences, you draw even closer to them. Most of the time, you never hear their story, so willingness is required of you to be open to their pain—to put the ego aside, to say a quick and silent prayer for them, to bless them as they go their way. Bless and release them, bless and release them. This is your pathway to peace.

Stage 4: Beyond Forgiveness—A truly wise person knows that there's nothing to forgive, and that everyone is *right* where they are. Period. Life happens. People act out of ego. People, including you, make mistakes. Life is. When you remove the emotional turmoil, expectations, judgment of self and others; and dial down the ego, forgiveness becomes unnecessary.

Internal change is more important than forgiveness—*your* internal thoughts and beliefs, not theirs. When you take your focus off other people—judging them, needing to make them wrong, competing with them, and *should-ing* on them, your consciousness becomes lighter and more expansive. You begin to focus more on yourself and start asking yourself questions like:

"Why did that upset me? Why am I so competitive? Why does it bother me when people don't like me? Why is it hard for me to say no? Why do I have so many expectations about others and myself? Why do I have so many opinions about everything? Why is my immediate reaction one of anger when someone hurts me? Why am I afraid of intimacy?"

The ego will rear its head. It doesn't want you to ask these types of questions. It wants you on mental auto-pilot, not self-reflecting. There's an old saying from the civil rights era, "You know you're doing right when they start shootin' at you." Similarly, you know you're on the right spiritual track when the ego resists. Self-understanding and the resulting internal change that results will lead you beyond forgiveness to a place of pure love.

This was Jesus' message, as well as the message of every true spiritual master—love is the answer, the end-all and be-all—the key. When we arrive at a state of consciousness where we are: always loving, always giving, always supporting, and always sharing; there's no need for forgiveness. Love overpowers the ego and its desire to be a victim.

One of India's spiritual masters is a woman named Mata Amritanandamayi, known throughout the world as Amma, or Mother, for her selfless love and compassion toward all beings. Her entire life has been dedicated to alleviating the pain of the poor, and those suffering physically and emotionally. In addition to doing good work for the poor in India, she travels and teaches, hosting gatherings of thousands. After her spoken message, people line up to hug her. She's known as the *hugging saint*. After a typical lecture, she hugs any attendee who desires her embrace, often hugging thousands over an eight to ten hour period. Here's her story, a testament to how much love a human can express:

Amma was born in a remote coastal village in Kerala, South India in 1953. As a small girl, she drew attention to herself with the many hours she spent in deep meditation on the seashore. She also composed devotional songs and could often be heard singing to the Divine with heartfelt emotion. Despite her tender age, her compositions revealed remarkable depth and wisdom.

When Amma was nine years old, her mother became ill, and Amma was withdrawn from school to help with household tasks and the care of her seven siblings. As she went door-to-door gathering food scraps from neighbors for her family's cows, she was confronted with the intense poverty and suffering that existed in her community and in the world beyond it.

Where Amma encountered people in need, she brought them food and clothing from her own home. She was undeterred by the scolding and punishment she received from her family for doing so. Amma also began to spontaneously embrace people to comfort them in their sorrow. Responding to her affectionate care, they began to call her Amma (Mother).

Amma was deeply affected by the profound suffering she witnessed. According to Hinduism, the suffering of the individual is due to his or her own karma—the results of actions performed in the past. Amma accepted this concept, but she refused to accept it as a justification for inaction. Amma contemplated the principle of karma until she revealed an even more profound truth, asking a question she continues to ask each of us today, "If it is one man's karma to suffer, isn't it our dharma (duty) to help ease his suffering and pain?"

With this simple yet profound conviction—that each of us has a responsibility to lend a helping hand to those less fortunate—Amma moved forward with confidence in her life of service and compassionate care for all beings, uniquely expressed by the motherly embrace she offers to all who seek solace in her arms.

Forgiveness—the Path to True Peace

Your True Self is constantly nudging you toward loving relationships—with others and yourself. Your Inner Teacher wants you to know the peace of God, your natural state. Inner peace and love are who you are. To realize this fact, a bridge has been built to get back to your home base of contentment. This bridge is forgiveness.

Forgiveness is not something that's activated by understanding it—you must *experience* it. Having an understanding of it means nothing—much like recognizing on a mental level the concept of hot versus the experience of burning your hand on a hot stove. Here's another example: You may comprehend the meaning of relief, but you *experience* it as you rest in the shade after a vigorous period of exercise and feel a cool breeze waft over you. That's the difference between understanding relief and experiencing it. Forgiveness is an action we take to experience peace.

You may have read many books about forgiveness, or perhaps you've heard ministers, trusted friends, or Facebook postings talk about forgiveness. Here's something you rarely read or hear:

The ego doesn't understand forgiveness at all. It wants you to see the *fault* in others before you forgive them, and then excuse it. This cannot be done. You cannot see an error and then close your eyes to it or pardon it. You cannot create and then deny your creation. The need to forgive is YOUR creation. If your inner-peace was symbolized by a sleeping baby, you're the one who awoke it with a loud noise.

The secret of forgiveness is to *not create the error* when you initially perceive it. The error is in your thinking.

There's the story of two monks walking through the forest on a beautiful, sunny day. One monk was the older, wiser teacher and the other, his novice. As they passed by a small village, a young woman stood next to a shallow stream, unable to cross it in her fine clothes without ruining them. The older monk offered his help, and she gladly accepted. He picked her up, carried her across the stream, and placed her on the opposite bank, safe and dry. The monks continued their journey through the forest. An hour later, the older monk sensed that his protégé was upset for some reason. He said to his young companion, "You have been unusually quiet and I sense you're troubled. What's wrong?" The younger monk said, "Master, I can't believe you picked up that young woman. You know it is not right to touch a female. Contact with the opposite sex is strictly forbidden in our order. How could you have done that?" The older monk replied, "I put that young woman down over an hour ago. You've been carrying her ever since."

The younger monk was upset and was judging his teacher. He was in need of forgiving his Master, and himself, but if he had not been negatively influenced by his own beliefs, *he wouldn't have been upset to begin with.*

By not creating the error in your own mind, forgiveness is not necessary.

When someone does something that hurts, angers, or disappoints you, look within and ask why. Your immediate reaction of anger or fear is an echo of a hidden belief. "Why am I reacting this way?" is always the first question you should ask yourself. What you disagree with and judge in others is what you disagree with and judge in yourself. We are all reflections of each other. If something doesn't exist in you then you don't recognize it in others, and vice versa.

Our need to forgive, to return to our home base of peace, lies in the letting go and releasing of our limiting beliefs. The ego's insistence that separation from Source is a reality is at the core of our untruthfulness to ourselves. The fact that we see *problems* at all is our problem.

Forgiveness entails accepting ourselves, others, and life in general as being exactly as it is at this moment. Recovering alcoholics call this *accepting life on life's terms.* You must start the forgiveness process by forgiving yourself. Your belief systems are in error, the way you perceive yourself and others is askew—but that doesn't mean you're bad or broken. It just means you've made a mistake. Mistakes can be corrected. Make a course correction and move on. Be kind and gentle with yourself in the process.

Observe your thoughts—every day, every minute. When you find yourself getting upset, ask why. Instantly analyze the reasons, dig deep in your mind for the core belief that's being tweaked. Let others be as they are. Accept them completely. Accept yourself completely.

If you slam on your mental brakes, but still screech past that point of anger or hurt, as you will in the beginning of your trip toward total acceptance and love, forgiveness is your bridge to return home. Say, *"I forgive this person for any perceived wrongdoing. I know he/she is doing their absolute best right here and now and I accept him/her as being exactly where they are in life."* Go on to say, *"I forgive myself for any perceived wrongdoing. I know I'm doing my absolute best right here and now and I accept myself as being exactly where I am in life."*

God knows you're already perfect. This Infinite, Universal, Creative Mind knows of the perfection of all Life, all of Its creations. It sees no error, no wrong, no bad-ness. It sees no need for forgiveness, and It wants this for you too.

The Power of "We"

Forgiveness

by
Nancee Noel, MA, LMFT

In your toolbox of life, forgiveness is a tool you can rely on to get the job done. It fits every situation, never fails when used properly, and results in joy, happiness, and peace.

You can use the tool of forgiveness anytime you have a negative emotional reaction to a person or situation, whether it's another driver, a politician, or the situation of *being forced* to wait in line.

Forgiveness heals the forgiver without changing the situation or the other people. It's always for the benefit of the forgiver. In true forgiveness, there's no blame, but a recognition that the other person is reflecting back to us something in ourselves that needs to be healed. Once the emotional reaction is replaced with gratitude for the information and the healing, true forgiveness has occurred.

To reach this point of gratitude, here are two methods that work for me.

One of the techniques I use frequently is to remind myself that the other person thinks differently than I do due to different upbringing and life experiences. If I had the same upbringing and experiences as them, I'd think and behave *exactly* as they do. As an adjunct to that idea, I bring to mind a quote from *Conversations with God* by Neale Donald Walsch: "No one does anything inappropriate according to his model of the Universe." This process moves my thinking from blame to at least neutrality, and hopefully all the way to brotherly love.

Sometimes I recite a version of the Hawaiian prayer, the H'oponopono. The version I use goes like this. (Note: I have added a few thoughts of my own—the prayer is underlined, the other words are my additions):

I am sorry that I have not seen you as a perfect son of God and one with me.
Please forgive me for my lack of vision and love.
I love you just the way you are.
Thank you for bringing me this opportunity to heal and grow in love.

I usually need to repeat the process several times before I can let go of all the negative emotions, truly feel love for the person, and be in a place of joy and gratitude. Saying it silently is fine, but this prayer has more power when spoken aloud.

This method can also be used to forgive ourselves for the perceived *stupid* mistakes we all make at times, falling short of how we would like to be.

Forgiveness requires a change of perception. You must change the way you perceive every negative encounter with others. Instead of seeing these situations as a chance to attack, vent, or prove you're right, see them as an opportunity to heal at a conscious and subconscious level.

If you need a good reason to change your perceptions, here it is: You reap the damage done by anger and other negative emotions, both physically and emotionally. By the same token, you benefit greatly from feelings of gratitude, joy, and peace. It's your choice. As *A Course in Miracles* says, "Choose again," to which I add . . . and again, and again, and again.

Love and Forgiveness Trump Attacking and Defending

In the classical period, the ancient Greeks and Romans were mighty warriors, as evidenced by the recent "300" films. They could definitely kick some major butt. These early soldiers were highly skilled with three primary weapons, one for defense and two for offense: the shield, spear, and sword. During battle, they would hold their shield close to their bodies to protect their vital organs and lash out with their offensive weapons, aiming primarily for their opponents' chest or neck. They were accomplished in both defense and offense.

So too is the ego—skilled in the arts of defense and offense. You're almost always in a mental state of defending yourself or attacking yourself or others. Isn't it confounding that the ego defends itself one minute and then attacks itself the next? A recovering alcoholic once said, "The voice that tells me it's okay to have just one drink is the same voice that tells me I'm not praying enough." As they say on Facebook, "WTF?!" The ego is cunning, baffling, and powerful.

Closely observe the ego-thoughts for an entire week and you'll be convinced. You're constantly defending yourself. A voice in your mind subtly says, "You're not doing enough, working hard enough, achieving enough, planning enough, organizing enough, saying enough, being cool enough, or just *being* enough." The constant and continuous message is, "you are not enough." The next set of voices in your mind, immediately take up the shield and a defensive stand. "Yes, I *am* working hard enough! Just last week I created a new report, I worked four hours of overtime, I re-organized my files." In whatever form the defensive thoughts take, they're fatiguing. Attack-defend, attack-defend, attack-defend, all day long.

These insane conversations in your mind often take on the voices of others. Your boss, spouse, or a friend criticizes you in your mind and you defend yourself. It's not your boss, spouse, or a friend criticizing you, it's the ego. Yet we entertain these looney mental exchanges, most of the time not even aware they're happening in our minds, and they cause us pain. They disturb our peace. It's hard to feel love for others if *they* are attacking you. It's hard to be at peace when you're in a defensive stance.

We attack others constantly too. The ego is a natural judge, but not one concerned with equity under the laws of nature. The ego just wants to feel better than others, it wants to win, it wants to be right, it wants to control. It does this by trying to place you above others. If you were completely unaware of your thoughts, the ego would run rampant with judgments of others—those stupid nimrods on the freeway, that clumsy and slow barista, the incompetent co-worker, the lazy spouse, the unfair college professor, the conservative or liberal idiots on social media, the evil terrorists, the moronic politicians—everyone is at the mercy of your judging ego.

Attack, attack, attack.

Yet when you attack, you feel a nagging sensation deep within your consciousness that something isn't right. When you're completely honest with yourself, you feel a tinge of guilt, uneasiness, pain—whatever you want to call it—whenever you attack someone. If you attack all day long, you wake up the next morning with an emotional hangover. You feel this pain when you attack because you intuitively know all living creatures are one, that we're all connected, at the spiritually sub-cellular level. Because you *are* one with all others, when you attack another, you attack yourself. That's why it hurts.

Your natural instinct is to Love, to come together with others, to support, to help, to be as One with others. Your True Self knows this; the ego resists it. Being aware of your thoughts is the first step in eliminating the attack-defend cycle. But just being aware of this pattern isn't enough. You need to make a commitment to see the world and others differently. You need to forgive yourself instead of defending, and love yourself and others instead of attacking. When you get more skilled at this, you'll experience an entirely new world.

The ego is likely to say, "Forgiving others is not as hard as forgiving myself. That's much harder." This is a lie posed by the ego. Forgiving yourself needs to replace defending yourself. The ego doesn't want to give up defending, that's how it stays in control. When you shed the light of love and forgiveness on yourself, the ego shrinks away like a puddle evaporating under the sunlight.

Do this: When you hear a defensive statement in your mind, replace it with, "I forgive myself for XYZ . . . and I love myself." Say, "I forgive myself for any *perceived* wrongdoing and I love myself." Do you see how the word *perceived* is important here? You're forgiving yourself, or others, for your misperceptions. You created the pain to begin with—forgiveness corrects that misperception.

A traditional Christian might say, "Blasphemy! Only God can forgive!" Well, God *is* forgiving when you forgive yourself. You are a creation of God, made in Its image. You're an individual expression of this Infinite Creative Consciousness. Your True Self, which *A Course in Miracles* calls, The Holy Spirit, is your direct link to God. This spark of

God within your consciousness is how you experience and communicate with God while having this human experience on the planet Earth. When you forgive yourself, it is your True Self speaking *for* God, *as* God.

Jesus said, "Those who live by the sword, die by the sword." He wasn't referring to actual *death*, he was speaking of *death of consciousness*—being in a darkened state within our minds. When you live by the sword, you're attacking others and yourself. You'll die by the sword (mentally) by feeling guilty because you've attacked.

The solution: Put away the sword and spear of attack, and let go of the shield of defense. Instead, love others and yourself, and forgive easily. The result will be peace, not war.

Forgiveness is Simple, but Not Always Easy: Jan's Story

Jan was getting a divorce from her husband Jacob and was not a happy camper. In fact, she was a raw nerve. Every little thing upset her. Jan cried easily and was prone to sentimentality when thinking of her twenty-five year marriage, which she thought was a happy and successful union. She didn't want a divorce. It all started when fifty-year old Jacob suddenly realized he was not happy and fulfilled and decided to leave the marriage—a classic mid-life crisis according to Jan's friends. Then Jan found out about his thirty-year old girlfriend and hit the ceiling. In fact, she became, quite figuratively, unglued. That's when the anger started. In June, she had loved her husband. By August, she was fantasizing about a horrific death for him. Her anger consumed her.

Jan was normally a happy and upbeat person, and so she had many friends and a very caring and attentive brother who offered their support and love. She had many sets of ears that would listen patiently as she told her story and expressed her anger. She was on the phone more than usual, talking to her friends and brother, but all this talking wasn't making her feel better. Her girlfriends cheered her on when she criticized her husband's girlfriend, whom they all knew from the manufacturing company where Jan and her friends were employed. Jan took pleasure in making fun of and condemning her husband and his new girlfriend, nicknamed, "The Slut," and Jan's girlfriends were excellent cheerleaders.

Jan and her husband had a fifteen-year old son, Jackson, and wanted to shield him from as much pain as possible. Jan told him about the divorce, but not much else. He seemed fairly happy living with Jan, as she tried to help him maintain his normal routine of schoolwork, baseball, football, and his church youth group. Jan and her husband were civil to each other for Jackson's sake, which included remaining friends on Facebook. Both Jan and Jacob were fairly regular Facebook users, and Jan would routinely check her husband's Facebook page to see his latest exploits. He was happy, which was unfortunate in her eyes, and he posted numerous comments about "The Slut," including detailed commentaries about their dates, trips, and daily interactions, complete with nauseating photos. Jan would fume, and then cry, and then fume some more. Then she'd get on the phone with her friends, or her brother, and be off and running again. This cycle went on for several months.

After the divorce was final, Jan felt numb for several more months, until she started to date and began feeling happy again. The anger and resentment she felt for Jacob still surfaced in her mind, though, and she felt and re-experienced it occasionally for many years. Jacob died of a sudden heart attack at age 62, and Jan thought this would bring her peace, but the resentments lingered for years.

Jan never learned about the miracle of forgiveness. She became fairly adept at lessening her anger, which was good. Otherwise, *she* might have been the first to have a fatal heart attack. But releasing her anger by thinking, feeling, talking, complaining, blaming, criticizing, crying, and even power walking or pounding her fists on her bed—none of these ever really released the pain. It was always there, and in fact seemed to intensify the more she talked about it. Jan's friends and family actually thought they were helping her by just listening—something they thought was an act of love.

Everyone in this situation was wrong. Release of pain comes through forgiveness.

No one mentioned the "F" word to Jan during her divorce, or even after it was final. Toward the beginning of her divorce, she would have bit the head off anyone who suggested that she forgive that bastard. That's because Jan believed that forgiveness meant condoning or admitting subtle approval of Jacob's behavior. She saw forgiveness as weakness, as giving in. But it could have been her greatest strength. Yes, Jan got good at lessening her pain, but never let it go through forgiveness.

Unless and until you forgive others, you will remain in pain. It will always be with you. Here's the key: Forgiveness means clearly realizing that it was all a self delusion—not the actions of others—but every angry or resentful thought and feeling after the other person seemingly hurt you. In Jan's case, she let the past define her present. The ego caught that football of hurt and ran with it—ran like hell, and hell is exactly what the ego miscreated for her. Every time Jan thought, felt, and talked about that pain, she reinforced it and kept it strong.

Forgiving means forgetting, plain and simple. You do not forget the experience, but you can forget the pain that you, and only you, have caused yourself. Forgiveness is not a one-time event, but a constant and consistent act you perform whenever the pain arises in your mind. If Jan had continuously said to herself, "I forgive Jacob and wish him well and I forgive myself for feeling angry," every single time the ego reminded her of her resentment, she could have totally released her pain many years earlier. In fact, it could have been erased from her mind a few weeks after he initially left her.

Forgive and forget your pain. Ask your True Self for help, and you'll receive it.

The Release and Forgive Exercise

This exercise could take several days, or longer, but don't draw it out more than three or four weeks. Set aside time every day to do some writing, be consistent. Be kind and gentle with yourself. Don't beat yourself up for not writing enough or not writing often enough. Push yourself gently, but don't make this painful. Be honest and forthright, urge yourself forward during each writing period. Don't get bogged down in emotion when writing. Don't get sucked into sadness, grief, guilt, or shame. That's the ego wanting you to cease. The ego hates this exercise with a purple passion. Don't listen to it.

Step One: For as far back as you remember to the current day, write down:

All Fears: Everything from the past, present, *or future* that you *fear*, including people, places, things, situations, institutions, activities, or responsibilities. Leave no stone unturned—if you think of something, anything in your life and feel the slightest twinge of fear, write it down. More often than not, we're afraid of ideas, concepts, and principles in addition to specific things or people. Here are some examples:

- I fear too much responsibility.
- I fear people getting too close to me.
- I fear being separated or cut off from people and life in general.
- I fear death.
- I fear what others think of me.
- I fear that I won't have enough money when I retire.
- Be specific, take your time, and search your mind.

Resentments and judgments: Write down all resentments and judgments you have of others. Who do you hate or dislike? Who pisses you off and pushes your buttons? Who did something to you that you cannot forgive? Who frustrates or irritates you? Write down who they are and what they did or why you dislike them. Don't hold back, and don't hesitate because you feel guilty for resenting or judging someone (e.g., I shouldn't feel that way about my mother). Examples:

- I resent my father because he drank too much and messed up the entire family.
- Rude drivers send me over the top.
- I can't stand that woman at the office because she's so arrogant.
- I resent my mother for trying to motivate me by making me feel guilty.
- I resent my wife because she's always nagging me.
- I can't stand all those pro-gun idiots and welfare reform nuts on Facebook.

Self-judgments, criticisms, anything negative you feel about yourself. Examples:

- I'm fat
- I'm weird
- I worry too much about being fat and weird
- I'm too shy
- I'm not very eloquent or articulate
- I want to be right too often.
- I come off as arrogant.
- I tend to control and manipulate when I really want something.

Guilt or shame: Write down any and all reasons for feeing guilt or shame. If you feel any guilt or shame at all, write it down. Examples:

- I shoplifted when I was ten.
- I had an affair.
- I criticize my spouse too much.
- I spread gossip at work.
- I was disloyal to a friend.

Is there anything else on your mind that burdens you? Write it down.

Step Two: Share your writing with a priest, minister, counselor, spiritual practitioner, or trusted friend.

Confidentiality is critical. Be sure you trust this person, and be aware of confidentiality limitations if you're confessing a crime. Read your writing aloud. Ask that they not interrupt or provide feedback. This is the process of release. You're letting this stuff go, not engaging in psychotherapy. Your attitude and approach to this step needs to be one of strength, honesty, and willingness to let it all go.

Step Three: Forgive yourself and others.

Now that you've unloaded it all, forgive. Forgive yourself and others you've talked about. Say:

"I forgive all the people I've talked about for any perceived or actual wrongdoing. I let them, their actions and words, and my perceptions of their actions and words go. I forgive them 100%, and I release all these perceptions, thoughts, and feelings from my mind, now and forever. I forgive."

Now do the same for yourself. Say:

"I forgive myself for any perceived or actual wrongdoing from my mental past, present, and future. I release all fear, worry, self-judgment, guilt, shame, regret, and any other perceptions, thoughts, or feelings not based in self-love, which is the essence of my being. I forgive myself now and forever."

Step Five: Continue to forgive yourself.

As any of these same fears, resentments, guilt, shame, etc., enter your mind forgive yourself, or others again. Release and forgive, release and forgive. Constantly. Continuously.

Useful Affirmations

The past is a done deal. I let it all go.

I live for today and let go of the past.

I live my life to the fullest and delight in others doing the same.

I forgive myself for any perceived wrongdoing. Anything and everything!

I let my parents or anyone from the past off the hook. I forgive anyone who I perceive ever harmed me. Anyone and everyone!

I forgive myself, I forgive you, I am for giving.

Each day is a blank slate and I'm writing with the Magic Marker of love.

I evolve from forgiveness to compassion and understanding of others and myself.

I am kind and gentle with myself and others.

I wipe the slate clean. I forgive, I forgive, I forgive.

Rhyming Affirmations

I live for today and let the past go,
I enjoy the present and watch my peace grow.

I forgive everyone, everyone in my life,
I release all resentments, all the anger, all the strife.

I forgive myself, for any perceived wrongdoing,
The love within, gives my mind a renewing.

I transform my resentments into compassion and love,
This new outlook fits me well, like a hand in a glove.

I am kind and gentle, especially with me,
Love boils up inside and sets me free.

CHAPTER TEN

Change

Nature will not let us stay in one place too long. She will let us stay just long enough to gather the experience necessary to the unfolding and advancement of the soul. This is a wise provision, for should we stay here too long, we would become too set, too rigid, and too inflexible. Nature demands change in order that we may advance. When the change comes, we should welcome it with a smile on the lips and a song in the heart.

—Ernest Holmes, *The Science of Mind*

Change is the greatest gift God gave to all that you would make eternal, to ensure that only Heaven would not pass away.

—*A Course in Miracles*

That feeling of uselessness and self-pity will disappear. We will lose interest in selfish things and gain interest in our fellows. Self-seeking will slip away. Our whole attitude and outlook upon life will change.

—*Alcoholics Anonymous*

Changing your Perception of Reality by Changing your Thoughts

There's one tried and true way to escape fear and all of its dastardly minions in your life, one way that always succeeds—to change the source of your perception. If you're like 99% of the planet's inhabitants, your perception of the outer world is one of fear, hostility, attack, and defense. You experience this within yourself in the form of self-judgment, self-induced fear, criticism, and condemnation. We're all alike in this regard, our minds operate pretty much the same way. If you're saying, "No, that's not me," that's the ego defending itself.

Your thoughts and beliefs are the source of your perception. This is the most important thing for you to know about yourself. Once you know this, you've identified the key that will open the door to happiness,

188

peace, and harmony in your life. When you realize that these attack thoughts are the source of your unhappiness, and you know that you don't want these thoughts, you simply need to let them go as they arise in your mind.

It's completely pointless to worry about or cry over all the negatives of this world, and it's foolish to attempt to change the external. Imagine a man sitting in front of the TV, trying to change the words coming out of an actor's mouth because the words upset the man. That's you trying to change the world. 12-Step recovery people talk about being powerless to change people, places, and things. The world is not the problem—it is only an effect. But changing your thoughts about the world—now there's something to sink your teeth into. By changing your thoughts, you're changing the cause—the effect changes as a result. As Wayne Dyer has said, "When you change the way you see the world, the world you see changes."

You may perceive the world or people in it as screwed up but you don't identify yourself as the *screwer-upper*, the source of your misery. You cannot escape from a miserable world (unless you'd enjoy being a cave-dweller), but you can escape the misery that you've created in your mind. Jesus referred to this as *salvation*, being saved from wrong thinking. When the cause of misery is gone, misery is gone. When the cause of fear is gone, fear is gone. When the cause of judgment of self and others is gone, judgment is gone. When you release and let go of these thoughts, your world changes, instantly.

We're not a prisoner of the world we see, because we can change its cause. The process is very simple. In fact, it begins with two easy steps:

1. Identify the thought or belief that's shaping your perception— the cause.
2. Let it go, release it, do not think about it anymore.

Can it get any easier than that?

Argh! These Voices in My Head!

Don't believe what you think. Well . . . don't believe *most* of it. The human mind is problematic and complex, and the ego is deceptive, confounding, and commanding, or, as *A Course in Miracles* suggests, insane.

You *people your consciousness* with figures from your past and you think they're real, you think they represent those actual people. They do not. These shadowy figures that float across your mind are only symbols of your fear, resentment, guilt, shame, or regret. They judge or attack you, so you think. But it's *you* who are doing the attacking and only you who is the victim of these constant attacks. When you attempt to communicate with these people in your mind, you are talking to yourself. When you judge others in your mind, you are judging yourself.

There's the story of a woman named Tina, who was consistently berated by her mother and always made to be in the wrong. Tina was occasionally complimented by her mother, but mostly judged as not good enough. After she graduated high school and left home, Tina's mother was often in Tina's mind, judging her, criticizing her, telling her all the things she was doing wrong with her life. When Tina got married a few years later, her mother-in-law was quite critical. Now, instead of her mother criticizing Tina in her mind, Tina envisioned her mother-in-law doing the criticizing. Tina's work supervisor sometimes appeared in her mind to criticize her about her work, although her actual supervisor did little criticizing in reality.

The ego was constantly judging and criticizing Tina, projecting fear and guilt onto others, putting familiar faces onto her judgment. Why others? Because if Tina suspected that it was *the ego* judging her, she would see the deceit and deception of the ego. The ego would show its hand.

The ego is sly. It hides behind the faces of others to poke and prod you.

You must see the insanity of this type of thinking. You must be awake and aware of your mind and see the destructiveness of any thoughts or beliefs related to fear, worry, guilt, shame, regret, and other thoughts not based in Love.

You must know your Truth.

Your Truth is that you're an individual expression of God. You lack absolutely nothing to be happy, loved, healthy, prosperous, and at peace at this moment. When you're more aware of your *thought life* and let go of untruths as they zip through your mind, regardless of whose face or voice the ego is using, you'll have fewer thoughts in general. As you then consciously generate Truthful thoughts and beliefs, those based in God/Love, you'll be claiming your inheritance as the child of an Infinite Loving Creative Consciousness.

You must do this if you wish peace.

You will. This is God's will. This is your will, when you're willing.

Your False Beliefs Are Holding You Back

Your thought and belief patterns based in fear, which you've accumulated since day one on this planet, are what hinder your enlightenment. The source of your beliefs—heredity and environment, are powerful forces, especially the environmental factors. Your belief systems originate from and are fed continuously by what you've learned and continue to learn from your parents, siblings, friends, intimate partners, teachers, ministers, and the world at-large (TV, movies, newspapers, the internet). As Psychology tells us, most beliefs we have about ourselves, and the world, were firmly entrenched by age five.

Your beliefs, in their entirety, comprise the ego. That's all the ego is, a collection of thoughts, ideas, beliefs, feelings, and mental images, nothing more. The ego is not the bad guy, the boogeyman, something to be feared or loathed, or something you can eliminate. It is not a separate part of you. You are not divided. It's just a massive collection, but these belief patterns are powerful because they're deeply rooted in your subconscious.

The ego is not what you are—it's what you believe you are. It's not based in Truth or Reality. It is a perception of you based on past experience and feedback from the external world. B.S. is a fitting acronym for your false Belief Systems. It's no mistake that the word *lie* is smack dab in the middle of the word *belief*.

Here are some samples of core beliefs that comprise the human ego. Many of these will ring true for you when you read them. All of these beliefs exist within you or someone you know. If you find yourself getting defensive, fearful, angry, or depressed while reading this list, there's your indicator light.

I am . . . incomplete, not good enough, inferior, unsuccessful, worthless, unlovable, not special, afraid, not safe, guilty, vulnerable, helpless, a victim, unwanted, alone, unimportant, defective, bad, imperfect, unattractive, flawed, stupid, awkward, fat, unclean, crazy, a failure, undeserving of love, weak, powerless, somehow less than, unable to say, "no."

The world is . . . against me, limited, unfair, a dog-eat-dog place, lacking in resources, a competitive marketplace, a dangerous and scary place, out to get me, uncooperative, full of separate personalities, full of evil or selfish people.

Like a computer's underlying operating system, false beliefs help you make sense of the world, drive you constantly forward, defend you, and serve as a kind of bubble that protects you from the world. But false is false. Just because you strongly believe that you're lacking in some way, and defend that belief through your thoughts, words, and actions, doesn't make it true. You're likely not even aware of your underlying false beliefs, which keeps them out of the realm of detection and elimination. It's like you have a pile of garbage darting around your subconscious mind—rubbish that's smarter than the smartest criminal mastermind, operating independently, pulling puppet strings, defending itself with ease, and escaping capture and banishment at every turn. But it's just a collection of beliefs.

A Course in Miracles teaches that if something is True (with a capital "T"), it is constant and unchanging, like God. Like Love. Like Peace. Like Joy. All these spiritual principles are constant, even if you're choosing not to experience them at any given moment. They're constant because they're attributes of God. Your core beliefs that are not based in love (most of them) are not constant and therefore not true. You don't need to change them, just let them go.

Another indication that a belief system is not true is that you defend it. The ego says, "This is my belief, I created it. I'm invested in it. It protects me and gives my life meaning, so therefore I'll defend it, sometimes vehemently." Picture a man who is obese. His obesity is the out picturing of his core beliefs, which are, "I am not enough," "I'm not that (mentally) strong," "It's hard to resist temptation, especially when it comes to cookies and gummy bears." These are just a few of the messages the obese man conveys to himself all throughout a given day. He is constantly defending and reinforcing his core beliefs.

Fear is not of God, and neither are the non-constants that underlie most of your thoughts on any given day—anger, resentment, guilt, shame, judgment of self and others, jealousy, envy, impatience, intolerance, yada, yada, yada. These non-constants, better known as mistaken perceptions, or lies posing as the truth, are the building materials of many of your beliefs. They're within the concrete mix of your subconscious building structure, but they can be torn down.

If you have the power, and you do, to create fantasy, illusion, and drama for yourself with your false beliefs as the seed, you also have the power to un-do them. It's the nature of who you are, a creative being mirroring the same creative forces as a Universal Creative Intelligence.

Change is hard. Undoing deeply rooted beliefs is like pulling weeds, except the weeds are small trees. They're not going to give themselves up easily. The ego is constantly trying to cling to its beliefs because it's made from them. By releasing and letting go of untrue core beliefs, you're deconstructing the ego. The ego's not crazy about this idea. It will resist.

Back in the 1850s, the well-traveled trails heading west to California and Oregon were lined with deep ruts. After years of covered wagons traveling the same road, deep grooves formed. The wagon wheels slipped easily into these ruts that guided the wagon toward a sure direction. They served a useful purpose in keeping the wagon steady and on-course. But if a wagon driver needed to steer out of a rut for some reason, like to defend the wagon train from a party of attacking Natives, the wagon resisted. The deeply rooted wheels struggled to maneuver out of the familiar ruts. It took great effort to free the wheels.

Your deeply rooted beliefs are like those ruts. They were formed at a young age, they've been reinforced millions of times over the years, and you tend to rely on them. Releasing them is a bit scary, and hard to maneuver.

Affirmative prayer is the solution. Like Superman, it swoops in to save the day. You must KNOW your truth, not just wish, hope, or plead to a God *out there*. For every false belief, there's a universal truth for you to affirm, and it's based on your inner divinity. You're not just reciting empty platitudes when you say, "I am a perfect creation of a Perfect Creator." You are speaking Truth.

Identify the core belief. Refute it. Release it. Replace it with the Truth. Do this every day, all day long. Like this:

False Belief: I am incomplete.
Truth: I am whole, perfect, and complete

False Belief: I am unloved.
Truth: I am love in expression. The love of God is always with me. I am loved, and I love others easily and with enthusiasm. I give love. I receive love.

False Belief: I am afraid.
Truth: I am loved, and I know all is well, right here and now. I release any thoughts of the future and know I am secure in God's love.

False Belief: I am not enough.
Truth: I am more than enough. I am a child of God, and as such, it is my birthright to have all the good things in life. God is constantly serving me more and more good and I accept it.

False Belief: I am powerless.

Truth: I am powerful. I have the power of a Universal Intelligence within me, I am made of it. This power courses through my body and mind and I use it for good.

Wake Up from "The Matrix"

The film "The Matrix" has a deeper spiritual meaning. To briefly summarize the plot: Humankind created a world of machines and robots infused with an advanced form of artificial intelligence. The machines become *too smart* and take over the world, imprisoning humans in life-sustaining pods. In these capsules, each human's brain is plugged into a mainframe computer that generates an artificial world, called the Matrix. Lying dormant in a pod, their brains connected to the Matrix, billions of humans think they're living their life normally, but are actually living an illusory existence. Occasionally, humans *wake up* from the Matrix because they question their existence, sensing there must be more to life. One such human is the main character, a young man named Neo. With the help of fellow rebels Morpheus and Trinity, Neo leads a group of humans who have escaped the Matrix and are determined to awaken others to free the world from the tyranny of the evil machines.

The primary theme here is the idea of waking up. Like the people in the film who are plugged into their limited world, most of us are not mentally awake and aware of actual Reality/God. This Infinite, Creative, Loving Intelligence is the one true, changeless, eternal, indivisible Reality in the universe. Each of us are individual expressions of It and mirror its creative ability. We create our external reality through our internal thoughts and beliefs, from the inside out.

Most of us don't realize that, like God, we are perfect just as we are and that we embody the same qualities as God. We don't need to seek out good—we already are the good that we seek.

We think we're separate from God. This thought stems from the human ego. Like the Matrix, it tries to convince us that there's a world separate from All-That-Is. In this separate world, which exists only in our minds, live the fear, guilt, hate, and false beliefs.

We've been hoodwinked. We're caught in a mental Matrix of our own making.

Neo, the character who intuitively knows that there must be more to life, is constantly seeking the truth. Neo means *new*. He is looking for new ways of thinking, new ways of perceiving the world, and new ways of being. If you re-arrange the letters of his name, Neo spells *One*, the idea that all of us together, in God, form the *one-ness* of existence.

Neo represents our intuitive drive to grow, expand, and become new. Christians call this being reborn. Jesus referred to it as the resurrection. Hindus call it seeking Nirvana, perfection. Buddhists refer to it as being *at one*.

Neo's mentor is Morpheus. The origin of this name, *amorphous*, means *to be without form* (Spirit), and the word *morph* means *change*. Morpheus represents our Higher Self, the True Self, what Christians refer to as the Holy Spirit. Our Inner Guide is our bridge to God, and if we choose to follow its lead, it will always guide us to God, to Love. Our greatest challenge in this life, and yet that which offers the greatest reward, is turning away from the external world (the Matrix) to listen and be guided by our True Self.

Another character, Trinity, represents the threefold nature of existence:

- God, Humans, True Self (Christians say Father, Son, Holy Spirit).
- It also represents the Creative Process: Seed, soil, plant.
- At the human level: Thought, subconscious mind, life circumstances.

In the film, the ego takes on many guises, from Agent Smith, to the Architect (the designer of the Matrix). The ego consistently lies to us, and wants us to believe that we're apart from God. It wants us to turn its attention to it and the many distractions that keep us from looking inward for the answers. The ego seeks to distract us from love itself, by trying to convince us that there are forces that oppose love: fear, resentment, guilt, shame, impatience, and judgment of self and others. Like the machines in the film, the ego is constantly trying to maintain the status quo and deny our innate love and one-ness.

The key is our free will, our power to choose.

In the film, free will is the anomaly that the machines could never control or predict. Neo made a conscious choice to wake up. He was offered one of two pills by Morpheus, who said:

"This is your last chance. After you take a pill, there's no turning back. If you take the blue pill, the story ends, you wake up in your bed and believe whatever you want to believe. If you take the red pill, you stay in Wonderland, and I show you how deep the rabbit-hole goes."

Neo chose the red pill.

Each of us can choose the red pill at any moment of the day. Unlike the film, this is not a one-time good deal. We can choose to be awake and alive at any time. We can choose to listen for the voice of God within ourselves whenever we desire. We can choose Love over fear. We can choose our True Self over the ego.

The choice is always ours.

The Power of "We"

Moving Forward

by
Judy Thompson, RScP

Change! It's a word we hear every day—the world is always changing, and we're part of that change. In our personal life, change is hard because we over-value what we have and under-value what we'll earn by letting go of what we have. Change is necessary to keep us moving forward and interested. Life without change would be static, unmoving, dull and boring. In other words, we'll continue to be stuck in the same life patterns and circumstances unless we modify our thoughts and beliefs. First-century B.C. philosopher Syrus said, "It's a bad plan that admits no modifications."

If change is a guaranteed constant and life is continuously evolving, why do we tend to resist creating our own good when the Universal Creator is always saying, "Yes?" In the words of Zig Ziegler, "We must give ourselves a check-up from the neck up" when we resist our good by indulging in what he called, "stinking thinking." As we grow into the spiritual beings we know we can become, we need to remind ourselves each day to continue with the process of releasing old and limiting beliefs and replacing them with new ones.

18th-century poet and transcendentalist Henry David Thoreau wrote, "As a single footstep will not make a path on earth, so a single thought will not make a pathway in the mind. To make a deep physical path, we walk again and again. To make a deep mental path, we must think over and over the kind of thoughts we wish to dominate our lives." Making a lasting change is like plowing the path—the more you use it, the easier it gets. Ernest Holmes, 20th-century philosopher and founder of Religious Science, wrote that change is a step-by-step process—it doesn't happen with a single thought, but with continuous thoughts—the releasing of old habits of thought creates new paths for our life.

Every day our cells renew, and every day our thoughts can be revitalized to create what we know is our truth—we are perfect, whole, and complete in the eyes of the Infinite. To keep our hearts centered we need only look into the mirror and see the miracles we are. In doing so, we allow ourselves to become magnets to the wonderful things the Universe has to offer.

Life isn't about finding. It's about realizing *what is* and creating more of what you want. Life is an experience to live to its fullest. Consider each day an opportunity of a lifetime. Start fresh! John F. Kennedy wrote that, "Change is the law of life and those who only look to the past or present are certain to miss the future."

Along with modifications to our thinking, we need to include time for meditation and prayer each day. When we take the time for daily meditation, we find the support and love of the Universal Source. We align our thoughts with this Power and begin to create a life we want. Keeping a journal puts our intentions in writing and makes our commitment stronger. When we write down an insightful message we receive during meditation, we can read it anytime we're drifting into old habits. In prayer, we consciously align our thinking with the Universal Mind and know that the transformation we seek is already taking place. The response of Spirit to us must be equal to our faith in It. It is always reciprocal, always mutual. It reflects back to us what we believe, just as the mirror we look into each day reflects our likeness.

Each day as you look in the mirror do you say, "WOW, YOU'RE LOOKIN GOOD?!" Or do you just grumble . . . or avoid looking? Do you see how a change in your thoughts can change your life?

If every day is an opportunity to start fresh, make that an affirmation: "Today I start fresh and accept the good that the Universe is willing to give. I SAY YES!"

Worship God, not gods

Are you worshipping gods or God? There are many gods on earth. Which are you worshipping? Money, status, power, entertainment? Do you invest your time and attention in seeking love or praise from others? Do you give adoration to sex, drugs, alcohol, nicotine, food, sickness or limitation, or a poverty consciousness? Are you invested in the accumulation of earthly information, or do you spend much of your time mesmerized by the so-called news of the world or the entertainment and sports media? Do you devote your waking hours to human politics or causes? How are you spending your time?

You're a Truth seeker. You desire a closer relationship and direct guidance from your True Self, your liaison with the Infinite. You seek ultimate Truth, not illusion. You desire a nourishing meal, not an unhealthy snack. How are you spending your time each day? A business leader once said that to determine what a person values, just look at his or her daily calendar. Our actions speak louder than words, beliefs, opinions, desires, hopes, or intentions. What are you doing to release limiting beliefs and realize the Truth?

From *A Course in Miracles*:

"God created love, not idolatry. All forms of idolatry are caricatures of creation, taught by sick minds too divided to know that creation shares power and never usurps it. Have no other gods before Him or you will not hear. Yet when they seem to speak to you, remember that nothing can replace God, and whatever replacements you have attempted are nothing."

This world is one of illusion, not Reality. God is Reality, and you are a creation of the Infinite. Your spiritual growth is an inner effort; you create your earthly life from the inside out. Your transformation is always about looking inward, not to the world of illusion. You may need to spend eight hours or more each day at a job to make money to buy food, clothing, and a roof over your head. If you're retired, be grateful. But beyond those eight hours, what are you doing? Which gods are you worshipping?

Also from *A Course in Miracles*:

"You do not realize how much you listen to your gods, and how vigilant you are on their behalf. Yet they exist only because you honor them. Place honor where it is due, and peace will be yours. It is your inheritance from your real Father. Only at the altar of God will you find peace. This altar is in you because God put it there. His Voice still calls you to return, and He will be heard when you place no other gods before Him."

Devotion to God and yourself as a creation of God implies a commitment. What will you commit to? Spiritual reading? Discussions of Truth within a spiritual community? Prayer and meditation? Self-observation and mindfulness? How about just *being*? The altar to God is within your consciousness. There are no sacrifices to make, just commitments to keep to yourself. Let your True Self be your guide.

Unlimited Growth Potential

There is no limitation outside our own ignorance, and since we can all conceive of a greater good than we have so far experienced, we all have the ability to transcend previous experiences and rise triumphant above them; but we shall never triumph over them while we persist in going through the old mental reactions.

—Ernest Holmes, *The Science of Mind*

A few years ago, researchers at Amherst College performed a fairly simple experiment with some very interesting results. They planted a squash seed and fed and watered the plant until it grew into a vine and produced a squash about the size of a person's head. Then they strapped a metal band around the squash with a harness to measure the pressure generated as the squash tried to grow. They expected the squash would exert as much as 500 pounds of pressure per square inch. They were right, after only one month.

The squash wasn't done growing after a month, though—it was still expanding. In two months, the pressure was up to 1,500 pounds. When it got to be 2,000 pounds of pressure, they had to reinforce the metal band. The experiment ended with the squash producing 5,000 pounds of pressure. But it didn't end because the squash quit growing—at 5,000 pounds it finally broke the metal bands that had been measuring its force and held it back. When they cut the squash open, they found it was full of thick, tough fibers, not normally found in squash. It had created these fibers to push against the metal restraint. They also discovered that the squash vine had produced an astounding 80,000 feet of roots to generate the life force it needed to grow.

You have unlimited spiritual growth potential. If a squash can do this, imagine what you can do! Your awareness and very essence as a spiritual being is predisposed to enlarge and increase. Within you, as in all living things, is an innate intelligence that desires to expand itself, and this growth is demonstrated differently for each individual. This is your nature.

Like a metal band constricting your mind, a part of you doesn't like or want to change. The ego detests straying from what's comfortable and familiar. The ego likes predictability, certainty, being in control. Change requires giving up control as you venture off into the unknown. The practice of *turning it over to God* is deplorable to the ego, yet this simple ritual of giving up the outcome and relying on divine guidance is a major leap forward.

When you run into a roadblock in your life, you're confronted with the opportunity to make a mental shift, to take a new road instead of the familiar path. Where does the other road lead? How long will it take? Is it dangerous? What you're not familiar with may instill fear in you. As a result, the ego acts out to prevent change, often without you consciously realizing it, and this can make your life unnecessarily miserable.

How can you see the world differently today? What types of mental shifts do you need to make to move over, under, or around fear, shame, guilt, impatience, sickness, a poverty consciousness, or judgment of self and others? How can you grow beyond the mental metal bands that are limiting you? Your only limitations are your thoughts and beliefs, and it's inevitable, like the growing squash, that you'll flourish beyond them.

As Jesus said, *"It is done onto you as you believe."* How much good can you conceive? If the principles of peace, joy, and love were represented as water in a ground well, what type of ladle would you use to dip it out? A teaspoon? A bucket? A large washtub? How much good you get within your consciousness, and therefore in your life, is dependent on your willingness and faith, and limited only by your beliefs in fear and separation from your Source.

Be open to change. Continually be receptive to new ways of thinking, believing, and feeling. Depend heavily on your True Self for inspiration, guidance, and wisdom. It will always lead you in the right direction. Your True Self gives you the power, strength, and desire to burst out of your old self to a new and improved you. There are no metal bands that can contain your growth.

Straying and Staying on your Spiritual Path

Student: I feel like I'm in a rut with regards to my spiritual growth. A few weeks ago I was doing lots of spiritual reading and meditating every day, and now, well, not so much. I just feel so unmotivated, spiritually speaking.

Teacher: How was it different a few weeks ago?

Student: Well, for one thing, I was in a class at my spiritual center, a ten-week class on affirmative prayer and meditation. We had fifty or sixty pages of reading each week, and we wrote out prayers for each class. Meditation too—we studied a different form of meditation every week and practiced it during class. That was cool. I liked that structure of being in class. It kept me on my spiritual path and *on the beam* so to speak.

Teacher: So you think the structure helped you?

Student: Absolutely. I was thinking of my spiritual growth in terms of "Star Trek," because you know I'm such a big fan of the series. When I'm not in a spiritual class, I feel like I'm on impulse drive—my progress is more or less at normal speed. When I'm in class though, it feels like my warp drive is activated and I'm going faster than light. You know, on Star Trek, when a ship is traveling at warp speed, it creates a sort of bubble of normal space-time, which surrounds the spacecraft so it feels normal even though it's traveling at immense speed. That's how I feel.

Teacher: Good analogy.

Student: Yeah, and I believe that every action I take toward a higher degree of understanding and awareness of my spiritual perfection is like laying another brick in the building of something. Every time I pray, every time I meditate, every paragraph I read in a spiritual book, and every time I think of God, another brick gets laid.

Teacher: What is the building?

Student: Heaven, I guess. The kingdom of heaven is within, right? Every step I take toward God puts me closer to perfect peace, love, and one-ness within my consciousness.

Teacher: Some would say you're already in heaven. Perhaps every step you take is like lifting the veil before your eyes a bit higher so you can see it more clearly.

Student: Wow, I've never thought of it that way.

Teacher: It seems you're a little hard on yourself, though, regarding your progress. When you feel unmotivated spiritually, what does that feel like?

Student: It feels crappy. It's like there's something I know I should be doing, but I'm not doing it. There's a sense of urgency, like I have a to-do list in my head, and I'm ignoring it. Then the ego steps in and tells me that I'm lazy, or a fake, or just not enough.

Teacher: Right, that's what you want to avoid. When those thoughts appear in your mind, you need to let them go immediately. Don't try to wrestle with them, just let them go.

Student: A lot of the time, I find myself defending myself in my mind, giving reasons and excuses why I'm not praying or meditating daily.

Teacher: It's an endless struggle, a constant skirmish if you decide to do battle with the ego. It's like trying to argue with a newspaper editor by writing letters to her newspaper. The editor buys ink by the barrel. In other words, the ego has all the time in the world to argue with you and actually loves it. Nothing tickles the ego more than you trying to defend or attack yourself or others. The secret is letting go, disengaging.

Student: But what if I'm really not doing enough praying or meditating?

Teacher: See, right there, that's the ego. You just need to let that go. You're right where you are. Or, to put it another way . . . you are right, where you are. Do you see how that pause after the word *right* makes a difference? There's no wrong here. Just keep on doing what you know is right for you and stop *should-ing* on yourself.

Student: Okay, I think I understand.

Teacher: Remember the story of the Prodigal Son?

Student: Hmmmm, well . . .

Teacher: Let's see if I can condense the story and apply it to you. The prodigal son asked his father for his inheritance so he could hit the road, experience life, and party. He did just that, eventually losing all his money. He had to work in a humiliating job and felt terribly guilty. He realized his life was better with his father, and when he finally returned home, he was ready to grovel and humbly work as one of his father's servants. When his father saw him, he ran out to greet him, hugging and kissing him. He ordered his servants to throw a huge celebration for his son. All along, the father knew his son would return, and when he did, he was welcomed back into the family.

Student: Okay, so how does that . . .

Teacher: You're the prodigal son. Whenever you're unmotivated toward your spiritual growth or veer off the path through unhealthy living or thinking, the ego wants you to feel guilty. When you return to right thinking, God is always there for you, welcoming you. This process could last for several years, months, weeks, or days, or it could be just a matter of minutes or seconds. Whenever you place your attention on God within, your True Self, It is right there with you, greeting you, hugging and kissing you.

Student: Wow!

Teacher: So don't give in to the guilt, fear, self-expectations, or whatever. Turn away from the ego's voice and think of God.

Student: It sounds too easy.

Teacher: It is.

Willingness is the Key to Change

You've heard the phrase, "A journey of a thousand miles begins with a single step." If the journey represents your spiritual growth, the single step is your willingness. One single decision on your part begins the process. At the macro level, you might say to yourself, "There must be a better way, there must be more to life than this." This is a simple statement sparked by a willingness to look, listen, and be open to something new. This type of life-altering realization might result in wholesale change in your life—deciding to attend a spiritual center on a regular basis, read more spiritual books, attend a spiritual retreat, or simply pray more.

At the micro level, willingness might demonstrate as a mental awakening during a typical day, when you catch yourself engaging in stinkin' thinkin'. Your willingness to be aware of and then change or re-direct your thoughts at any time is a result of the willingness seed.

Your willingness is a result of your free will. You're a spiritual being, completely free. You can choose life or death at any moment. You can choose happiness or misery, mental wealth or poverty, peace or anger, love or fear. All these choices are yours as a thinking spiritual creature.

This power and freedom you have to make choices is a true gift. Many people don't use it or are even aware they possess this power—their lives are driven by other people, life circumstances, and their over powering, deceitful, selfish ego—they are convinced by their false selves that they have no choices, that they're victims, or that they simply can't control their thoughts. "That's just the way I am," or "That's the way life is," are typical taglines of those who think they're choice-less.

That's not you! Your willingness to grow, expand, and experience more light and love fuels your freedom.

You can change your mind at will. Poof! Just like that. Your willingness to change, to release from your mind what you know isn't true—this is how enlightenment happens.

From *A Course in Miracles*:

"Healing is a sign that you want to make whole. And this willingness opens your ears to the Voice of the Holy Spirit, Whose message is wholeness. He [the Holy Spirit, your True Self] will enable you to go far beyond the healing you would undertake, for beside your small willingness to make whole He will lay His Own complete Will and make yours whole. What can the Son of God not accomplish with the Fatherhood of God in him? And yet the invitation must come from you, for you have surely learned that whom you invite as your guest will abide in you."

When you decide to sidle up to and get cozy with your True Self, you're choosing wisely. You don't have all the answers; none of us do, but your True Self does. It knows all. Your True Self is your bridge to God. It's a radio transmission wave that God uses to communicate with you and vice versa. Your willingness to listen to it, to be led by it, to subjugate yourself completely to it, is the golden key to the city of happiness, love, and peace. If that sounds over-dramatic, this will blow your mind: Your True Self knows the meaning of life.

What IS the meaning of life? Well, your True Self knows it even if you don't. Think of your True Self as a wise, experienced teacher that you venerate. You're the initiate and your True Self is the master. It's God's voice, for God's sake. It knows all, is all good, loves you unconditionally, and its sole purpose is to guide and lead your thinking—to get you to remember who you are.

But your True Self will be silent until you turn to it. It doesn't teach you involuntarily. It's not a nagging spouse or parent that tries to *force* you to do well, or clenches your jaw shut involuntarily when you're about to say something stupid.

Your willingness activates it.

The 12-Step program has helped millions of people recover from alcoholism and a variety of other addictions. It's a spiritual program. No one would argue that point. Step three of the twelve steps is, "Made a decision to turn our will and our lives over to the care of God as we understood Him." In the book *Twelve Steps and Twelve Traditions*, a foundational book for anyone working a 12-Step program, here is what it says about willingness:

"To every worldly and practical-minded beginner, this Step looks hard, even impossible. No matter how much one wishes to try, exactly how can he turn his own will and his own life over to the care of whatever God he thinks there is? Fortunately, we who have tried it, and with equal misgivings, can testify that anyone, anyone at all, can begin to do it. We can further add that a beginning, even the smallest, is all that is needed. Once we have placed the key of willingness in the lock and have the door ever so slightly open, we find that we can always open it some more. Though self-will may slam it shut again, as it frequently does, it will always respond the moment we again pick up the key of willingness."

Your Spiritual Growth is Unstoppable

"It is our light, not our darkness, that most frightens us. Our deepest fear is not that we are inadequate. Our deepest fear is that we are powerful beyond measure. It is our light, not our darkness, that most frightens us. We ask ourselves, who am I to be brilliant, gorgeous, talented and fabulous? Actually, who are you not to be? You are a child of God."

—Marianne Williamson

The shapers and molders of early Christianity worked hard to de-emphasize the divinity of humans, placing special emphasis on God the Father and his Divine Son Jesus, but relegating humans to a lowly, sinful state. The Gnostic gospels, on the other hand, tell a different story.

Discovered in Egypt in 1945, the Gospel of Thomas was pretty much given the cold shoulder at the First Council of Nicaea in AD 325 and subsequently ignored by Bible scholars. To paraphrase St. Thomas, "Jesus taught that 'knowing yourself' and realizing your divinity was the key to the kingdom."

Of course, in the New Thought philosophy of today, we understand that knowing yourself is to have awareness of your divine distinctiveness. Ancient Greek Gnostics said the same thing. "Know yourself," is a traditional Greek maxim. Gnosticism downplays the material world, emphasizing Reality as your Divine spirit, identical in its nature and quality with God.

You are a powerful being! You are a spark of God, imbued with the same creative abilities as the Infinite.

Just as the early Bible scholars did, the ego ignores, diminishes, and even vehemently denies your divinity. It needs your attention to maintain control, it doesn't want you seeking and following your True Self. The ego is like the maniacal power monger who says, "Stick with me, because everyone else is against you."

You have an instinctive drive for renewal—you will never be the same as you release the old and embrace the new. There's a Power and Presence in this universe that's all good. It's within you, and as you embrace It, you cannot help but transform your mind, expand your awareness, and build a strong, collaborative relationship with your True Self.

Transformation can bring with it intense change, something the ego resists. It can be downright scary, especially if it happens quickly. There's the story of a young woman who found a *Science of Mind* spiritual center and was ecstatic. She couldn't believe there were other people in this world that thought as she did. She had no knowledge of the existence of New Thought churches. For the first few months attending services and classes, she felt like she was on a high, and everyone in her life commented on her new glow. But the ego resisted change, and she reverted back to unhealthy habits for a few months. She eventually realigned her thinking back to a higher plane and became active at church again. Two steps forward, one step back. It's important to realize the ego's resistance and lovingly ignore it. The one step back is optional.

Your change and growth is inevitable and unstoppable. As you release limiting beliefs like the layers of an onion being peeled away, you discover that Perfect, Loving core. At first it might just be glimpses during meditation, prayer, or while in service to others. You'll experience that sense of *one-ness*, and it'll become stronger as you continue to rely on your True Self for guidance.

Here are the telltale signs of spiritual growth: Your life becomes simpler, containing less drama and more silence. You feel better about yourself, experiencing less anger, frustration, agitation, and fear, and more serenity. Then the comments from friends and family start rolling in. "You seem different. You're much happier these days, aren't you? I can tell."

Like Jesus' resurrection, as the old self dies, and as false and limiting beliefs fade away, your core divinity shines forth. You begin to see God in everything and everyone, and you come to fully understand the idea that there's only One Life, God. Being reborn means aligning with the Christ (savior) Consciousness within your mind. Jesus was fully aligned with the Christ Consciousness, just as you will be. As Jesus said in John 14, "Whoever believes in me (within your consciousness) will do the works I have been doing, and they will do even greater things than these."

This fact is inevitable. Your spiritual growth is unstoppable.

Spiritual Evolution

You are in a constant state of evolving spiritually. How many times have you heard the phrase, "The only thing constant is change?" Well, that little bit of wisdom isn't completely accurate. God is constant, unchanging, and without opposite. God is always there for you, always available, always ready to respond to you. But the sentiment is accurate, your *consciousness* is always growing and evolving. With each passing moment, you never quite perceive yourself and the world the same way.

Think about the evolution of the collective human thought over the last 500 years, and what change has occurred. Less than 200 years ago, England banned slavery, followed by the U.S. thirty years later. Can you imagine the mindset of someone who believed that owning a human being was morally acceptable? Our planetary collective consciousness is a set of shared beliefs, ideas and moral attitudes, which operate as a unifying force for us. It has transformed profoundly over the last 100 years, influenced by religion, science, philosophy, psychology, sociology, anthropology, and most recently, technology out the wazoo. Our consciousness as a species has evolved, becoming more fine-tuned to universal principles like freedom, equality, love, and expressions of happiness and joy. Humans, in general, are more moral, cultured, and civil than they were a few hundred years ago, a reflection of our collective spiritual growth and awareness.

The next stage in human spiritual evolution is the transition from ego-centered individualization manifesting as separate being-ness, to the universal truth of the unity of all life. This spiritual truth that *we are all one* is coming to fruition. We are growing together, coming to realize what it means to be related to each other on a spiritual level. We see it in New Thought religions and philosophies, we see it in governments, social welfare, and non-profits, and we even see it in Facebook memes. The vegetarian and vegan movement over the last 50 years is a testament to this. It's not just a move toward healthier food sources, but a reminder of the gnawing moral imperative related to animal rights and our barbaric practices of raising animals en masse to slaughter and eat. Yes, we are one with the animals, fish, insects, and all other life forms too. We are completely dependent upon each other, because we're all one.

But collective evolution is just an effect, not a cause in itself. Evolution begins with personal involution, the seed thoughts within our minds that move us forward and manifest as written words, speech, and behavior. It takes one person to begin to think differently for a change to occur on a global scale. As the popular phrase goes, "be the change you wish to see."

There's a passage from the first chapter of the Book of John in the Bible that underlines your personal spiritual involution. More than a few Bible readers have scratched their heads reading this passage—the deeper, metaphysical meaning gives us confirmation of our inner truth:

"Dear friends, now we are children of God, and what we will be has not yet been made known. But we know that when Christ appears, we shall be like him, for we shall see him as he is. All who have this hope in him purify themselves, just as he is pure."

Now is the keyword in that first sentence. You are a *child* of the Infinite. You are an individual expression of the One. You are one with God and in God, right here, right now. Not later, not in some distant future, not after you search for God, not after you read a gazillion spiritual books, or meditate until your mind reels. Right now, you are a divine, creative, perfect expression of the One. You are one with God whether you know it or not. So you must know it because that's Reality with a capital "R."

The second half of that first sentence is: "And what we will be has not yet been made known." The process of your spiritual evolution is always taking place, you are constantly unfolding into the next higher expression of yourself. What wonderful news! You're a work of art that is relentlessly painting itself. You have no way of knowing what you'll be like next year, only that you *will* be different. The more willing you are to change, to embrace new ideas about the nature of Reality, the more you will evolve. Your growth, for the most part, may just entail letting go of old, limiting beliefs. Change comes not just from seeking the new, but also from releasing the old.

"When Christ appears," taken literally, tells of a second coming, but the King James version of this same passage doesn't mention Jesus at all. It reads, "But we know that, when He shall appear, we shall be like Him; for we shall see Him as he is." The deeper, metaphysical meaning of this passage is more telling. It highlights your divine nature, your *Sonship*. It's saying that as you evolve and become more aware of Reality, you will recognize your own Christ Consciousness. Your True Self will point you to your divine nature. This Christ Mind is an ideal to aspire to, as Jesus did. The man named Jesus was completely aligned with his Christ Mind. As you follow your True Self daily, as you identify more closely with it rather than the ego, you *see Him as he is.* You recognize right-mindedness—love, joy, peace, understanding, harmony, and strength—and this Christ Mind becomes your default mode. You identify less and less with fear, judgment of self and others, resentment, and selfishness. You'll be in your *right mind.* As a wise Christian Scientist once said, "you will 'realize' your *real I,* you will see yourself with 'real eyes.'"

Here's a beautifully written version of this passage from the book of John, from Eugene Peterson's paraphrased Bible entitled *"The Message:"*

"But friends, that's exactly who we are: children of God. And that's only the beginning. Who knows how we'll end up! What we know is that when Christ is openly revealed, we'll see him—and in seeing him, become like him. All of us who look forward to his Coming stay ready, with the glistening purity of Jesus' life as a model for our own."

Isn't this a delightfully paraphrased version of this passage? Doesn't this idea of *seeing Christ* take on an entirely new meaning and power for you when you see the Christ within you? Imagine Paul Revere shouting, "The Christ is coming, the Christ is coming," but not somewhere out there, in the external world. The Christ comes in your own mind as you're aware of it and embrace it. As you evolve from that state of unconsciousness or unawareness to one of the certainty of your divine, creative nature, God can do nothing for you until you consciously cooperate and align yourself with It.

The flipside is: as you turn within and align yourself to God, anything and everything is possible. I *know* you're allied with your True Self, right here, right now, always and forever.

Your Spiritual Mind Treatment

I can think of no better way to close out this book than with a Spiritual Mind Treatment for you, the reader. Here we go:

God is. God is all. God is the all in all. This Infinite, Creative, Universal Intelligence is the source and sustainer of all living creatures and all of creation throughout the known and unknown universes. This Eternal Intelligence is all good, all loving, all powerful, and always creating. It is True Reality, Love, Truth, Light, Peace, and Joy. This God Essence and Energy is all that is life affirming and life expanding. Spirit is without opposite, indivisible, the One Power. It is all knowing, all seeing, and everywhere present at all times. It is beyond time and space. It is the One Universal Mind. It is All That Is.

This Infinite Intelligence is who I am. I am made of It, I am an individual expression of It. It is the source of my being. As a spiritual being, I am surrounded and enveloped by It. It permeates every fiber of my being. And as this Spiritual Essence is within me, so also do I live within It, It being the All, and I being part of that All. I live and move and have my being within God. As a wave is to an ocean, so I am to the Infinite. God Is within me and I am within It. As this is the truth about me, I know this to be the truth of the person reading these words. I know for you that you are an individual expression of this Infinite Loving Intelligence. It is the source of your being. As a spiritual being, you are surrounded and enveloped by It. It permeates every fiber of your being. You live and move and have your being within God. As a wave is to an ocean, so you are to the Infinite. God Is within you and you are within It. You and I and all of Life are one with God. We are all One. And in this absolute certainty of Oneness, I speak these words for you, the reader.

I know for you that you are whole, perfect, and complete. Whole, perfect, and complete. You lack nothing to be the perfect you that you are. You have all that you need, and all that you desire you already are. You are love, you are peace, and you are joy. You are patience, understanding, harmony, strength, courage, openness, willingness, and you have an enthusiastic zest for life. All that is good in life, you are. All that is life enhancing, you are. These principles are your birthright, because you are a direct reflection of the Infinite. You are a vehicle for Spirit to express through and Spirit is All Good. You are constantly and continuously moving toward and attracting Divine Right Action in your life. Your spiritual growth and understanding are unstoppable and inevitable. I know for you that you consistently turn to your True Self for guidance and action. You know beyond all doubt that your True Self is your source and supply and whatever you think you need at any given moment, it supplies for you: love, care, protection, strength, guidance, wisdom, insight, and clarity. Whatever you need, you have. Whichever divine principle you embrace, you are. I know for you that your union with your True Self is natural and effortless all throughout your day. You keep your mind open to love and you embody and express it easily. You know your own truth and without difficulty or uncertainty, you identify thoughts and beliefs that are ego based and therefore not based in truth. You easily release them as they enter your mind and return back to your True Self in consciousness. You are led to the light as you turn to it. And you turn to it, again, and again, and again, always and forever. You are one with God.

I give thanks for this Truth about you, revealed through me by a Loving Infinite Essence. With gratitude I release these words into the Law, knowing they have no choice but to manifest exactly as I've spoken them.

And so it is. Amen. Right on!

WORKS CITED

A Course in Miracles : Combined Volume. Mill Valley, CA: Foundation for Inner Peace, 2007.

Alexander, Eben. *Into the Afterlife : A Neurosurgeon's Near-Death Experience and Spiritual Awakening.* London: Piatkus, 2012.

Baer, Greg. *Real Love: The Truth about Finding Unconditional Love and Fulfilling Relationships.* New York: Gotham Books, 2004.

Brown, Brené. *The Gifts of Imperfection: Let Go of Who You Think You're Supposed to Be and Embrace Who You Are.* Center City, Minn: Hazelden, 2010.

Chödrön, Pema. *The Places that Scare You: A Guide to Fearlessness in Difficult Times.* Boston: Shambhala, 2002.

Emerson, Ralph Waldo, and Edward Waldo Emerson. *The Complete Works of Ralph Waldo Emerson.* Centenary ed. Boston: Houghton, Mifflin and Harcourt, 1903.

Holmes, Ernest. *Can We Talk to God?* Deerfield Beach, FL: Health Communications, Inc., 1992

Holmes, Ernest. *The Science of Mind.* New York: G.P. Putnam's Sons, 1997.

Hotchkiss, Burt. *Your Owner's Manual.* Sweet Home, OR: B. Hotchkiss, 1992.

Peterson, Eugene H. *The Message.* Colorado Springs, CO: NavPress, 2004.

Rhinehart, Luke. *The Book of EST.* New York: Holt, Rinehart and Winston, 1976. Communications, 1999.

Taylor, Jill Bolte. *My Stroke of Insight: A Brain Scientist's Personal Journey.* New York: Viking, 2008.

Twelve Steps and Twelve Traditions. New York: Alcoholics Anonymous World Services, 1981.

Walsch, Neale D. *Conversations with God: An Uncommon Dialogue.* New York: G.P. Putnam's Sons, 1996.

Wikipedia contributors, "Mata Amritanandamayi," *Wikipedia, The Free Encyclopedia*

Williamson, Marianne. *A Return to Love: Reflections on the Principles of a Course in Miracles*. New York: HarperCollins, 1996.

World Services, Inc. *Alcoholics Anonymous: The Big Book --4th Ed.* New York City, NY: Alcoholics Anonymous World Services, 2001.

ABOUT THE AUTHOR

Mark Reed is a deeply loved and loving spiritual practitioner, counselor, teacher, and prayer, licensed by the Centers for Spiritual Living. He is a dedicated student of "The Science of Mind," "A Course in Miracles" and the 12 Steps, and has taught many classes on affirmative prayer, oneness, mental discipline, ego relinquishment, visioning, meditation, and spiritual development. He's a veteran web designer, email marketing pioneer, inspiring Facebook presence and blogger, and has written a myriad of spiritual self-help articles for publication. His interests are helping others know their own spiritual truth and writing about himself in the third person. Mark's spiritual home is the West Valley Center for Spiritual Living in Peoria, AZ and he and his beautiful wife Dora reside in nearby Avondale. You can contact Mark at follow.the.true.you@gmail.com and pursue your "True You-ness" at facebook.com/followthetrueyou.

Made in the USA
San Bernardino, CA
18 June 2015